THE LEGO® IDEAS BOOK

YOU CAN BUILD ANYTHING!

FAN BUILDERS: Sebastiaan Arts, Tim Goddard, Deborah Higdon, Barney Main, Duncan Titmarsh, Andrew Walker

AUTHOR: Daniel Lipkowitz

THE LEGO® IDEAS BOOK
CONTENTS

Introduction 4
Brick Tips 6

Planes, Trains & Automobiles
Start Up Your Engines 10
Cars 12
Monster Trucks 14
Trucks 16
Ice Cream Van 18
Small Vehicles 20
Around the World 22
Classic Trains 24
City Trains 26
Aeroplanes 28
Hot Air Balloon 30
Helicopter 31
Boats 32
Fishing Boat 34
Meet the Builder: Barney Main 36

Town & Country
Bricks for Building 42
Family House 44
Ground Floor 46
Top Floor 48
Microbuildings 50
Train Station 52
Station Buildings 54
Inside the Station 56
Country Barn 58
Farmyard Life 60
Down on the Farm 62
Bridges 64
Bigger Bridges 66
Meet the Builder: Deborah Higdon 68

Out of this World
Stellar Pieces 74
Hover Scooter 76
Space Walkers 78
Spacefighter 80
Small Spaceships 82
More Small Spaceships 84
Microships 86
More Microships 88
Small Transporters 90
Moon Miner 92
Robotic Vehicles 94
Jetpacks 95
Rocket 96
Aliens 98
Meet the Builder: Tim Goddard 100

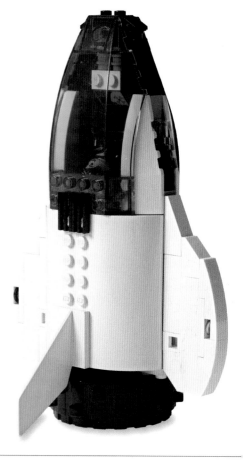

In Days of Old

Pieces of History 106
Castle 108
Drawbridges 110
Portcullis 112
Castle Doors 114
Traps 116
Knightly Steeds 118
Wagons & Carts 120
Dragons 122
Battering Rams 124
Laying Siege 126
Cannons & Catapults 128
Micromedieval 130
Meet the Builder: Sebastiaan Arts 132

A World of Adventure

Bricks for Adventure 138
Pirate Ship 140
A Pirate's World 142
Shipwreck 144
Pirate Island 146
Viking Longship 148
Viking Village 150
Jungle Rope Bridge 152
Into the Jungle 154
Wild Animals 156
Robots 158
Creature 'Bots 160
Real-World Robots 162
Meet the Builder:
Duncan Titmarsh 164

Make & Keep

Useful Pieces 170
Desk Tidies 172
Truck Tidy 174
Minifigure Display 176
Boxes 178
Treasure Chest 180
Picture Frames 182
Mosaics 184
3-D Mosaics 186
Classic Board Games 188
More Board Games 190
Building Reality 192
Your Own Designs 194
Meet the Builder: Andrew Walker 196

Acknowledgements 200

INTRODUCTION

Building with LEGO® bricks is huge fun and endlessly creative. With a bucket of bricks and a bit of practice, you can build just about anything! But even the best builders need some inspiration. That's where this book comes in! In its pages, you will discover a dazzling array of ideas for all ages and abilities.

2x2 SLOPE

The models created by the featured LEGO® fans are for inspirational purpose only and are built from the fans' own collections; therefore, the LEGO elements used for the models may vary in age, colour, condition and availability.

THE LEGO® BRICK

The starting point of all LEGO® models is the LEGO brick. The basic LEGO brick has two simple components: studs on one side and tubes on the other. The studs of one brick lock into the tubes of another. The LEGO Group call this bond "clutch power"! LEGO bricks come in many shapes and sizes, but all bricks have the ability to connect to another.

2x4 BRICK

2x3 PLATE (FLAT, WITH STUDS)

2x2 TILE (FLAT, WITHOUT STUDS)

LEGO® TECHNIC RIGHT ANGLE AXLE CONNECTOR

SPECIAL PIECES As well as bricks, you can get customised pieces such as propellers, flames and loudhailers. LEGO Technic pieces are useful because they include gears and axles. All these pieces interconnect with regular bricks.

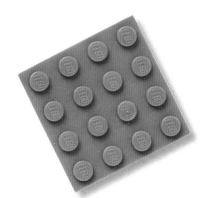
4x4 PLATE

SCALE Before you build a model, decide what scale to build it in. In "minifigure scale", your minifigures must be able to sit inside a spaceship or enter a castle through the door!

FLAME

If you don't have a lot of bricks, you could try building in "microscale". Regular bricks have different purposes: a flag piece can become a spaceship wing, or a tiny 1x1 slope can become a cockpit viewscreen!

PROPELLER

You might even want to try a bigger scale to create a LEGO sculpture.

MINIFIGURE-SCALE CASTLE GATEHOUSE

LOUDHAILER

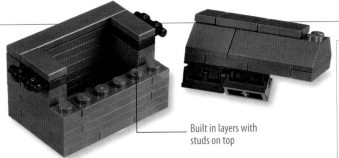

Built in layers with studs on top

STUDS ON TOP
Most LEGO models are built in layers from the bottom upwards. The pieces are arranged with the tubes facing down and the studs facing up. This is the simplest way to build and many great creations can be made in this way.

STUDS ON THE SIDE
Some bricks have studs on more than one side. These clever bricks allow you to build things on the side of your models or upside down! They also help create a smooth effect.

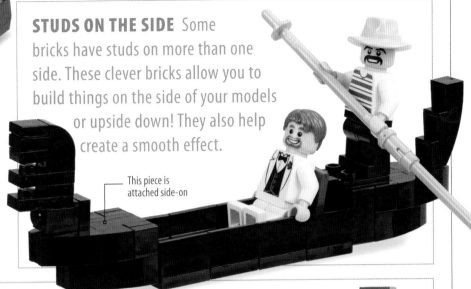

This piece is attached side-on

USEFUL PIECES FOR BUILDING ON THE SIDE

These two pieces connect together, allowing you to clip another brick onto the pin (side-on)

1x1 BRICK WITH 1 SIDE STUD

1x2/1x4 ANGLE PLATE

1x2 HINGE BRICK AND 1x2 HINGE PLATE

LEGO TECHNIC HALF PIN

1x2 BRICK WITH HOLE

1x4 BRICK WITH SIDE STUDS

HOW TO USE THIS BOOK
The ideas in this book will inspire you to create many more models of your own. We don't show building steps or brick lists because it's unlikely you will have all the bricks for each model. Here's how the pages work.

BUILDING BRIEF
The building brief is the start point for a model. But remember: if briefed to build a small spaceship, the model you create would be different to anyone else's model. And that's fine!

LABELS
The labels point out interesting details on a model: important bricks, building techniques and functions. They also suggest changes you could make and different bricks you could use.

MAIN MODEL
The main model is often shown from different angles so you can see just how it's made. But don't just try to copy it. Use it to fire up your imagination – then adapt it to your own collection of bricks.

ALTERNATIVE MODEL
The alternative models show different (sometimes simpler) ways of achieving a building effect, using alternative bricks.

CONSTRUCTION BOX
The pictures in boxes show some of the construction secrets of the main model – they show it taken apart to explain a useful building technique that you can use in your own models.

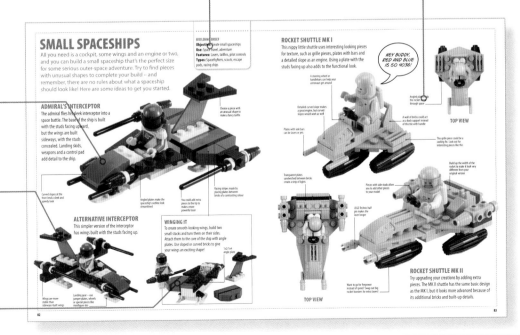

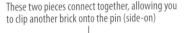

BRICK TIPS

Every LEGO® builder has his or her own way of doing things, but here are some useful tips to get you started. Of course, the most important thing to remember is to just use your imagination and...get building!

INSPIRATION IS EVERYWHERE! JUST LOOK OUT OF THE WINDOW – OR AT THE WINDOW!

RESEARCH Check out real-life examples or photographs of the kinds of thing you want to make to get good building tips and ideas.

MIX AND MATCH YOUR BRICKS Mix up all your LEGO sets and use space pieces for house builds or LEGO® CITY pieces for fantasy builds.

KEY PIECE You could start your build by finding an unusual or interesting shaped piece and think of different ways of using it.

PLAN (OR DON'T BOTHER!) Sometimes it helps to plan out your build in advance and gather all the bricks you need. Other times it's good to just jump right in and start building!

SORT YOUR BRICKS Whether it's by colour or type, it could save you lots of time when you're building.

PURPOSE When you're building, think about the purpose or function of your model.

PLAY POTENTIAL Don't forget that you will want to play with your models. Make sure your minifigures have brick studs to stand or sit on. Build a range of models to expand your play. Think of multiple play scenarios for your models!

WHO SAYS THAT GIRAFFES HAVE TO BE YELLOW AND BROWN? USE YOUR BRICKS TO COME UP WITH YOUR OWN COLOUR SCHEME.

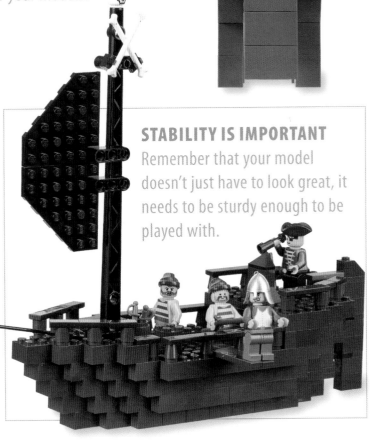

STABILITY IS IMPORTANT Remember that your model doesn't just have to look great, it needs to be sturdy enough to be played with.

BE CREATIVE WITH YOUR BRICKS You can use different bricks to achieve similar effects. If you don't have cabbages for your farm truck, but you have some yellow bricks, then you've got straw bales!

DON'T WORRY IF YOUR BUILD GOES WRONG It's all about finding your own way of doing something. If things do go wrong, just take your model apart and begin again! There's usually more than one way to solve a building problem.

YOUR MODEL MIGHT TURN OUT VERY DIFFERENT FROM HOW YOU IMAGINED— AND MAYBE EVEN BETTER!

IT'S ALL IN THE DETAIL Use details to bring your models to life and give them the finishing touch, from lights on cars and spaceships to flowers in gardens.

Up, up and away! This biplane is bright, colourful and has double wings, for twice as much building fun. (See pp. 28–29)

PLANES, TRAINS & AUTOMOBILES

It's time to get going! How do you want to travel – by land, sea, air, road or rail? Will your model have two wheels, four wheels, wings, propellers or sails?

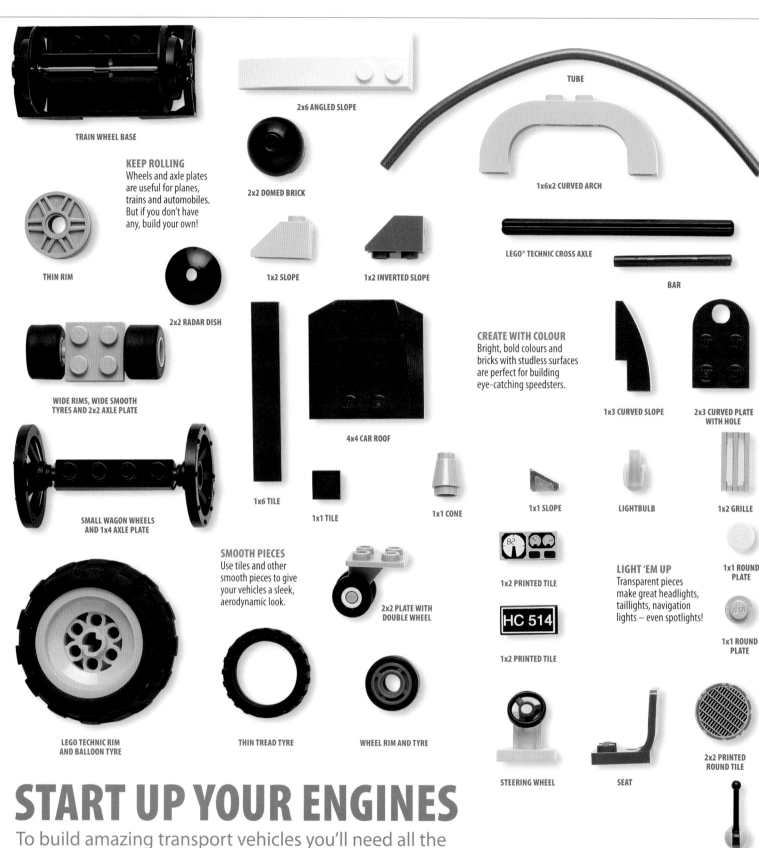

TRAIN WHEEL BASE

2x6 ANGLED SLOPE

TUBE

KEEP ROLLING
Wheels and axle plates are useful for planes, trains and automobiles. But if you don't have any, build your own!

2x2 DOMED BRICK

1x6x2 CURVED ARCH

THIN RIM

2x2 RADAR DISH

1x2 SLOPE

1x2 INVERTED SLOPE

LEGO® TECHNIC CROSS AXLE

BAR

WIDE RIMS, WIDE SMOOTH TYRES AND 2x2 AXLE PLATE

CREATE WITH COLOUR
Bright, bold colours and bricks with studless surfaces are perfect for building eye-catching speedsters.

1x3 CURVED SLOPE

2x3 CURVED PLATE WITH HOLE

4x4 CAR ROOF

SMALL WAGON WHEELS AND 1x4 AXLE PLATE

1x6 TILE

1x1 TILE

1x1 CONE

1x1 SLOPE

LIGHTBULB

1x2 GRILLE

SMOOTH PIECES
Use tiles and other smooth pieces to give your vehicles a sleek, aerodynamic look.

2x2 PLATE WITH DOUBLE WHEEL

1x2 PRINTED TILE

LIGHT 'EM UP
Transparent pieces make great headlights, taillights, navigation lights – even spotlights!

1x1 ROUND PLATE

HC 514

1x2 PRINTED TILE

1x1 ROUND PLATE

LEGO TECHNIC RIM AND BALLOON TYRE

THIN TREAD TYRE

WHEEL RIM AND TYRE

2x2 PRINTED ROUND TILE

STEERING WHEEL

SEAT

START UP YOUR ENGINES

To build amazing transport vehicles you'll need all the basics – wheels, axles, propellers. But don't just stick to LEGO® car or airplane sets! Look through your entire collection and choose some really exciting pieces to give your models an unusual shape or imaginative detail. Here are some good bricks to look out for.

JOYSTICK

BARRED WINDOW WITH 4 CONNECTIONS

1x2 GRILLE SLOPE

1x1 BRICK WITH 1 SIDE STUD

1x2 PLATE WITH VERTICAL BAR

1x2/1x4 ANGLE PLATE

ANGLE PLATES
Angle plates are great for attaching grilles and lights to the front or back of your model.

1x2/2x2 ANGLE PLATE

1x1 PLATE WITH SIDE RING

2x2 BRICK WITH SIDE PINS AND AXLE HOLE

1x1 PLATE WITH VERTICAL CLIP

1x1 BRICK WITH VERTICAL BAR

1x2 HINGED BRICK AND 1x2 HINGED PLATE

HINGED PLATES

1x2 PLATE WITH HANDLED BAR

1x1 HEADLIGHT BRICK

SKELETON ARM

1x2 PLATE WITH LEGO TECHNIC BEAM

1x2 PLATE WITH HANDLED BAR

2x2 TURNTABLE

1x2 JUMPER PLATE

1x2 CURVED HALF ARCH

LEGO TECHNIC T-BAR

1x2 TEXTURED BRICK

CHOOSE BRICKS FROM ACROSS ALL YOUR LEGO SETS TO BUILD UNIQUE VEHICLES

1x1 PLATE WITH HORIZONTAL CLIP

LEGO TECHNIC HALF PIN

TRAIN BUFFER

LEGO TECHNIC HALF BUSH

2x2 TILE WITH PIN

2x4 WHEEL GUARD

WHEEL GUARDS
Ready-made wheel guard pieces can help construct the base of your model. Choose printed pieces to add detail! (See Hot Rod, p.15)

2x4 WINGED WHEEL GUARD

2x2 BRICK WITH WHEEL ARCH

PROPELLER WITH 4 BLADES

1x2x2 LADDER

1x2 PLATE WITH SIDE BARS

2x2 PLATE WITH FRONT GRILLE

1x6 CURVED BAR WITH STUDS

NEW PURPOSE
Try to think of exciting new uses for your pieces. This webbed radar dish (below) makes a great propeller! (See Swampboat, p.23)

2x4 WHEEL GUARD

PROPELLER WITH 3 BLADES

A CLEAR PLACE TO START
Windscreens and windows are a good starting point for a vehicle. They can help determine the size of your model.

1x2x2 WALL ELEMENT

LEGO TECHNIC WIDE RIM

6x6 WEBBED RADAR DISH

CURVED WINDSCREEN

1x4x3 WINDOW FRAME WITH WINDOW GLASS

2x4x2 WINDSCREEN

CARS

It's time to hit the road! Before building a car, think about where you're going. For city driving, you could make a compact auto to fit a single minifigure. For off-road vehicles, add some rugged, outdoor features. Whatever you build, make sure the driver fits inside and the wheels can spin freely!

DOORLESS ENTRY

Doors can be tricky to build, but even if you leave doors out, you can still make a handle using a headlight brick and a 1x1 tile. You could make a petrol cap too!

Roof pops off to let driver in and out

Hood ornament on 1-stud jumper plate

Same piece for front and rear windscreens

REAR VIEW

License plate. You could also use a printed tile

Side mirror, made from plate with side ring. You could attach a 1x1 slope, plate or tile instead

Taillights – transparent tiles built into body of car can be any colour

CITY CAR

To navigate the narrow streets of a bustling city, design a compact car. Build the basic shell first, and then add details like a front grille, headlights and licence plate.

WISH I COULD FEEL THE BREEZE THROUGH MY HAIR...BUT IT'S PLASTIC!

Take off roof and rear windscreen to make a convertible!

1x2/2x2 angle plate

AUTO ANATOMY

This car was built on a base of overlapping rectangular plates with axle plates underneath to attach the wheels. The front details are mounted on an angle plate.

UNDER THE HOOD

The front is held together by an assembly of bricks, clips and sideways building. When you build in multiple directions, the more points of contact you have and the better it holds together.

CARGO SPACE

This car has front and back seats and a small boot to store anything your minifigure might need on the road. You could take out the rear seats to make a larger boot.

Roof lights for foggy nights. Use transparent red pieces for hi-tech night vision!

Pack a spare tyre for emergencies on the back or in the boot

1x1 slopes mirror shape of front of roof

OFF-ROAD CAR

For a more complex car, create something with a special purpose, like driving across rough terrain! This auto was built from the top down, with the roof, hood and windscreen pieces picked out first and then the rest constructed to fit them.

Put transparent slopes on their side for a different effect

Brick-built wheel guards. Make sure the tyres have clearance to turn!

Use different colour bricks in the car's body to add decoration, stripes, dirt or camouflage

MONSTER TRUCKS

Who says that cars and trucks have to be down-to-earth? With a few special pieces and lots of imagination, you can turn your creation into the craziest car around. From towering turbo trucks to super-fast speedsters, these over-amped autos rule the road, the ring and the racetrack!

Elastic band

LEGO Technic half beam

IN SUSPENSE

To make the springy suspension, the wheels are attached to pivoting LEGO Technic half beams. Elastic bands pull the beams toward the centre, so when a wheel is pushed out of position, it springs right back in again.

Boosters made from wheel rims – or use jet engines to go even more over the top!

REAR SIDE VIEW

SKELETON TURBO

Don't let the cheery yellow fool you – this monster means business! It is built around a working suspension system that lets each oversized wheel move independently to conquer or crush any obstacle in its path.

Use curved and bumpy pieces as debris to test suspension

Rollcage built with clips and robot claws

Build a row of bars to clip on mirrors, chains and spikes

Chunky grille made from barred window

Vented engine made from 1x1 round plates

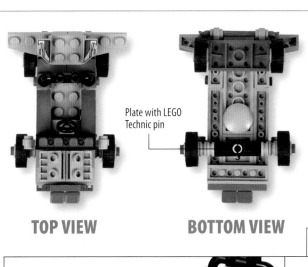

TOP VIEW

Plate with LEGO Technic pin

BOTTOM VIEW

Covered engine cowling built with hinged bricks

Decorated spoiler detail on wheel guard

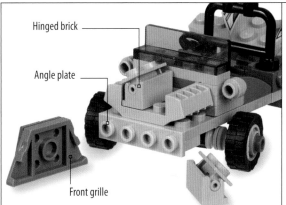

Hinged brick

Angle plate

Front grille

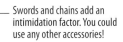

MUSCLE POWER

Two hinged bricks placed back-to-back in a plate with side vents make an exposed four-cylinder racing engine. An angle plate holds the front section in place.

HOT ROD

This speedster's front wheels are clipped to a plate with a LEGO Technic pin on its underside so the axle can turn from side to side. An angle plate under the front of the car keeps the axle from turning all the way around.

Swords and chains add an intimidation factor. You could use any other accessories!

Find new uses for stickers, like this skull decal

NOBODY'S STEALING MY PARKING SPACE AT THE OFFICE TODAY!

The ultimate hurdle...can your creation overcome it?

Using big wheels on smaller vehicles gives monster truck proportions

FRONT VIEW

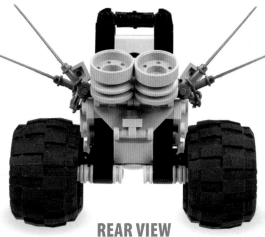

REAR VIEW

TRUCKS

Big trucks, little trucks, construction trucks, farm trucks, highway trucks with box trailers, fuel tanker trucks and postal delivery trucks – as long as it has wheels and carries cargo, it's a truck. They might drive cross-country or work at the docks, they might have four wheels or eighteen, but if you have the pieces, you can build them!

BUILDING BRIEF
Objective: Build trucks
Use: Hauling all kinds of loads
Features: Wheels, strength, size, cargo space
Extras: More wheels, moving functions, detachable trailer

TRANSPORT TRUCK

A truck doesn't have to be big to be packed with details. Grey, brown and tan bricks make this classic hauler look well-worn and rustic. It may be carrying cabbages now, but its wooden-slat bed can haul just about anything!

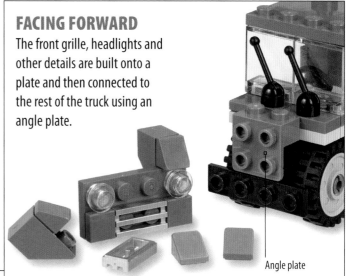

FACING FORWARD

The front grille, headlights and other details are built onto a plate and then connected to the rest of the truck using an angle plate.

Angle plate

Slopes create an angled front

Wooden cargo bed made with stacked headlight bricks and long tiles

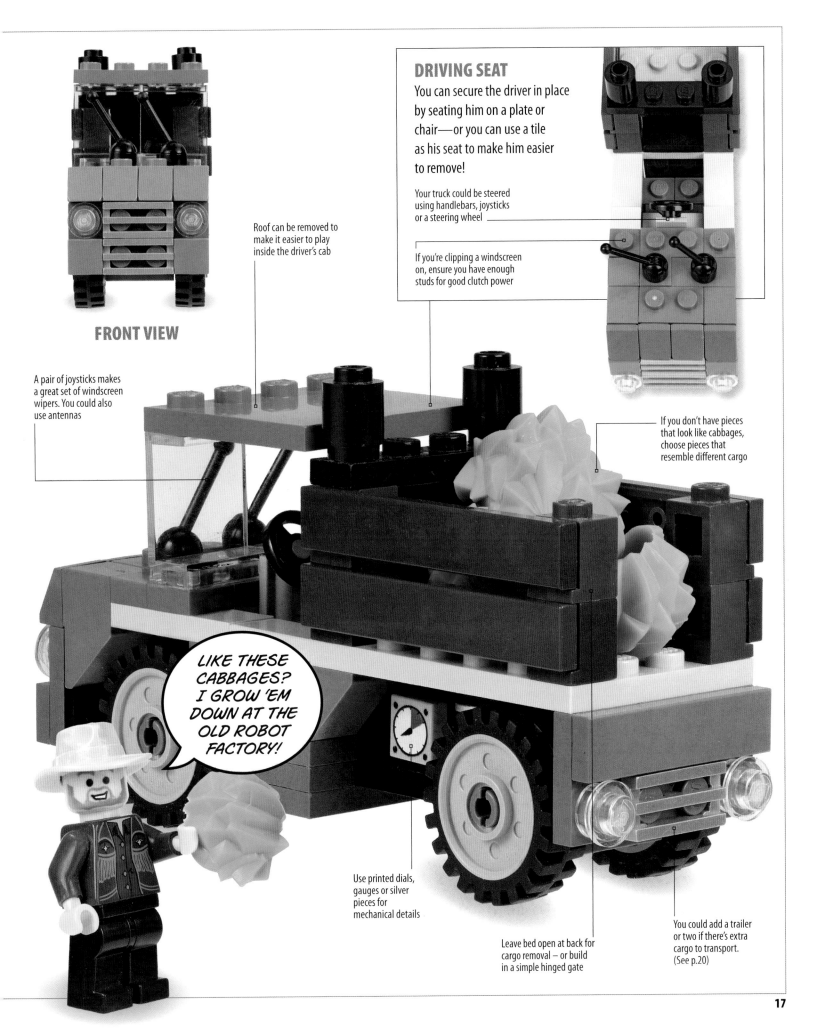

FRONT VIEW

DRIVING SEAT
You can secure the driver in place by seating him on a plate or chair—or you can use a tile as his seat to make him easier to remove!

Your truck could be steered using handlebars, joysticks or a steering wheel

If you're clipping a windscreen on, ensure you have enough studs for good clutch power

Roof can be removed to make it easier to play inside the driver's cab

A pair of joysticks makes a great set of windscreen wipers. You could also use antennas

If you don't have pieces that look like cabbages, choose pieces that resemble different cargo

LIKE THESE CABBAGES? I GROW 'EM DOWN AT THE OLD ROBOT FACTORY!

Use printed dials, gauges or silver pieces for mechanical details

Leave bed open at back for cargo removal – or build in a simple hinged gate

You could add a trailer or two if there's extra cargo to transport. (See p.20)

ICE CREAM VAN

On a hot summer's day, the sight of a friendly ice cream van is always welcome! Make your van fun and colourful with decorative pieces. Don't forget to stock the back with plenty of frozen treats so you can serve all your customers some tasty ice cream!

BUILDING BRIEF
Objective: Make ice cream vans
Use: Transportation, selling treats
Features: Window, removable roof
Extras: Goblets, pieces to personalise your van

CHOOSE YOUR FLAVOUR

The ice cream van has an iconic shape. Use curved half arches at the front of the van to achieve this look. Add tiles to the top of the roof to make it smooth, but don't worry if you don't have enough tiles; exposed studs are okay too.

BOTTOM VIEW

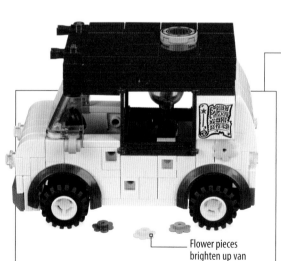

Flower pieces brighten up van

MAIN ATTRACTION

To attract potential customers, make your van eye-catching! You could attach flowers or other accessories to the side of your van with a headlight brick. Coloured round plates could look like scoops of ice cream.

Roof made from plates topped with tiles

Air vent keeps the inside of your van cool

Printed scroll pieces make great menus. What's on offer today?

MY ICE CREAMS ARE SPECIAL. WHY? THEY DON'T MELT!

Built-in window acts as serving hatch

Red wheel arches match the red roof. You could use your favourite colours

FRONT VIEW

REAR VIEW

Roof lifts off so you can serve the ice cream from inside the van!

A layer of tiles, with just a few exposed studs, allows the roof to be detached easily

Ice cream machinery is made from a goblet and a domed brick

Use a grille or tile for a licence plate

Add interesting pieces to the front of your truck. These goblets make cool ice cream cones

If you don't have a windscreen, just leave the front open

Curved half arches give a rounded front

LEGO Technic half pin

STREETS AHEAD

The front of the van is attached using bricks with holes and LEGO Technic half pins. You could even add a printed tile to make your van stand out even more. Don't forget to add headlights and a bumper!

Remember to leave enough space around the wheels so they can move

SMALL VEHICLES

They're bigger than bicycles but smaller than cars!
Small vehicles serve all kinds of purposes for all sorts
of drivers, from navigating across bumpy terrain to
cruising over a golf course. They can park in small
spaces, pass through narrow gaps and fit inside your
pocket. Here are some ideas to get you started!

IF YOU'RE GOING TO GO EXPLORING, DON'T FORGET YOUR HAT!

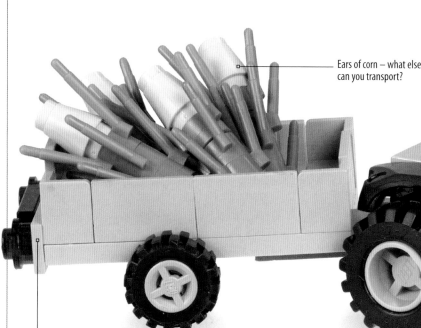

Ears of corn – what else can you transport?

Grille attached with minifigure angle plate

Angle plate holds taillights and licence plate in place

Brown bars makes the front grille look chunky and hard-wearing

QUAD BIKE

Take your adventures off-road by building
an all-terrain vehicle with a compact, tough
shape and four big wheels. Add an easy-to-
attach trailer for special expeditions!

Standing driver has good control of the vehicle, but you could make it a seated vehicle

Make sure wheel guards are raised enough so wheels can turn

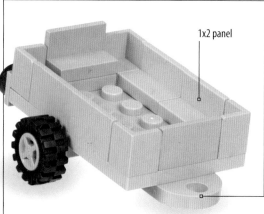

1x2 panel

2x3 curved plate with a hole hooks over the vertical bar on the truck to attach trailer

TRAILING BEHIND

This trailer is built around a
4x6 plate mounted on two
wheels. The walls are made
from thin panels, which
leave as much space for
cargo as possible.

1x2 plate with vertical bar attaches trailer

REAR SIDE VIEW

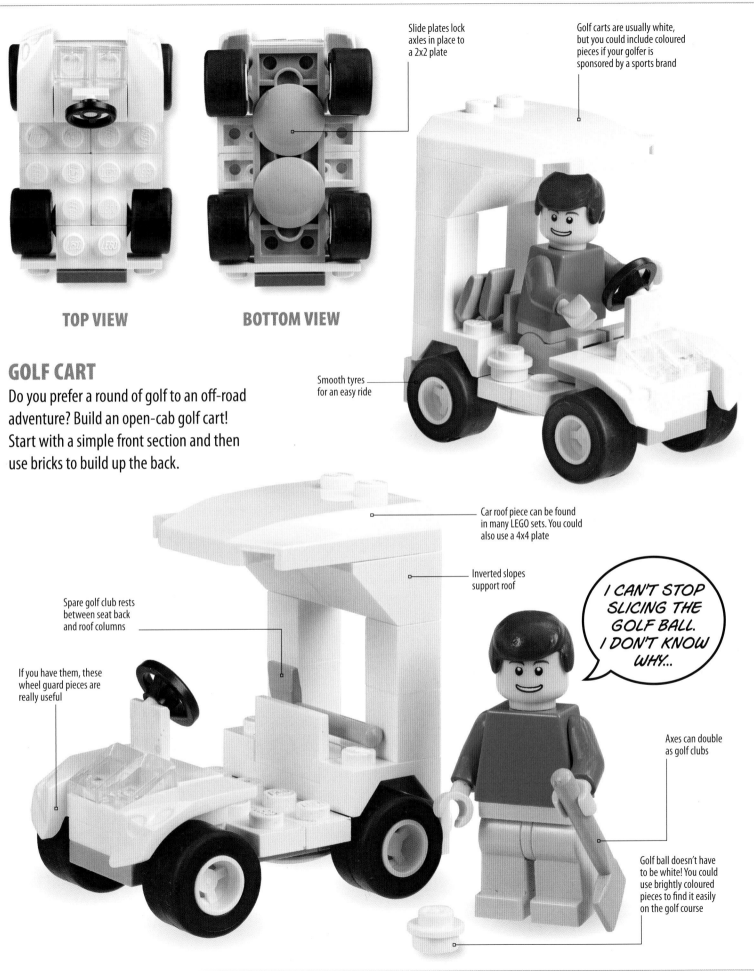

Slide plates lock axles in place to a 2x2 plate

Golf carts are usually white, but you could include coloured pieces if your golfer is sponsored by a sports brand

TOP VIEW

BOTTOM VIEW

GOLF CART

Do you prefer a round of golf to an off-road adventure? Build an open-cab golf cart! Start with a simple front section and then use bricks to build up the back.

Smooth tyres for an easy ride

Car roof piece can be found in many LEGO sets. You could also use a 4x4 plate

Inverted slopes support roof

Spare golf club rests between seat back and roof columns

If you have them, these wheel guard pieces are really useful

I CAN'T STOP SLICING THE GOLF BALL. I DON'T KNOW WHY...

Axes can double as golf clubs

Golf ball doesn't have to be white! You could use brightly coloured pieces to find it easily on the golf course

AROUND THE WORLD

From the rickshaws of Asia and the gondolas of Italy to the swampboats of the Florida Everglades, the world is chock full of transport vehicles designed to navigate different environments and terrains. What other exotic forms of transport can you think of? Look out for ideas on your next holiday!

BUILDING BRIEF
Objective: Build international transport vehicles
Use: Carrying a driver and passengers
Features: All kinds of form and propulsion
Extras: Environments, local buildings, landmarks

HURRY UP! I'VE GOT A GONDOLA TO CATCH.

THIS JOB MAY NOT PAY MUCH, BUT IT'S GREAT EXERCISE.

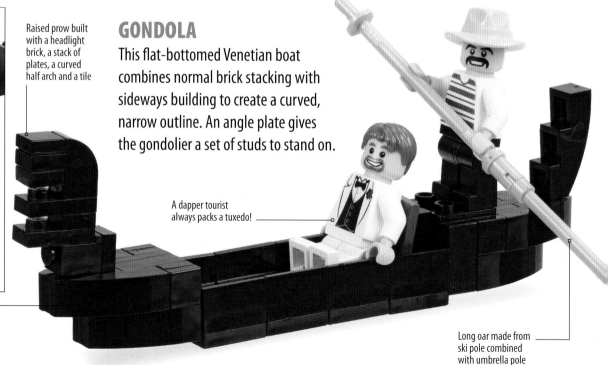

Ski pole holds up the roof

Wheels similar to wagon wheels are often used on rickshaws, even today

Make sure the bars are the right width apart that the driver can hold them both at the same time!

RICKSHAW

The base of this foot-powered rickshaw is built on its side, so the bars and wheels can be attached. Make sure the canopy is positioned high enough so that the minifigure passenger can fit in.

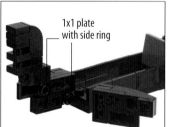

1x1 plate with side ring

Raised prow built with a headlight brick, a stack of plates, a curved half arch and a tile

BOAT BRICKS

Two plates with a side ring hold the curved sides together at the front of the gondola. One of them also attaches the curved sections to the main body of the boat.

GONDOLA

This flat-bottomed Venetian boat combines normal brick stacking with sideways building to create a curved, narrow outline. An angle plate gives the gondolier a set of studs to stand on.

A dapper tourist always packs a tuxedo!

Long oar made from ski pole combined with umbrella pole

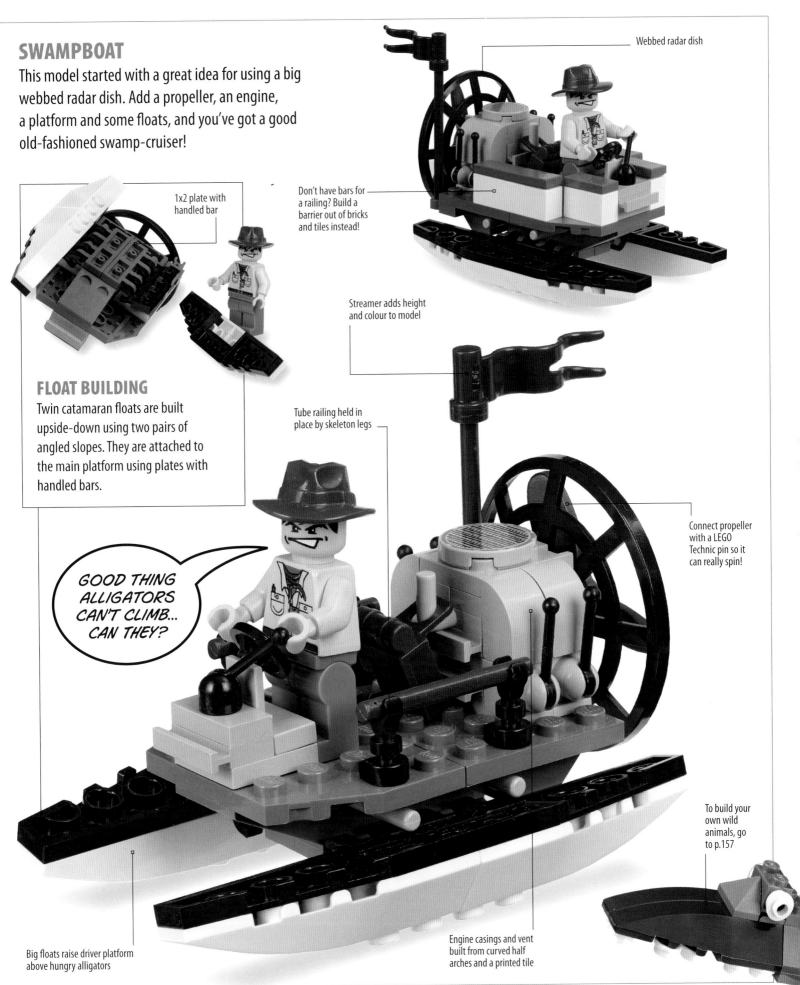

SWAMPBOAT

This model started with a great idea for using a big webbed radar dish. Add a propeller, an engine, a platform and some floats, and you've got a good old-fashioned swamp-cruiser!

Webbed radar dish

Don't have bars for a railing? Build a barrier out of bricks and tiles instead!

1x2 plate with handled bar

FLOAT BUILDING

Twin catamaran floats are built upside-down using two pairs of angled slopes. They are attached to the main platform using plates with handled bars.

Streamer adds height and colour to model

Tube railing held in place by skeleton legs

Connect propeller with a LEGO Technic pin so it can really spin!

GOOD THING ALLIGATORS CAN'T CLIMB... CAN THEY?

To build your own wild animals, go to p.157

Big floats raise driver platform above hungry alligators

Engine casings and vent built from curved half arches and a printed tile

CLASSIC TRAINS

To build an old-style train, you don't need a lot of special parts! Find some pictures of steam trains for reference and choose the perfect pieces from your LEGO collection. Then, get building – all you need is a little loco-motivation!

STEAM ENGINE

The key to building a steam locomotive is capturing the shape of the classic train engine: a cylinder with a smokestack in front, a box for the engineer's cabin, and wheels underneath.

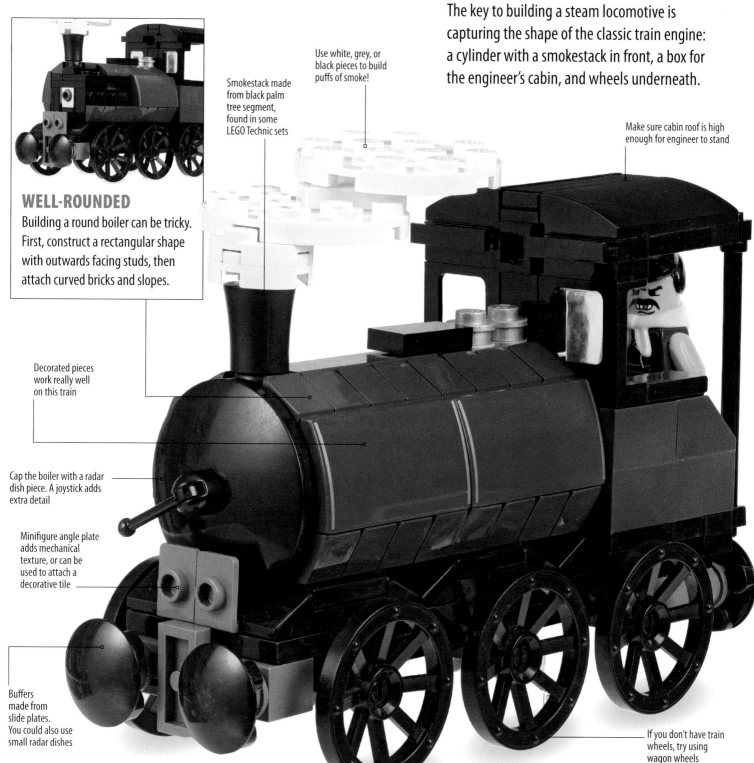

WELL-ROUNDED

Building a round boiler can be tricky. First, construct a rectangular shape with outwards facing studs, then attach curved bricks and slopes.

Use white, grey, or black pieces to build puffs of smoke!

Smokestack made from black palm tree segment, found in some LEGO Technic sets

Make sure cabin roof is high enough for engineer to stand

Decorated pieces work really well on this train

Cap the boiler with a radar dish piece. A joystick adds extra detail

Minifigure angle plate adds mechanical texture, or can be used to attach a decorative tile

Buffers made from slide plates. You could also use small radar dishes

If you don't have train wheels, try using wagon wheels

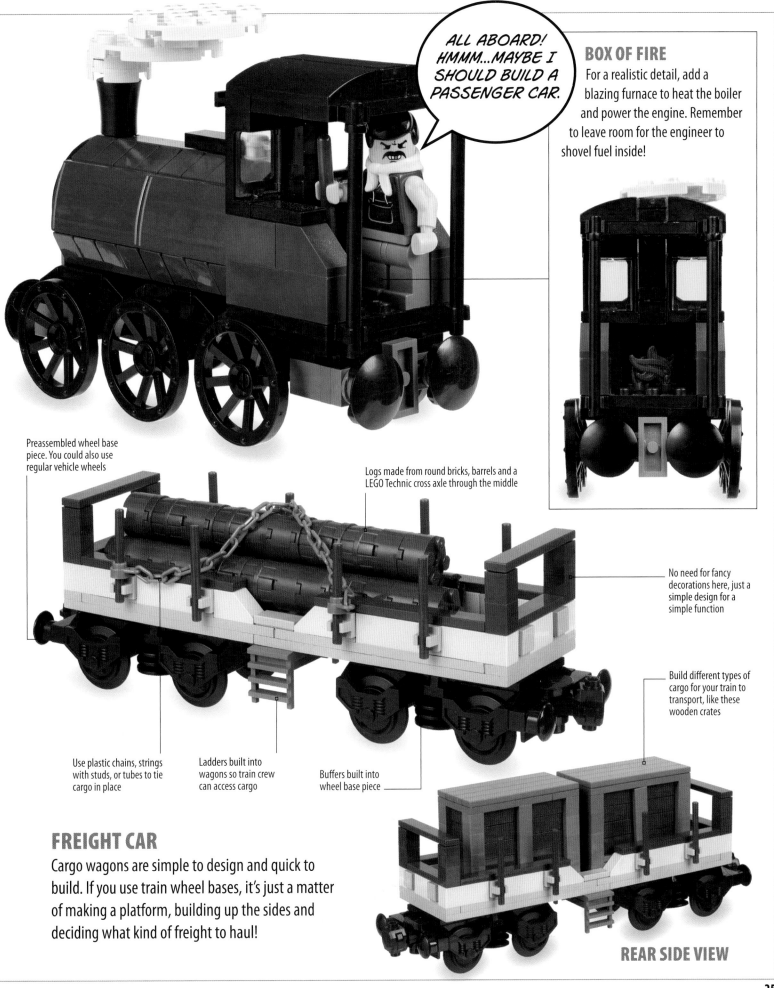

ALL ABOARD! HMMM...MAYBE I SHOULD BUILD A PASSENGER CAR.

BOX OF FIRE
For a realistic detail, add a blazing furnace to heat the boiler and power the engine. Remember to leave room for the engineer to shovel fuel inside!

Preassembled wheel base piece. You could also use regular vehicle wheels

Logs made from round bricks, barrels and a LEGO Technic cross axle through the middle

No need for fancy decorations here, just a simple design for a simple function

Use plastic chains, strings with studs, or tubes to tie cargo in place

Ladders built into wagons so train crew can access cargo

Buffers built into wheel base piece

Build different types of cargo for your train to transport, like these wooden crates

FREIGHT CAR
Cargo wagons are simple to design and quick to build. If you use train wheel bases, it's just a matter of making a platform, building up the sides and deciding what kind of freight to haul!

REAR SIDE VIEW

CITY TRAINS

Trains run through many modern cities, from above-ground commuter lines to trains in tunnels beneath the streets. They are built for speed and efficiency, so they usually have a compact, tube-shaped profile. Match the colours of your favourite city's trains or try building a super-streamlined bullet express!

BUILDING BRIEF
Objective: Build modern city trains
Use: Urban transportation, commuting
Features: Boxy shape, multiple doors, plenty of sitting and standing room
Extras: Bogies, passengers, tunnels, station platforms, rain shelters

BUILD-A-BOGIE

The wheeled undercarriage seen on modern trains is known as a bogie. If you don't have train pieces, try making a bogie using LEGO Technic half pins, radar dishes and tiles. You can even link train cars together by adding ball-and-socket joints or plates with vertical bars and holes.

Turntable lets the section swivel, but keeps the wheels lined up as it goes around curves

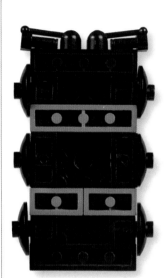

BOTTOM VIEW

Wheels are made using radar dish pieces held on by LEGO Technic half pins. Can you think of a way to make them rotate?

LEGO Technic half pin

Joysticks, binoculars or antennas can represent braking pins and beams

OPEN-TOP TRAIN

The sections of roof between the doors can be removed easily for quick access to the train's interior.

Curved slopes are perfect to get the shape of this train

Vertical hand rails are a common feature of underground trains

TUNNEL TRAVEL

This train is designed to travel smoothly underground. The distinctive roof is built from curved slopes, with transparent slopes used at the top of the doors.

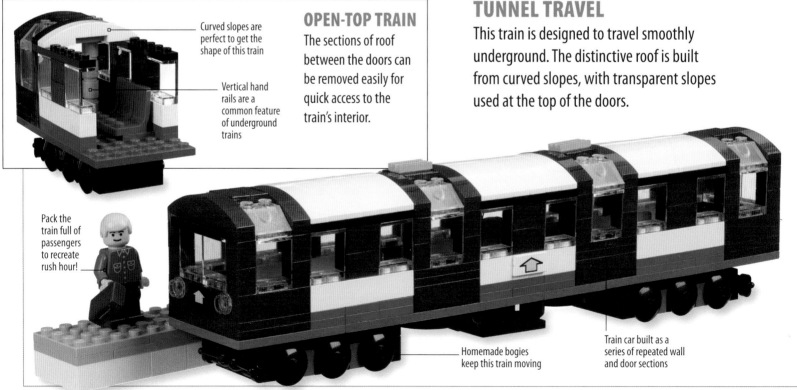

Pack the train full of passengers to recreate rush hour!

Homemade bogies keep this train moving

Train car built as a series of repeated wall and door sections

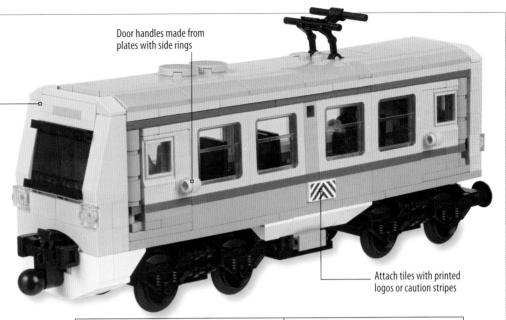

MIND THE GAP

The windscreen is built onto hinged bricks and plates, which creates a sloping angle at the front of the trolley car. The gaps on either side are hidden by tall slopes.

Door handles made from plates with side rings

Attach tiles with printed logos or caution stripes

Tall slope

Hinged brick

POWER SOURCE

Above-ground trains use roof-mounted devices to collect electricity from overhead power lines. It's easy to build one – you just need some bar pieces and robot or skeleton arms!

Create doors in a different colour so they stand out from rest of car

1x1 plate with horizontal clip

Round bricks give door room to swing open

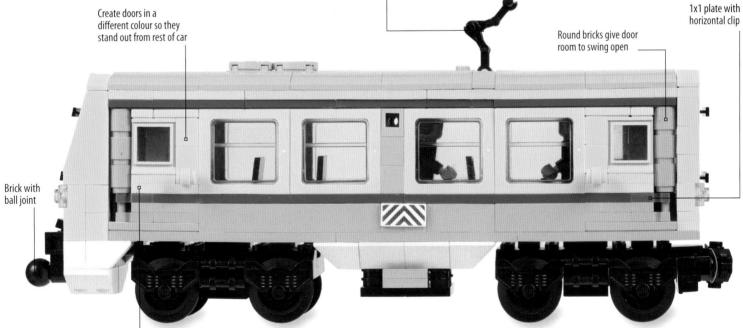

Brick with ball joint

ALL ABOARD!

The doors of the train open and close, thanks to two plates with horizontal clips that are built into each door. The clips attach to a vertical bar, which acts as a hinge. You could also use hinged plates or bricks.

ABOVE-GROUND TRAIN

This overground train is built on six-stud-wide plates and rolls on wheel base pieces. Cars can be connected with ball-and-socket joints, so your train can follow curves in the track!

AEROPLANES

There's a whole sky full of aeroplanes for you to build!
You can make a vintage plane with an open cockpit, an
ultra-modern passenger jet or anything in between.
Big planes, little planes, biplanes, triplanes – even cargo
planes with loading ramps and space inside to carry your
auto models. Grab your bricks and prepare for take-off!

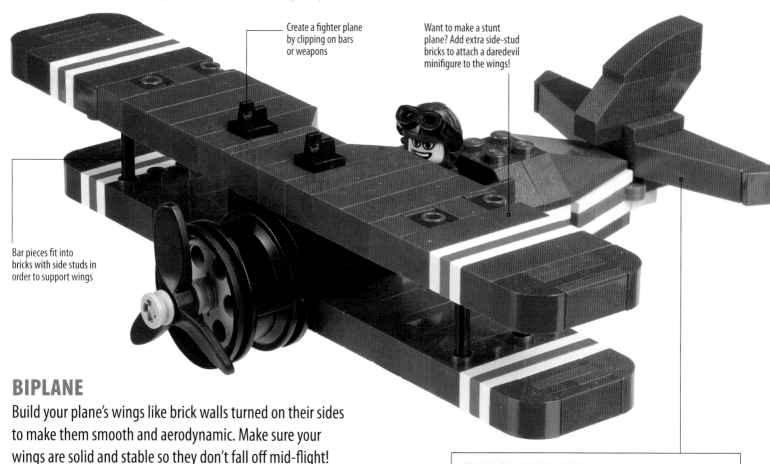

Create a fighter plane
by clipping on bars
or weapons

Want to make a stunt
plane? Add extra side-stud
bricks to attach a daredevil
minifigure to the wings!

Bar pieces fit into
bricks with side studs in
order to support wings

BIPLANE

Build your plane's wings like brick walls turned on their sides
to make them smooth and aerodynamic. Make sure your
wings are solid and stable so they don't fall off mid-flight!

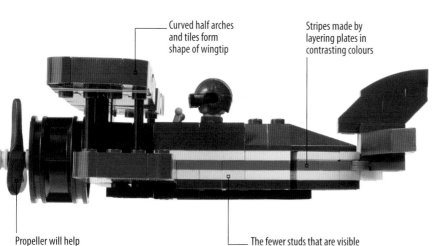

Curved half arches
and tiles form
shape of wingtip

Stripes made by
layering plates in
contrasting colours

Propeller will help
your aeroplane
take flight!

The fewer studs that are visible
on your plane model, the more
aerodynamic it looks

TALE OF A TAILFIN

Build one tailfin with slopes and curved slopes.
Then create two sideways tailfins and attach them using
back-to-back pairs of headlight bricks and jumper plates.

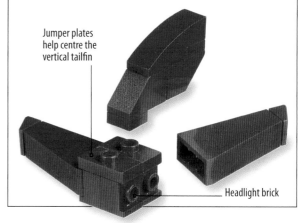

Jumper plates
help centre the
vertical tailfin

Headlight brick

MICROPLANE

You don't need to build a big model to make a big plane. Microscale aeroplanes are easy to create and look great. Just make sure you include the key features that make your plane recognisable!

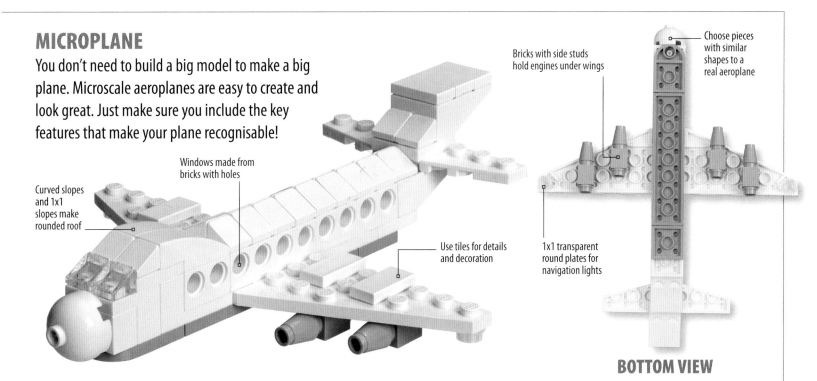

Windows made from bricks with holes

Curved slopes and 1x1 slopes make rounded roof

Use tiles for details and decoration

Bricks with side studs hold engines under wings

Choose pieces with similar shapes to a real aeroplane

1x1 transparent round plates for navigation lights

BOTTOM VIEW

Plates at bottom lock plane body together

BOTTOM VIEW

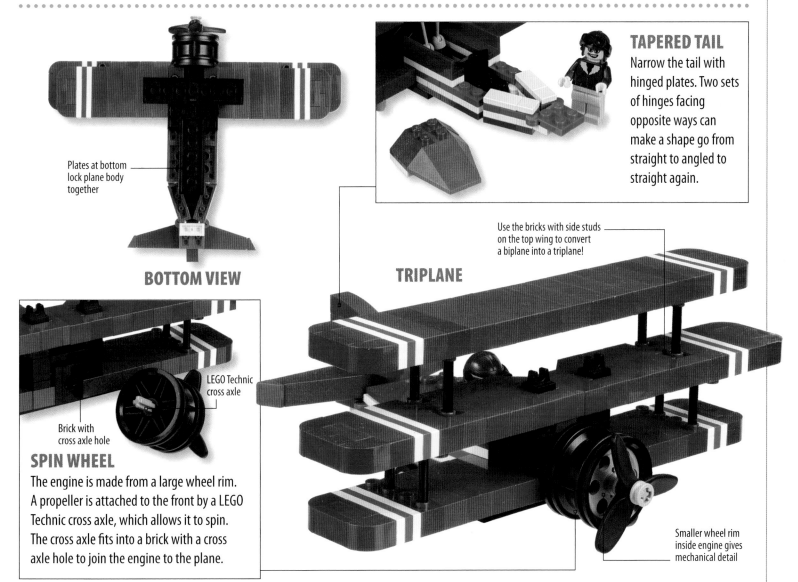

TAPERED TAIL
Narrow the tail with hinged plates. Two sets of hinges facing opposite ways can make a shape go from straight to angled to straight again.

Use the bricks with side studs on the top wing to convert a biplane into a triplane!

TRIPLANE

LEGO Technic cross axle

Brick with cross axle hole

SPIN WHEEL
The engine is made from a large wheel rim. A propeller is attached to the front by a LEGO Technic cross axle, which allows it to spin. The cross axle fits into a brick with a cross axle hole to join the engine to the plane.

Smaller wheel rim inside engine gives mechanical detail

HOT AIR BALLOON

The most important thing to remember about a hot air balloon is its shape. You may think of a balloon as a sphere, but it's really more like a lightbulb shape. The second most important thing is stability: round shapes need lots of bricks, so make sure they're all locked together securely!

BUILDING BRIEF
Objective: Build hot air balloons
Use: Leisurely trips through the sky
Features: Brightly-coloured balloon top, hanging basket
Extras: Passengers, sandbags, blazing burner

BRICK BALLOON

Build a balloon shape one layer at a time, starting at the bottom and building upward. Overlap the bricks to keep the outline as round as possible. The basket is made from a plate built up with rows of bricks, plates and tiles.

Make a swirl by moving the colours one stud over on each new layer

Add a burner flame to keep the balloon aloft

WAIT...HOW DO I GET BACK DOWN AGAIN?

Long axles attach basket to balloon

Ballast sacks made from plates with vertical clips on blank minifigure heads

1x1 round bricks are good for a wicker texture

HEAVIER THAN AIR

Build your balloon from the bottom up, gradually stepping outwards and then sharply inwards toward the top. To cut down the weight, make the balloon's centre hollow and strengthen it with crossed bricks inside.

HELICOPTER

Helicopters come in all shapes and sizes, and are designed for lots of different jobs. Decide what kind you want to make before you start building: A lightweight news chopper with a camera? A rescue copter with lots of cargo space? Big helicopters can have multiple rotors on top to keep them flying high!

BUILDING BRIEF
Objective: Create helicopters
Use: Controlled hovering flight, transport
Features: Top rotor, tail rotor, cockpit, skids, landing gear
Extras: Cameras, rescue equipment, additional rotors

Boosters or rockets can be held together with a bar or antenna through the middle

Intakes built from harpoons inserted into radar dishes, round bricks and domed bricks

RESCUE COPTER

This emergency chopper's bright colour makes it easy to spot out at sea. Its body is built thinner and thinner toward the tail, tapering from six studs wide to only two.

Add small tools and weapons to equip your chopper for rescue!

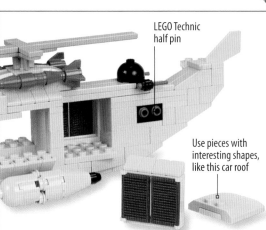

LEGO Technic half pin

Use pieces with interesting shapes, like this car roof

SIDE VIEW

To shape the side of your helicopter, use 1x2 bricks with holes with LEGO Technic half pins in them to secure angled pieces. Windows and slopes add detail too.

Big window shutters make an easy-to-open cargo hatch

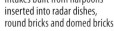

Swap intakes for round transparent plates to make spotlights for nighttime rescues!

Row of 1x1 slopes creates a sleek angled side

Unusual pieces like telescopes and steering wheels used as rescue equipment

COPTER COMPONENTS

Choose your windscreen first and use that as a guide for the helicopter's dimensions. A spacious cockpit with side windows gives your crew a wide view for spotting trouble.

BOATS

What kind of boat do you want to build? Whether you'd prefer a pocket-sized microship or a minifigure-scale vessel with a detailed interior, here are some maritime models to get you started. Build a speedboat for zipping around the bay, or a luxury cruise liner for sailing the seas – just don't forget to give your masterpiece a name!

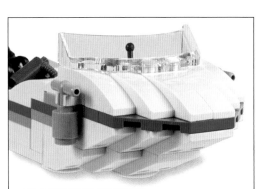

ABOVE THE WAVES
Use two layers of inverted slopes on the bottom of the prow and a layer of curved slopes on top for a streamlined shape!

A LEGO Technic axle connector forms the base of this rooftop radio mast

SPEEDBOAT

This flashy boat's main body is built from white plates, with a tan floor for colour contrast. Blue plates create a wave pattern for a really aquatic look! The cabin roof can be removed, with 1x1 slopes filling the gaps left by the support columns.

Hinged brick and plate allows motor to tilt up and down

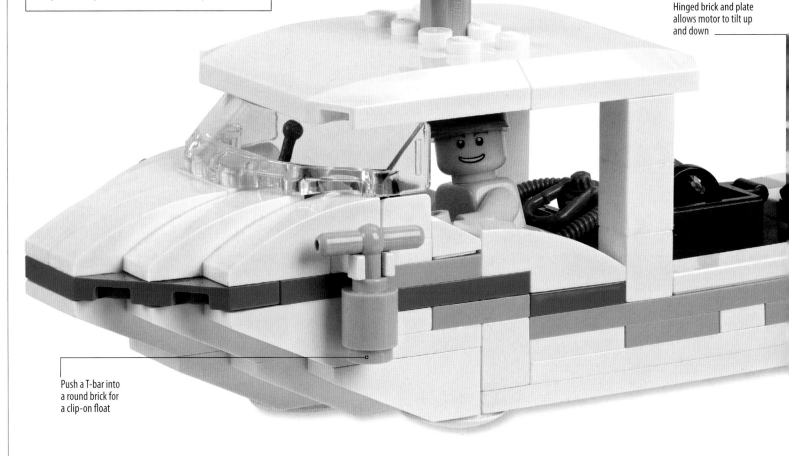

Push a T-bar into a round brick for a clip-on float

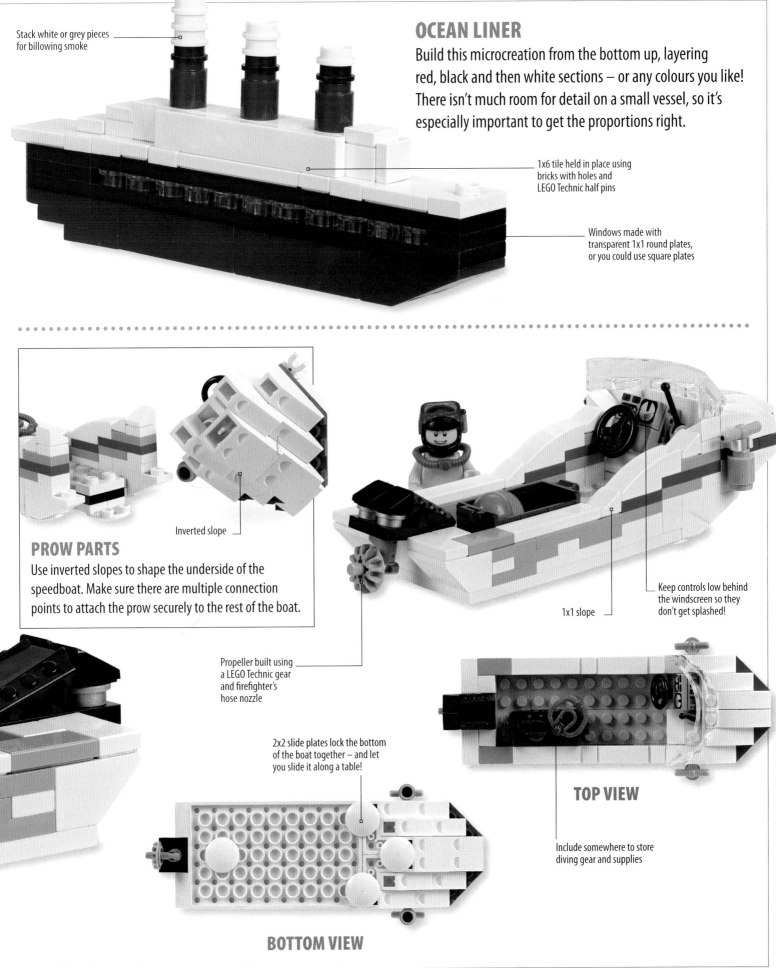

Stack white or grey pieces for billowing smoke

OCEAN LINER

Build this microcreation from the bottom up, layering red, black and then white sections – or any colours you like! There isn't much room for detail on a small vessel, so it's especially important to get the proportions right.

1x6 tile held in place using bricks with holes and LEGO Technic half pins

Windows made with transparent 1x1 round plates, or you could use square plates

Inverted slope

PROW PARTS

Use inverted slopes to shape the underside of the speedboat. Make sure there are multiple connection points to attach the prow securely to the rest of the boat.

Keep controls low behind the windscreen so they don't get splashed!

1x1 slope

Propeller built using a LEGO Technic gear and firefighter's hose nozzle

2x2 slide plates lock the bottom of the boat together – and let you slide it along a table!

TOP VIEW

Include somewhere to store diving gear and supplies

BOTTOM VIEW

FISHING BOAT

You don't need lots of special pieces to build a fishing boat. You can create the perfect seafaring vessel with some of your own bricks and plenty of imagination. Start with the hull and a cabin, then add nautical details like rigging, anchors and radio equipment. You don't even need to build a whole boat – just build the part that floats above the waves!

GONE FISHING

The toughest part of making a boat without specialised hull pieces is getting the shape right. This model uses hinged pieces to make the shape for the hull, and has lots of improvised building. The front mast was originally the centre of a spiral staircase!

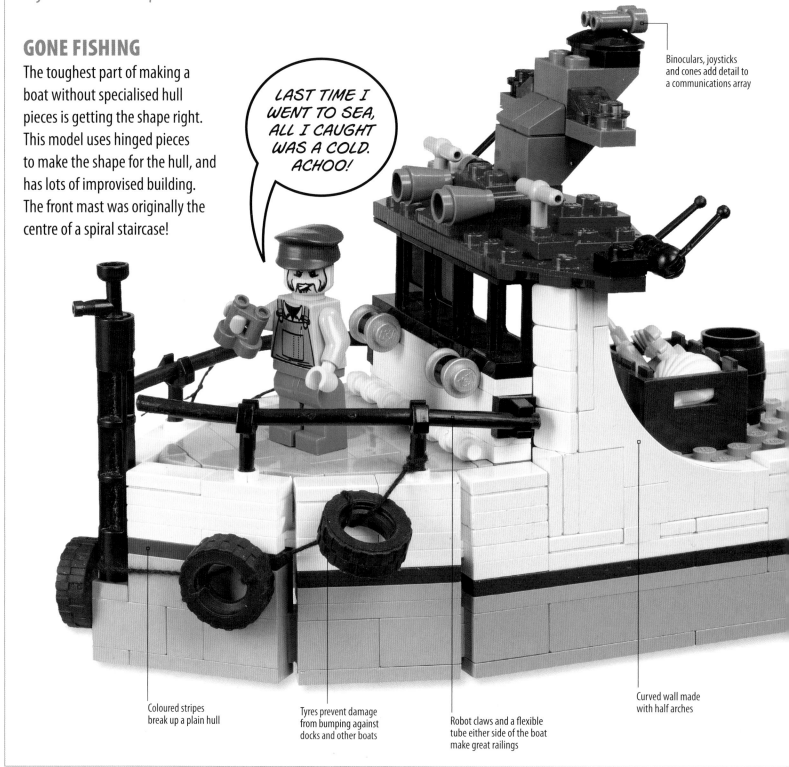

LAST TIME I WENT TO SEA, ALL I CAUGHT WAS A COLD. ACHOO!

Binoculars, joysticks and cones add detail to a communications array

Coloured stripes break up a plain hull

Tyres prevent damage from bumping against docks and other boats

Robot claws and a flexible tube either side of the boat make great railings

Curved wall made with half arches

34

BOW BUILDING

Connecting sections of bricks with hinged bricks gives the boat its pointed bow. The forward deck is a wall built sideways from the body of the boat. Slopes help shape the deck so it fits into the angled curve of the hull.

Tall slopes give forward deck an angled shape

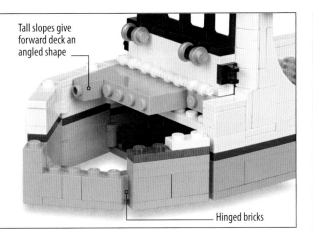

Hinged bricks

BELOW DECK

If you're only building the part of the boat that sticks out of the water, not the whole thing, feel free to leave the bottom open – as long as the hull holds together!

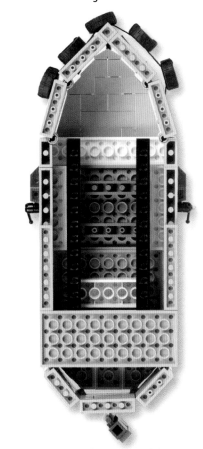

Warning lights made by mounting transparent cones on poles

CRUISE CONTROL

A boat's control cabin is usually loaded with dials, levers, lights, radios and receivers. Fill yours with as many technical-looking pieces as you can!

Working winch built with LEGO Technic pieces and a chain

You can't steer a boat without a rudder!

Fill barrels and crates with fish, crabs, clams... anything you like!

MEET THE BUILDER

BARNEY MAIN

Location: UK
Age: 18
LEGO Speciality: Pirates, transport

How old were you when you started using LEGO bricks?

I was 18 months old when I got my first LEGO® DUPLO® set, but moved on to LEGO sets shortly afterwards – and haven't stopped since then!

Which model were you most proud of as a young LEGO builder?

A model of a Viking warrior's head called "Infuriated Isaac" that I built when I was nine years old. It was featured in the *LEGO® Magazine*, as "Designer's Choice", which I was very proud of!

This pirate ship flies through the skies, catching lightning using the nets on the back. It was inspired by the movie *Stardust*, but I added a whole load of my own ideas, such as the lightning-sharks!

Both the blades of the windmill and the wooden boarding on the sides are made by "stepping" plates, and putting tiles on top. It's a very versatile technique, and has a lot of applications.

What are you inspired by?

Anything and everything! The basic idea for a model stems from all sorts of things – discovering a cool part combination, films and literature or seeing something in real life. Often I see something that I'd like to replicate, such as a style of stonework, but only recall it a couple of months later when I'm building and decide to put it in! Sometimes if I'm entering a contest with a specific theme, I do my research more thoroughly: I once had to build a model of my own Dr Seuss story, so I read through a lot of his books again to get the style right. That said, my finished models rarely look anything like my initial idea – I just go with the flow, really, and let the model itself dictate how it's going to look!

What is the biggest or most complex model you've made?

I built a big battle scene from the movie *The Chronicles of Narnia: Prince Caspian*. The battlefield was actually raised off the ground so that I could build the tomb inside the mountain, and also the sink-hole that opens up in the ground in the movie. It was really fun making all the Narnian mythical creatures – griffins, centaurs, satyrs – as well as making the famous cracked Stone Table and the siege weapons.

If you had all the LEGO bricks (and time!) in the world, what would you build?

That's a tough one. I enjoy building at real-life scale, so maybe something like a full-size version of myself! I'm also a big fan of the musical *Les Misérables* and would like to do a large, detailed version of the iconic barricade scene.

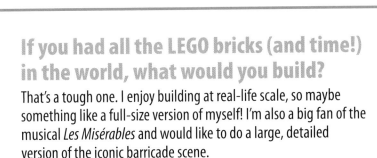

Models that use only a few colours can look really stylish, but multicoloured models are fun too!

Condensing the various scenes from Charles Dickens' *A Christmas Carol* into one model was a big challenge, as was capturing the characters in minifigure form! Lots of different colours and textures are used to help differentiate the different scenes, and the roof is made out of diving flippers!

The water here is built by turning a wall on its side to get a nice smooth surface. I left holes where I wanted the boats to go. There are loads of different parts supporting the inside of the cliff —pillars, castle towers, LEGO Technic bricks and so on — but you can't see them!

What is your favourite creation?

I really like my life-size version of the Three Blind Mice from the nursery rhyme. I think I captured the mice's expressions, the carving knife and all the gory details really well! The cheese was made from Modulex, which is a miniature LEGO brick from the 1960s used for architectural modelling!

What are some of your top LEGO tips?

Brick separators are incredibly useful! I have three lying around in case of an emergency, and it saves having to bite the bricks or ruin your fingernails. As for building, just use what bricks you have, and be creative! Think about what parts you have a lot of – if you've got lots of green bricks, why not make a giant frog? Or if you've got lots of white horns, how about a dragon, using the horns for its spine?

How much time do you spend building?

Normally an hour or two a day.

Although this pirate hideout was designed as a static display scene, it's useful to think about the backstory: Why is the soldier being made to walk the plank? Who hid all the treasure here? Why are the pirates battling each other?

What is your favourite LEGO technique or technique you use the most?

I love coming up with innovative ways to make roofing. For example, diving flippers make a great-looking Gothic tiled roof. I bought 250 black flippers specifically for this!

How many LEGO bricks do you have?

Not enough! At the last count, around 15,000 pieces (although that was a fair few years back).

"Infuriated Isaac"
Barney Main, 9

Building a head is quite similar to building the hot air balloon on p.30, but with added details and facial features. The key to a character is often getting detail around the eyes right – Infuriated Isaac has a very shifty expression!

I JUST GO WITH THE FLOW, REALLY, AND LET THE MODEL ITSELF DICTATE HOW IT'S GOING TO LOOK!

The big challenge for this castle was the steep grassy slopes up to the keep, which were done using hinged bricks and plates. The battlements have some intricate detailing, and the castle even has its own toilet!

What things have gone wrong and how have you dealt with them?

Something I find challenging is being colour-blind. It can be very difficult to distinguish colours, and I have no concept of whether they clash or not. Also, only having a student budget, I don't have nearly the amount of bricks I'd like. I frequently have to make compromises with the size and colour of models, which is why there's normally a lot of grey in them! However, not having enough bricks can be beneficial, as it forces you to innovate and come up with new ways of doing things.

What is your favourite LEGO brick or piece?

That's tricky! There are a lot of parts that I invariably use, but I'll have to go with the headlight brick. It's really useful for turning bricks on their sides or upside down, and you can attach both bricks and bars to it. But be warned – it is actually slightly thicker than a brick, as the stud on the side sticks out a bit, and this can make building with it tricky sometimes.

What do you enjoy building the most?

I don't normally build transport, so this project was venturing into new territory for me. I love pirates and castles – but anything that is green, brown, grey and gritty suits my taste. Urban streets are also fun to do, as there's so much scope for colour and texture. I'd like to get good at making spaceships, but find them really difficult to build, as I always want to add sails or battlements!

Do you plan out your build? If so, how?

Not really! I sometimes do a rough sketch but generally I just start building and hope it goes to plan! I tend to think about the next step in a model when I'm not building, and I've been known to wake up during the night with an idea what to do next! Naturally, I implement it immediately...

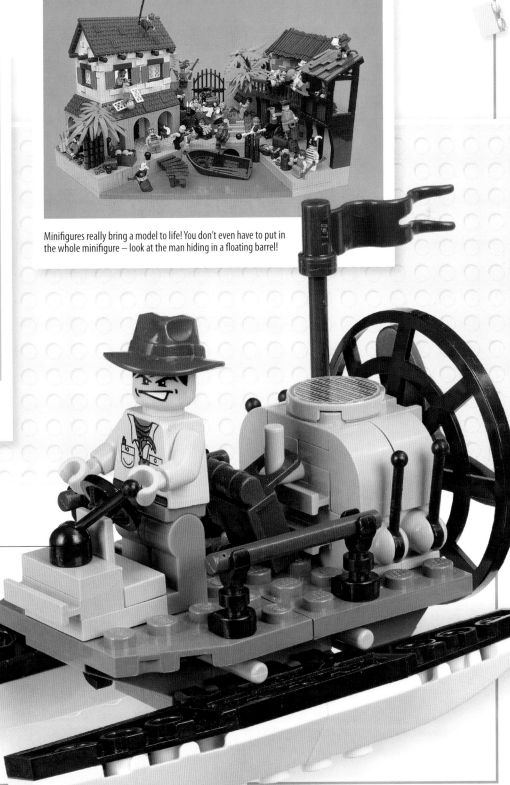

Minifigures really bring a model to life! You don't even have to put in the whole minifigure – look at the man hiding in a floating barrel!

This museum is compatible with LEGO® Modular Buildings, such as Café Corner. It is, however, considerably more dilapidated, with its broken windows and grimy streets.

You can build things that you see around you, things that you may only have seen in books or photographs – like this swampboat – or creations that come entirely from your imagination!

TOWN & COUNTRY

What kind of structures does your LEGO®
world need? Will you build a place for
your minifigures to live, work or just
somewhere for them to hang out and
have fun? You need to get building!

Home sweet home! Your buildings
can be simple or complex, big or small.
This is the top story of a large family
residence. (See pp.48–49)

4x5 DOOR

**1x2x3
WALL ELEMENT**

**1x1x2 HINGE BRICK
AND WINDOW SHUTTER**

HOME ESSENTIALS
Door and window pieces are useful for building houses. Mix and match colours and styles if you don't have enough of one!

1x6 TILE

2x4 PLATE

2x2 TILE

2x2 TILE

2x3 PLATE

1x6 ARCHED FENCE

1x2x2 WINDOW FRAME

6x6 TILE

BUSH

**2x3 CURVED PLATE
WITH HOLE**

DO IT YOURSELF!
If you haven't got a ready-made piece, try to recreate it yourself.

LUGGAGE CART

BALL JOINT

USE REAL BUILDINGS AS INSPIRATION. THEN ADD SOME IMAGINATION!

FLOWER

FLOWER

1x1 CORNER PANEL

**FLOWER WITH
OPEN STUD**

SMALL TREE

**BARRED WINDOW
WITH 2 CONNECTIONS**

CARROT

CHERRIES

BAMBOO PLANT

FLOWERS AND STEM

TAP

USE WHAT YOU HAVE
Be innovative with your bricks. If you don't have a ladder, turn this barred window (above) on its side! (See Children's Bedroom, p.49)

1x2 PLATE WITH SIDE RAIL

1x2 TEXTURED BRICK

CRATE

THE GREAT OUTDOORS
Remember to build both indoor and outdoor spaces to make your scene as realistic as possible.

LARGE PLANT LEAVES

TELESCOPE

1x4x1 LATTICE FENCE

1x4x2 LATTICE GATE

1x4x2 BARRED FENCE

1x8 PLATE WITH SIDE RAIL

ORNAMENTAL ARCH

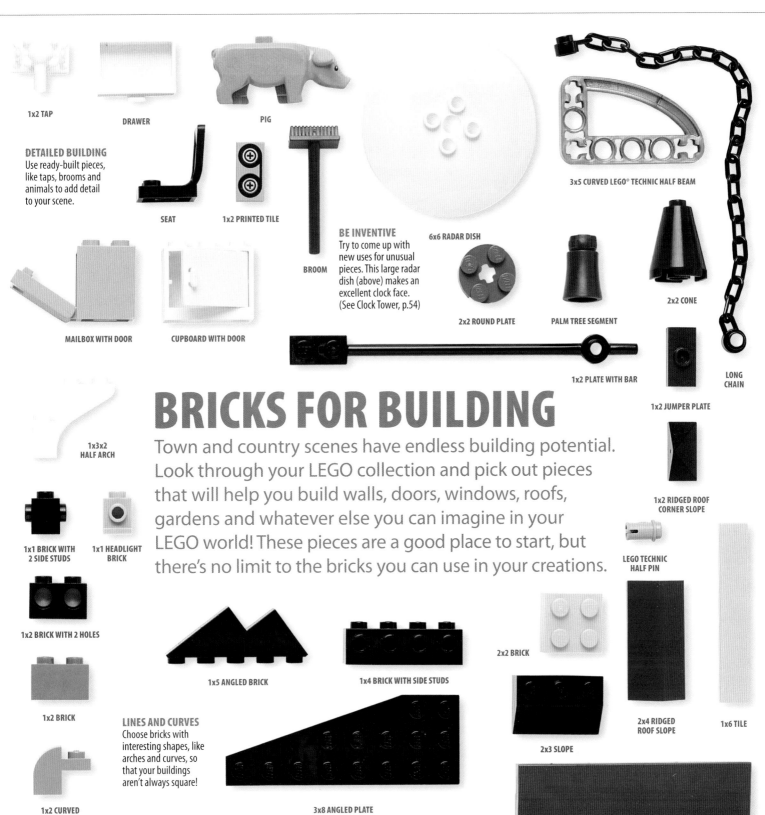

1x2 TAP

DRAWER

PIG

DETAILED BUILDING
Use ready-built pieces, like taps, brooms and animals to add detail to your scene.

SEAT

1x2 PRINTED TILE

BROOM

BE INVENTIVE
Try to come up with new uses for unusual pieces. This large radar dish (above) makes an excellent clock face.
(See Clock Tower, p.54)

6x6 RADAR DISH

2x2 ROUND PLATE

PALM TREE SEGMENT

3x5 CURVED LEGO® TECHNIC HALF BEAM

2x2 CONE

MAILBOX WITH DOOR

CUPBOARD WITH DOOR

1x2 PLATE WITH BAR

LONG CHAIN

1x2 JUMPER PLATE

1x3x2 HALF ARCH

BRICKS FOR BUILDING

Town and country scenes have endless building potential. Look through your LEGO collection and pick out pieces that will help you build walls, doors, windows, roofs, gardens and whatever else you can imagine in your LEGO world! These pieces are a good place to start, but there's no limit to the bricks you can use in your creations.

1x2 RIDGED ROOF CORNER SLOPE

LEGO TECHNIC HALF PIN

1x1 BRICK WITH 2 SIDE STUDS

1x1 HEADLIGHT BRICK

1x2 BRICK WITH 2 HOLES

1x5 ANGLED BRICK

1x4 BRICK WITH SIDE STUDS

2x2 BRICK

1x2 BRICK

LINES AND CURVES
Choose bricks with interesting shapes, like arches and curves, so that your buildings aren't always square!

2x3 SLOPE

2x4 RIDGED ROOF SLOPE

1x6 TILE

1x2 CURVED HALF ARCH

3x8 ANGLED PLATE

1x12x3 ARCHED BRICK

1x2x3 INVERTED SLOPE

6x8 RAMP

FAMILY HOUSE

Town construction is all about making detailed models of real buildings – and what could be better than making a home for an entire LEGO family? Plan out your bricks before you start, to see which colours you have the most of. Do you want matching doors and windows? Two floors or three? This is your house – the design is up to you!

BUILDING BRIEF
Objective: Build big family houses
Use: Sleeping, cooking, living, dining
Features: Must be strong and sturdy, removable roof
Extras: Furniture, satellite dish, front and back gardens

If you don't have enough roof pieces and slopes, use plates and hinges to build an opening roof!

You could make each floor a different colour

HOUSE BUILDING

Start your house with a basic brick outline, and decide where you want to put the doors and windows before you make the walls. Plan the layouts of your rooms as you build so everybody has enough space – and remember, you'll want to add furniture, so leave space for that too!

Garden – use flowers, trees and colourful 1x1 plates to design your outdoor space

There are many different types of doors and windows. Will you stick to one style for your family house – or mix and match?

Real lawns aren't totally flat, so use a few plates to add depth

You could build a bigger yard, and add sheds, swings or even a swimming pool!

44

EASY ACCESS

Make each floor removable by lining the tops of the walls with tiles. Use just a few plates with exposed studs to hold the next level in place.

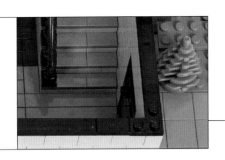

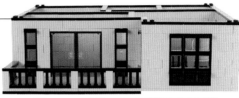

Inner walls built into outer walls for strength to support upper levels

EXPLODED VIEW

Choose where to place your staircase before finalising the room layout

Each row of roof tiles is supported by a layer of bricks underneath

Each floor is about seven or eight bricks high

Textured bricks add detail and decoration

Balcony railing made from barred fence

BRICKS IN THE WALL

If you don't have enough of one colour, build walls with stripes or other patterns. You could try to replicate the look of real bricks — or use crazy colours!

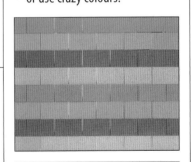

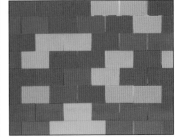

Front walkway, built with tiles. You could add a welcome mat too!

GROUND FLOOR

What does a minifigure family need? Take a look at real houses to decide what rooms and furniture you want. The ground floors of most houses have a front hall, dining room and kitchen, but maybe you want to build a playroom or den as well?

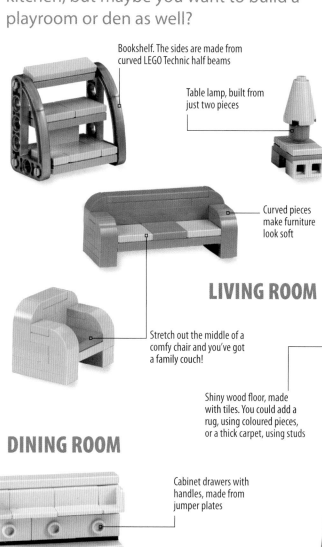

Bookshelf. The sides are made from curved LEGO Technic half beams

Table lamp, built from just two pieces

Curved pieces make furniture look soft

LIVING ROOM

Stretch out the middle of a comfy chair and you've got a family couch!

Shiny wood floor, made with tiles. You could add a rug, using coloured pieces, or a thick carpet, using studs

DINING ROOM

Cabinet drawers with handles, made from jumper plates

Make extra tile tablecloths for special occasions

Table legs made from telescopes

KITCHEN

THIS PLACE HAS EVERYTHING PLUS THE KITCHEN SINK!

Stove, built from a mailbox and two printed videotape tiles

FURNITURE

When building furniture, look at your pieces in new ways. Turn them around or upside-down and see if you can discover part of a chair, lamp or sofa. Remember to build your furniture to minifigure scale!

STAIRS

The stairs in this house use a long rubber piece for the handrail, supported by skeleton legs. If you don't have these pieces, you could use 1x1 bricks in alternating colours and 1x1 slopes.

TOP FLOOR

Every member of the family is an individual, so all the bedrooms in the house should be distinct too. Make each one show the interests and personality of whoever sleeps there. You could also put in a guest room, storage room or games room!

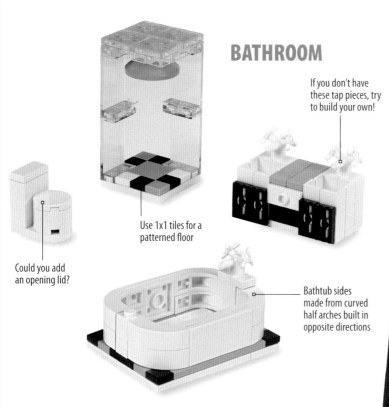

BATHROOM

If you don't have these tap pieces, try to build your own!

Use 1x1 tiles for a patterned floor

Could you add an opening lid?

Bathtub sides made from curved half arches built in opposite directions

TOP FLOOR FURNITURE

When you're building the same piece of furniture a few times, try to make each item unique. Experiment with sizes, colours and styles, and think about how a child's furniture is different from an adult's!

LAMPS

Modern floor lamp made with two radar dishes and an antenna

Crystal lamp base made with transparent plates

Master bedroom doors open out onto balcony

Long tiles create wooden plank effect

For stability, build the balcony directly into the floor of the top story

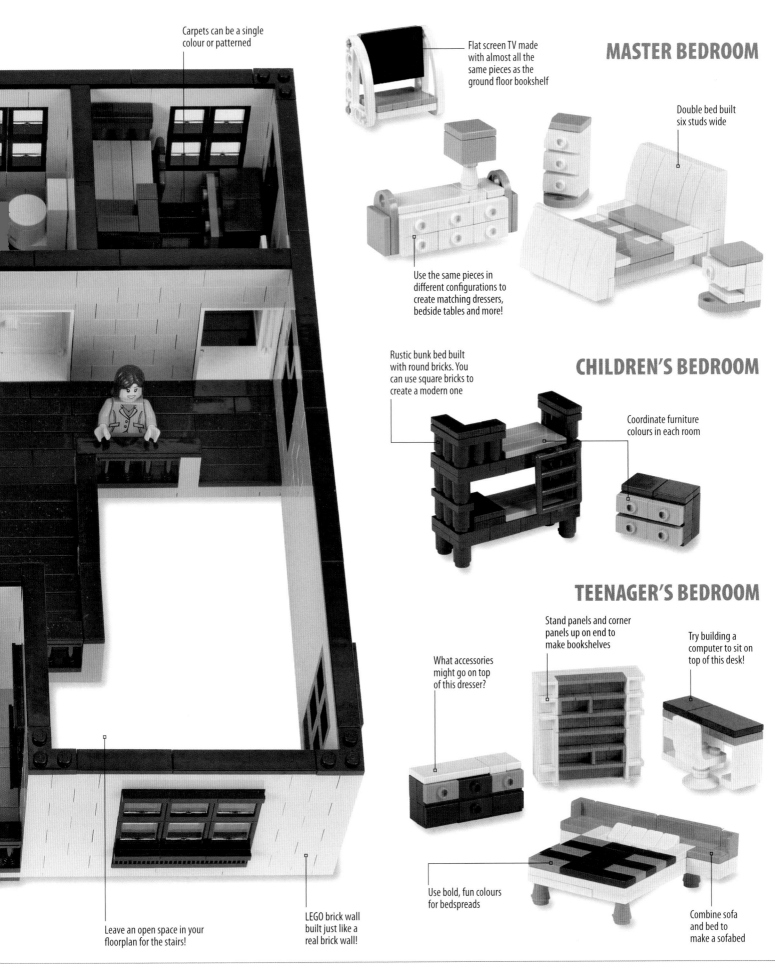

Carpets can be a single colour or patterned

Flat screen TV made with almost all the same pieces as the ground floor bookshelf

MASTER BEDROOM

Double bed built six studs wide

Use the same pieces in different configurations to create matching dressers, bedside tables and more!

Rustic bunk bed built with round bricks. You can use square bricks to create a modern one

CHILDREN'S BEDROOM

Coordinate furniture colours in each room

TEENAGER'S BEDROOM

Stand panels and corner panels up on end to make bookshelves

Try building a computer to sit on top of this desk!

What accessories might go on top of this dresser?

Use bold, fun colours for bedspreads

Leave an open space in your floorplan for the stairs!

LEGO brick wall built just like a real brick wall!

Combine sofa and bed to make a sofabed

MICROBUILDINGS

Want to build a whole town or city, but don't have much space? Try creating microbuildings! With just a handful of standard bricks, a few special pieces here and there and lots of imagination, you can build a landscape that is tiny, but hugely impressive!

LIGHT AND COLOUR

Use transparent plates to create the look of stained-glass windows. You may not be able to capture the intricate detail of the real thing, but the idea will shine through!

Simple colour scheme

Add details to break up plain facades

1x1 slopes look more in-scale than big roof pieces

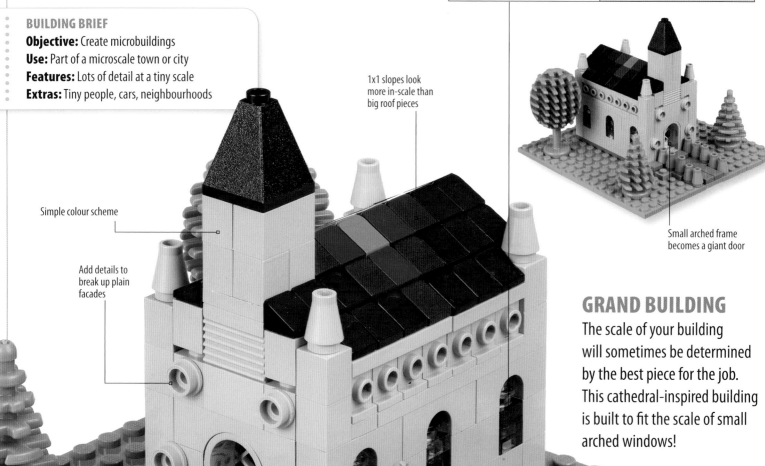

Small arched frame becomes a giant door

GRAND BUILDING

The scale of your building will sometimes be determined by the best piece for the job. This cathedral-inspired building is built to fit the scale of small arched windows!

1x1 green cones make great hedges and trees

RAISE THE ROOF

The building's roof is built up one row at a time using 1x1 slope pieces, arranged in a simple pattern. Each row is one plate higher than the last one.

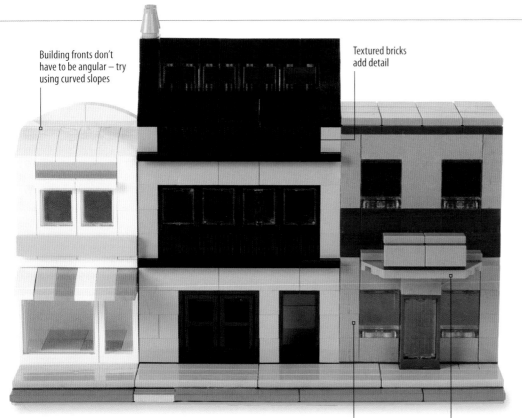

Building fronts don't have to be angular – try using curved slopes

Textured bricks add detail

CANAL HOUSE

Photographs can help you design locations from a particular time or place, like this Dutch canal house. Keep the proportions as close as possible to the real thing.

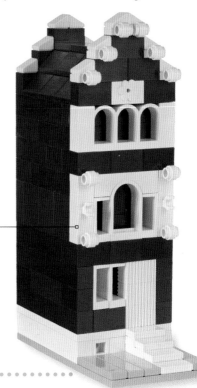

STREET STORES

For a row of buildings, start with a street base, made of plates and tiles. Create each building separately and then attach it to the base. Give each one its own distinct lines, like the green and orange store's curved roof.

Try to choose interesting colour combinations

Add awnings and overhangs to entrances

Building and trim have contrasting colours

Add simple decorative details, but don't overdo it

REAR VIEW

MICROHOUSE

Don't just build a boring box for your microscale house. Experiment with different shapes and pieces! Pick out your windows and doors first so you know how big to make the rest of the building around them.

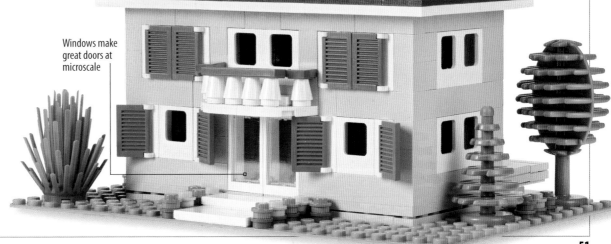

Same roof pieces as on big houses – just fewer of them!

Windows make great doors at microscale

TRAIN STATION

A train station is a functional building, but that doesn't mean it has to look boring! Try to design your station in an unusual shape, and give it some interesting features, like arched doorways, striking brickwork or a unique roof. You could even build a removable roof so you can access the interior for rebuilding and play.

BUILDING BRIEF
Objective: Build train stations
Use: A place for passengers to get tickets and wait for their trains
Features: Ticket desk, indoor and outdoor waiting areas
Extras: Trains, signal lights, signs, train tracks

Roof built in an elongated hexagonal shape

GETTING INTO SHAPE

Building a roof in an unusual shape can be tricky, so focus on this aspect of the model first. When the roof is complete, build the walls to fit.

I'M LATE! DO LEGO TRAINS RUN ON TIME?

ARCHES

Two half arches form the top of a fancy doorway, while a single half arch piece can be used to support part of the roof.

Elevate the main building on a platform to draw attention to it

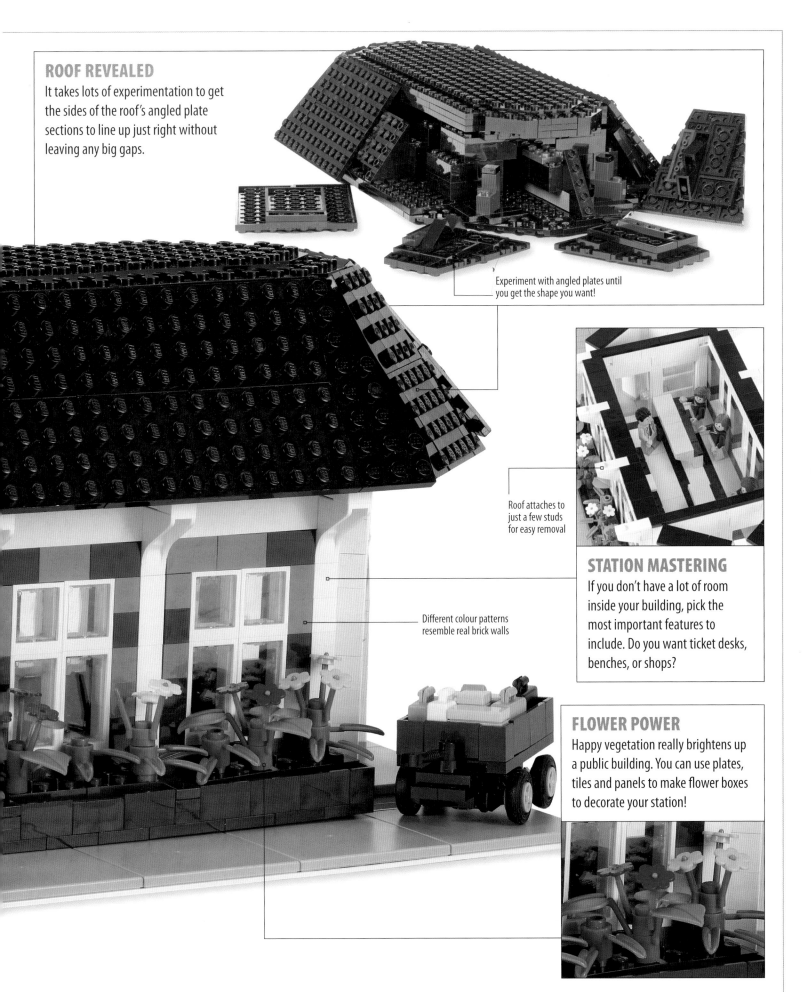

ROOF REVEALED

It takes lots of experimentation to get the sides of the roof's angled plate sections to line up just right without leaving any big gaps.

Experiment with angled plates until you get the shape you want!

Roof attaches to just a few studs for easy removal

Different colour patterns resemble real brick walls

STATION MASTERING

If you don't have a lot of room inside your building, pick the most important features to include. Do you want ticket desks, benches, or shops?

FLOWER POWER

Happy vegetation really brightens up a public building. You can use plates, tiles and panels to make flower boxes to decorate your station!

STATION BUILDINGS

It takes more than one building to make a train station! Look at real stations to get ideas about what else your scene could include. Each building should be different from the others, but perhaps you could incorporate common elements into each of them so they all fit together.

BUILDING BRIEF
Objective: Make more buildings for your train station
Use: Keeping the trains on schedule
Features: Matching colour schemes, useful station functions
Extras: A method of connecting the buildings together

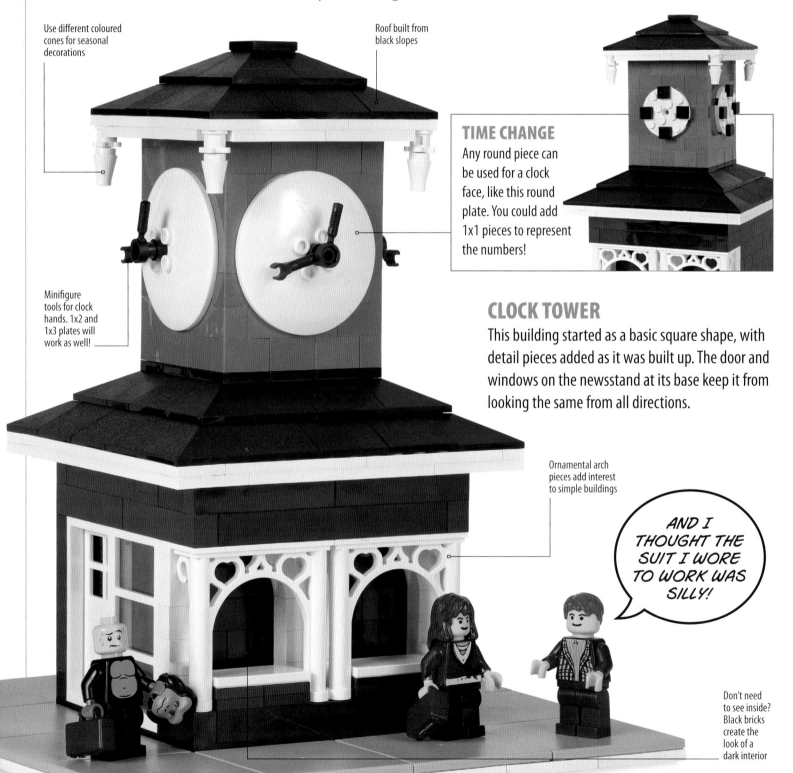

Use different coloured cones for seasonal decorations

Roof built from black slopes

TIME CHANGE

Any round piece can be used for a clock face, like this round plate. You could add 1x1 pieces to represent the numbers!

Minifigure tools for clock hands. 1x2 and 1x3 plates will work as well!

CLOCK TOWER

This building started as a basic square shape, with detail pieces added as it was built up. The door and windows on the newsstand at its base keep it from looking the same from all directions.

Ornamental arch pieces add interest to simple buildings

AND I THOUGHT THE SUIT I WORE TO WORK WAS SILLY!

Don't need to see inside? Black bricks create the look of a dark interior

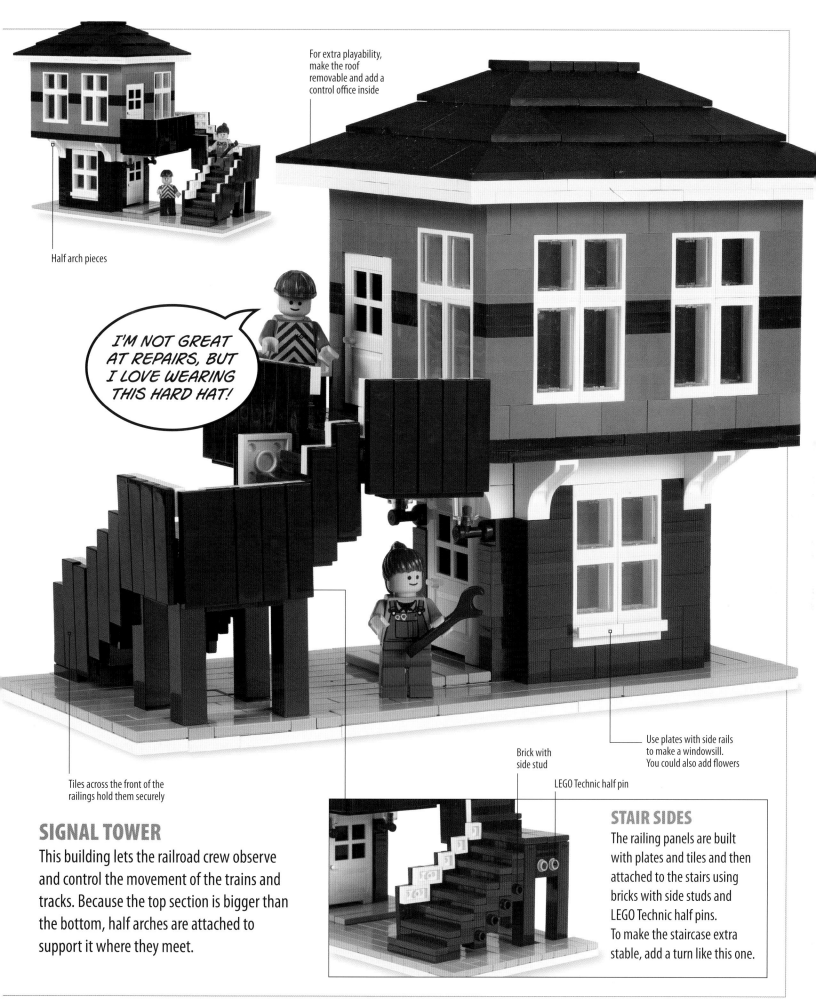

For extra playability, make the roof removable and add a control office inside

Half arch pieces

I'M NOT GREAT AT REPAIRS, BUT I LOVE WEARING THIS HARD HAT!

Tiles across the front of the railings hold them securely

Use plates with side rails to make a windowsill. You could also add flowers

Brick with side stud

LEGO Technic half pin

SIGNAL TOWER

This building lets the railroad crew observe and control the movement of the trains and tracks. Because the top section is bigger than the bottom, half arches are attached to support it where they meet.

STAIR SIDES

The railing panels are built with plates and tiles and then attached to the stairs using bricks with side studs and LEGO Technic half pins. To make the staircase extra stable, add a turn like this one.

INSIDE THE STATION

There are lots of great things you can build inside your train station, from rows of seats and departures desks, to check-in counters and x-ray scanning machines. You could also build waiting rooms, machines and ticket counters for a bus station – or even an airport. Now all you need to do is get your minifigures ready to travel!

DEPARTURES

This is the departure gate, where passengers hand over their tickets before boarding the train. The simple desk is made from red and white pieces, with no sideways building.

You could use transparent pieces to cover the studs and act as desk lights

BUT I CAN'T SIT NEXT TO HER – WE'RE WEARING THE SAME TORSO!

TICKET COUNTER

White bricks with tiles on top make this ticket counter look sleek and hi-tech. Computer screens are positioned at an angle on jumper plates, and the keyboards are attached with a clip and bar hinge so they can be positioned at an angle.

This ticket counter could also be an airport check-in desk!

You could build the computer desks in the colours of your railway company

Same-colour minifigure torsos look like uniforms

SORRY, BUT MY THREE INVISIBLE FRIENDS ARE SITTING HERE.

SITTING AROUND

Build your waiting area for as many passengers as you like. These red seats clip onto a 2x12 plate. The feet are 1x2 jumper plates with 1x1 round plates on top. Don't forget to add a small side table. Remember: it's all about the details!

2x2 tile used as tabletop

Jumper plates evenly spaced out

X-ray machine – grey tiles, small panels and cones make it look functional

SECURITY ALERT!

Security is an important feature in airports and some train and bus stations. Make sure your x-ray machine is the right size to scan LEGO luggage, and that the body scanner is tall enough for a minifigure – and his hat – to walk through!

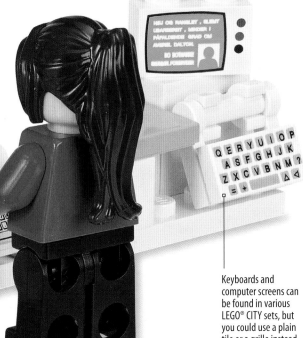

Keyboards and computer screens can be found in various LEGO® CITY sets, but you could use a plain tile or a grille instead

X-ray scanner, made from specialised angled pieces. A stack of 1x2 bricks with slopes on the top corners would work just as well

COUNTRY BARN

Want a break from the hustle and bustle of the big city? Head out to the countryside and build yourself a farm, starting with a good old-fashioned barn. Make it big and sturdy, with plenty of room for animals, crops and equipment inside. Farming life is hard work, but building it can be lots of fun!

BUILDING BRIEF

Objective: Build barns for your farms

Use: Storage of food, tools and livestock

Features: Opening doors, lots of space

Extras: Farming equipment, granary, farm animals

BARN RAISING

The roof is the trickiest part of this model, so build it first, leaving a narrow groove in the underside so it can slot securely onto the barn walls and be removed easily. Match the trim around the doors and windows to the colours of the roof.

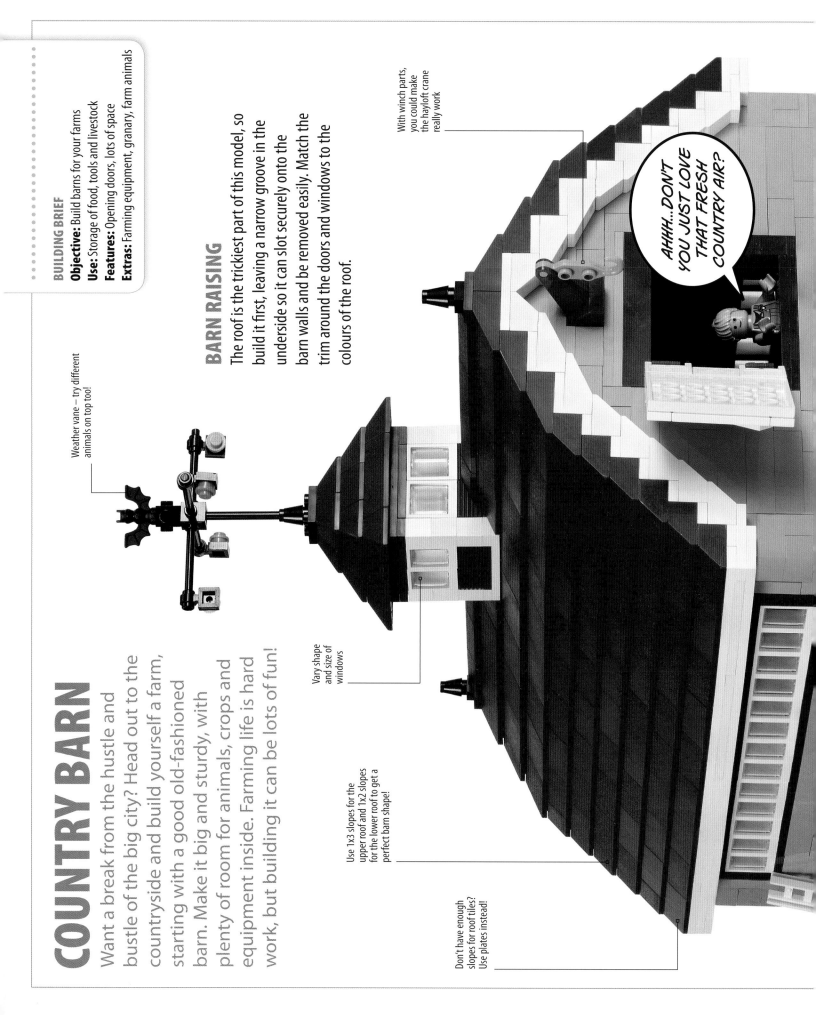

Weather vane — try different animals on top too!

With winch parts, you could make the hayloft crane really work

Vary shape and size of windows

Use 1x3 slopes for the upper roof and 1x2 slopes for the lower roof to get a perfect barn shape!

Don't have enough slopes for roof tiles? Use plates instead!

AHHH...DON'T YOU JUST LOVE THAT FRESH COUNTRY AIR?

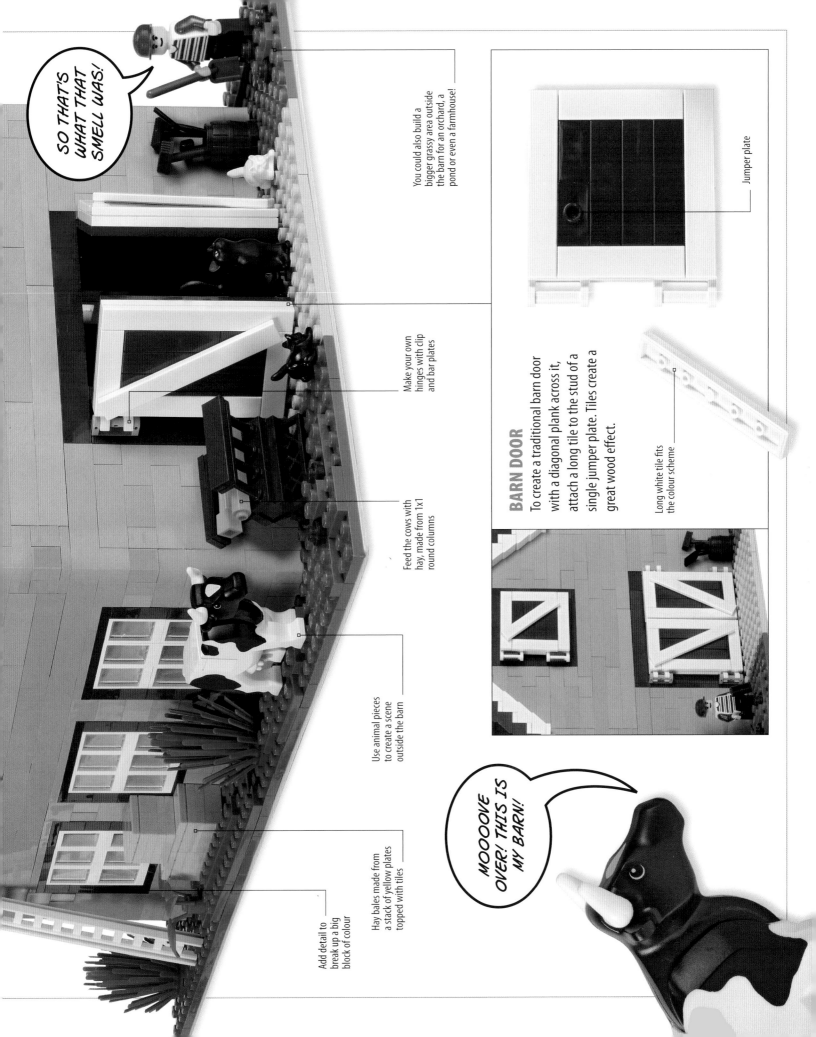

SO THAT'S WHAT THAT SMELL WAS!

You could also build a bigger grassy area outside the barn for an orchard, a pond or even a farmhouse!

Make your own hinges with clip and bar plates

Feed the cows with hay, made from 1x1 round columns

Use animal pieces to create a scene outside the barn

Hay bales made from a stack of yellow plates topped with tiles

Add detail to break up a big block of colour

Jumper plate

BARN DOOR

To create a traditional barn door with a diagonal plank across it, attach a long tile to the stud of a single jumper plate. Tiles create a great wood effect.

Long white tile fits the colour scheme

MOOOOVE OVER! THIS IS MY BARN!

FARMYARD LIFE

With the right bricks and pieces, you can create a whole farm for those hard-working minifigures. Think about what kind of farm you want to run – a dairy farm, an orchard, a ranch – and bring it to life!

BUILDING BRIEF

Objective: Build whole farms

Use: Milking, sowing, feeding, harvesting

Features: Coops, pens, orchards, natural surroundings

Extras: Tractor, field, stable, pen, farmer's house

Some duck houses are built on an island in the middle of a pond. Where will yours go?

COOL COVER

The angled roof of this duck house is made from large ramp pieces, which are built up and locked together with basic plates. You could even attach the roof with a clip and bar hinge so you can play inside!

HOLD ON? THIS IS NICER THAN MY HOUSE!

BRICK FOWL

If you don't have the right LEGO animal, make your own! This duck is made using a few simple colours and pieces, like clip-plate wings and a bill made from a 1x1 cone.

DUCK HOUSE

A duck house doesn't have to be a plain, white hut! Design an unusual roof, add lattice windows or build it on a raised platform so the ducks can wander underneath.

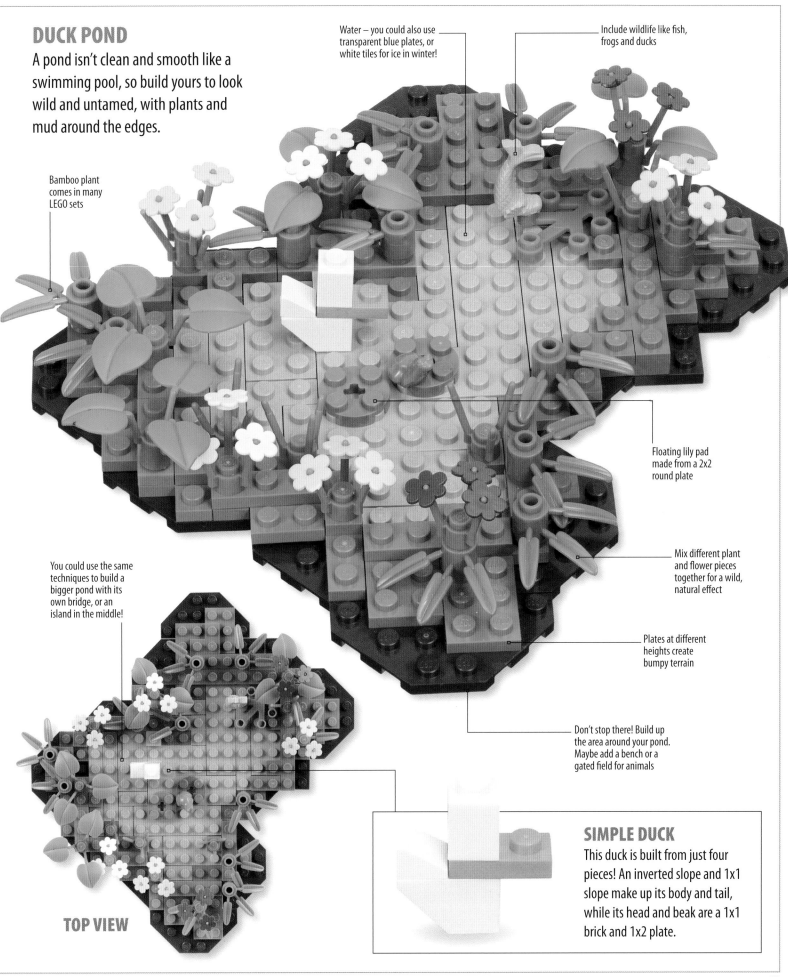

DUCK POND

A pond isn't clean and smooth like a swimming pool, so build yours to look wild and untamed, with plants and mud around the edges.

Water – you could also use transparent blue plates, or white tiles for ice in winter!

Include wildlife like fish, frogs and ducks

Bamboo plant comes in many LEGO sets

Floating lily pad made from a 2x2 round plate

You could use the same techniques to build a bigger pond with its own bridge, or an island in the middle!

Mix different plant and flower pieces together for a wild, natural effect

Plates at different heights create bumpy terrain

Don't stop there! Build up the area around your pond. Maybe add a bench or a gated field for animals

TOP VIEW

SIMPLE DUCK

This duck is built from just four pieces! An inverted slope and 1x1 slope make up its body and tail, while its head and beak are a 1x1 brick and 1x2 plate.

DOWN ON THE FARM

To bring your farm creations to life, think about the small details: What does a shed's roof really look like? How can you build a realistic gate? What fruit will be growing in your orchard? Don't stop until you're really happy with your model!

TIN ROOF

Long, grey plates with side-rails look like a sheet of corrugated metal when attached side-by-side.

Roof is attached to shed with a 1x6 jumper plate

A plate hung diagonally adds decoration

THAT'S A WHOLE LOTTA FARM TO WATER. I'LL NEED A BIGGER CAN.

TOOL SHED

To make your doors (or windows) look smaller than they are, build a doorway the size you want, then place the door behind it so it opens inwards.

DON'T HOG ALL THE FOOD HAMLET!

A clean, square fence on rough, uneven terrain makes a good visual contrast

PIGPEN

You don't want farm animals to run wild and eat your crops, so build some enclosures! Instead of a single-piece base, this sty has layers of plates to give its surface some depth.

Mud doesn't stay inside boundaries, so let it flow out past the fence

Gate made from lattice gate attached upside-down

BRICK FRUIT
If you don't have pieces of LEGO fruit, make your own! Round or square red bricks make great apples, or use yellow for lemons. Can you think of any other pieces to use?

You could add flowers to your trees too!

Palm tree segments come in many LEGO sets – or you could use round bricks

ORCHARD
You could build a well-tended orchard with rows of straight, matching trees – but your farm will look more natural if your tree trunks and branches are different shapes.

Build a strong, wide base to support a tall tree

Why not build a whole vegetable patch with rows of lettuces, carrots and tomatoes?

If it's autumn, your tree may have fewer leaves on it

Carrot growing out of the ground is really a 1x1 brick topped with a 2x2 plate!

2x2 round plate

EASY AS ONE, TWO, TREE
Building your own trees is easy! Stack round brown bricks or plates on a sturdy base for the trunk, then add plant leaves or any green pieces as leaves.

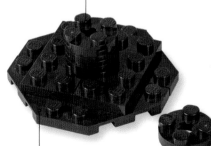

Use green plates if you want your tree to have a base of grass

BRIDGES

It's easy to snap some plates together and call it a bridge, but if you really want to cross a gap with style, try making a bridge that looks like the real thing – and works like it too. Here's a great way to build a gentle humpback bridge for a park or country river crossing.

BUILDING BRIEF
Objective: Build bridges
Use: Crossing streams, rivers and ditches
Features: Strength, stability, walls, railings
Extras: Cars, pedestrians, tollgates, nighttime lights

HUMPBACK BRIDGE

To build this picturesque bridge, start with a central arch. Make a solid base around the arch shape, building steps into it to create height. Then use slopes and tiles to create a smooth finish.

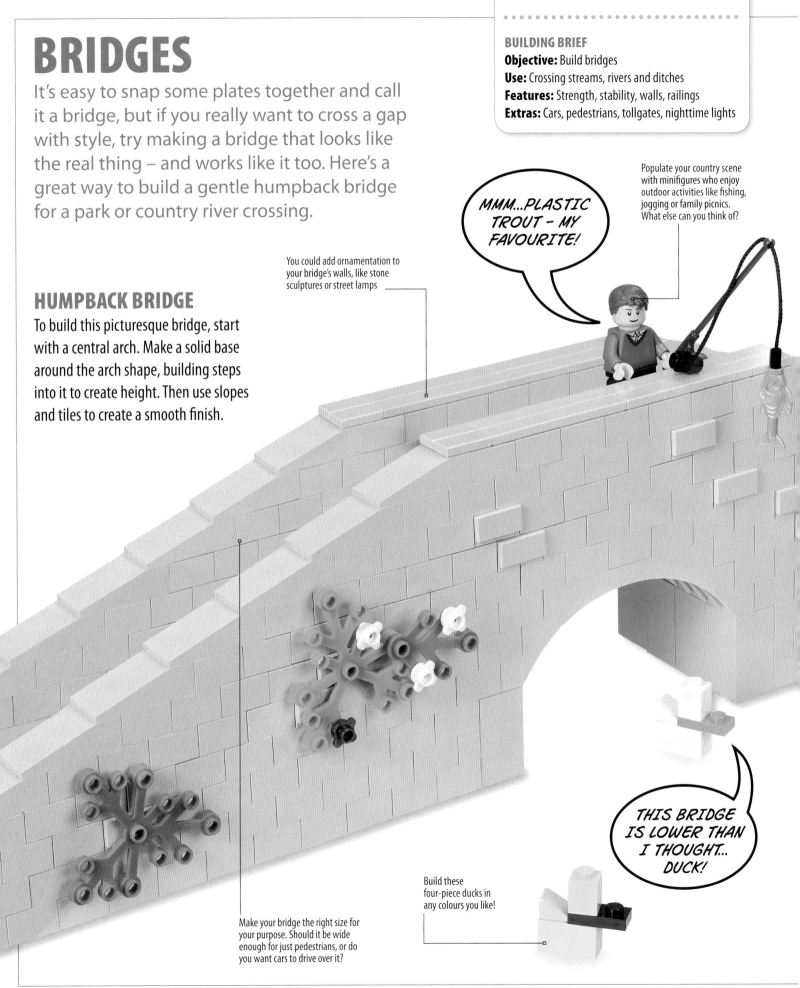

You could add ornamentation to your bridge's walls, like stone sculptures or street lamps

MMM...PLASTIC TROUT – MY FAVOURITE!

Populate your country scene with minifigures who enjoy outdoor activities like fishing, jogging or family picnics. What else can you think of?

THIS BRIDGE IS LOWER THAN I THOUGHT... DUCK!

Build these four-piece ducks in any colours you like!

Make your bridge the right size for your purpose. Should it be wide enough for just pedestrians, or do you want cars to drive over it?

MINI ARCH

The arch is built just like the ones on the big model, but with fewer bricks. Use smaller arch pieces for even tinier bridges.

MICROBRIDGE

You can build a bridge in microscale, too! Try to include all the key features of a bigger model, like arches, support columns, railings and a smooth pathway across.

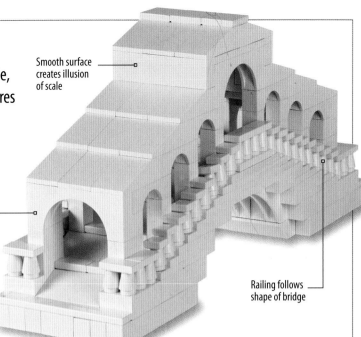

Smooth surface creates illusion of scale

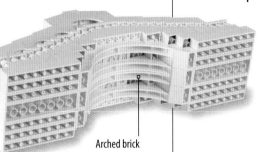

Arched brick

All-white bricks look like polished marble

Railing follows shape of bridge

Use slopes to make the walls follow a gentle curve. You could also use plates to build gradual steps

You could also make a base for your bridge to sit on. Build it up with grass, trees flowers and a river

Attach plant leaves and flowers to jumper plates built into the bridge walls

Your bridge doesn't have to be built out of tan bricks. Use brown pieces for a rustic wooden bridge, or grey for old stone

BULGING BRICKS

To make some of the stones bulge out from your wall, include headlight bricks among your 1x2 bricks and attach 1x2 tiles to them.

BIGGER BRIDGES

For larger spans of water, you need a bigger bridge! Large bridges usually have more arches to support their length and weight. They're made out of the strongest materials around, so use lots of grey bricks to mimic stone, or LEGO Technic elements for metal girders.

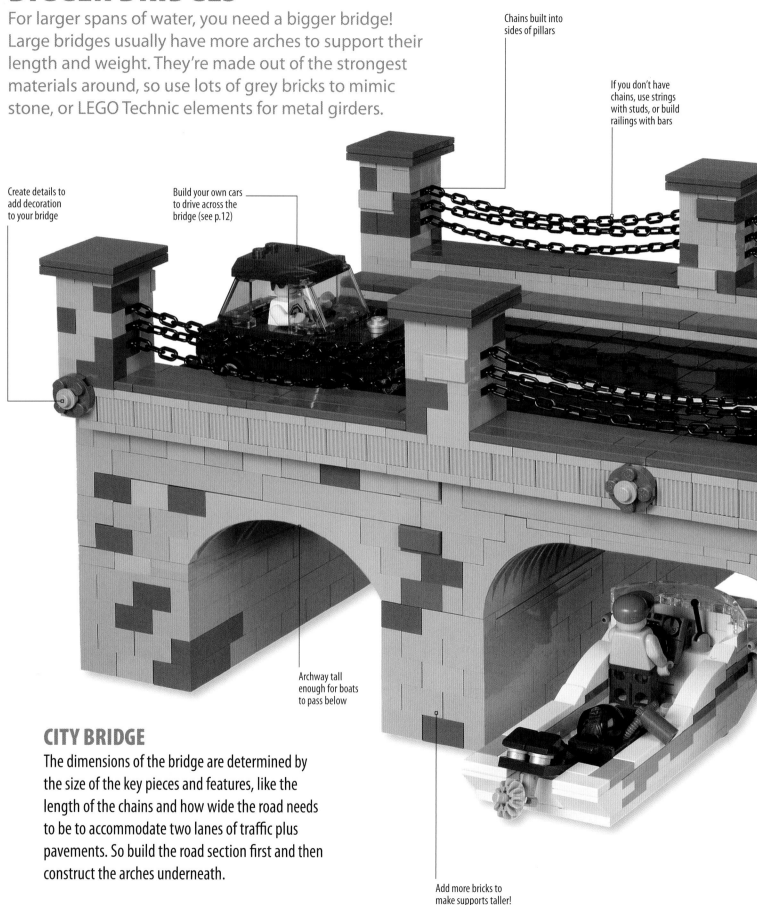

Chains built into sides of pillars

If you don't have chains, use strings with studs, or build railings with bars

Create details to add decoration to your bridge

Build your own cars to drive across the bridge (see p.12)

Archway tall enough for boats to pass below

CITY BRIDGE

The dimensions of the bridge are determined by the size of the key pieces and features, like the length of the chains and how wide the road needs to be to accommodate two lanes of traffic plus pavements. So build the road section first and then construct the arches underneath.

Add more bricks to make supports taller!

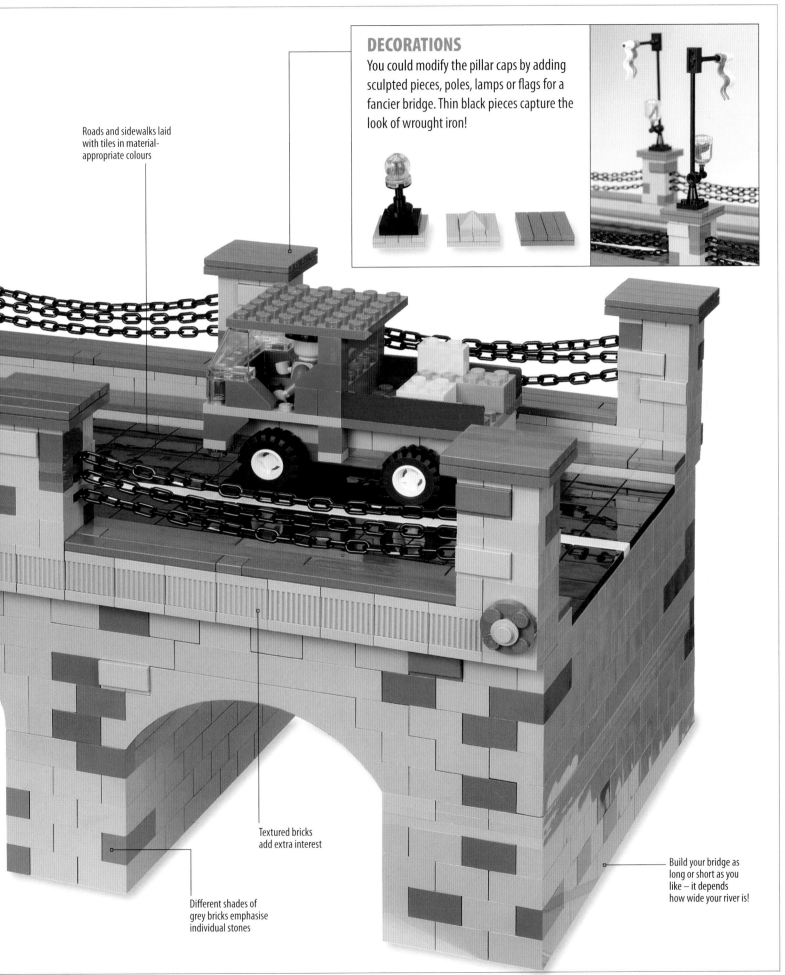

Roads and sidewalks laid with tiles in material-appropriate colours

DECORATIONS

You could modify the pillar caps by adding sculpted pieces, poles, lamps or flags for a fancier bridge. Thin black pieces capture the look of wrought iron!

Textured bricks add extra interest

Different shades of grey bricks emphasise individual stones

Build your bridge as long or short as you like – it depends how wide your river is!

MEET THE BUILDER

DEBORAH HIGDON

Location: Canada
Age: 52
LEGO Speciality: Architecture, furniture

Which model were you most proud of as a young LEGO builder?

I don't remember being particularly proud of one model, but I do remember building houses – I loved the roof pieces and the doors and windows. In a box of things from my childhood, I still have pieces of a large fireplace that I built for my dolls, with candlesticks and a hand-drawn fire. I didn't like playing with dolls as much as I liked building furniture and houses for them!

This is a model of some buildings in the French village of St Paul de Vence. It was my first MOC to win a big competition at a LEGO fan festival.

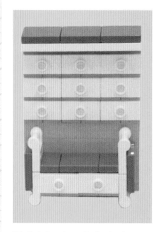

This little bench was built after I saw a picture of a real bench in a Dutch museum. I liked the style and colour and thought I could model it in LEGO bricks.

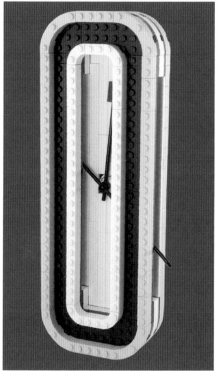

This MOC is based on a modern design I saw on the internet. I changed the colours and some parts of the design to make it work in LEGO bricks. And yes, it really does tell the time!

What is the biggest or most complex model you've made?

Mechanically, a sliding house was the most complex. It appeared to be a huge challenge but it was a simple solution in the end. I hid a motor in the "basement" and had the sliding roof of the house simply sit in a channel and be dragged along. At first, I thought of all kinds of complicated ways to get it to slide, but an AFOL (Adult Fan Of LEGO) friend and I talked about it, and he helped me come up with that simple solution. It doesn't always have to be complicated, sometimes we just think it does!

What is your favourite LEGO brick or piece?

That's really hard to choose but I think my favourite LEGO pieces are tiles. I wish they were all made in every colour, every size! I like them because they really help to make a smooth piece of furniture look almost real. They also help to add small details, which are important when modelling houses and furniture.

If you had all the LEGO bricks (and time!) in the world, what would you build?

I've got a lot of ideas in my head so I don't know where I'd start! On my list of MOCs (My Own Creations) to do, there's a minifigure scale Garden of Versailles in France with all the buildings, fountains and flower beds. I have also thought about a minifigure scale of a Greek fishing village in a mountain like the microscale one I made. But I'd need more than all the LEGO bricks and time in the world – I'd need a new house with an enormous LEGO room and the largest building table in the world!

What things have gone wrong and how have you dealt with them?

Things have fallen apart because I didn't build them strongly enough, especially when I have to travel with my MOCs. Occasionally, things fall on the floor and I have to rebuild them but sometimes I can't remember how I solved a particular problem so I have to rethink. I'm determined to make my ideas work. It takes a lot of patience and determination to rebuild, but it will always be worth it in the end. Often it turns out better than the original!

Another doorway from the series. I thought this could be the entrance to an old castle or manor house.

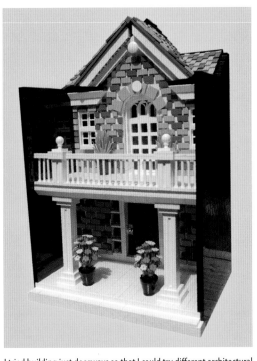

I tried building just doorways so that I could try different architectural styles without making the whole building. A grey stone doorway like this would be attached to a very big old stone house.

Microscale Rialto Bridge: this famous bridge crosses a canal in Venice, Italy. I wanted to build something like it and I wanted it to look like marble or very white stone, so I used just one colour

I LIKE LOOKING AT VERY ORIGINAL FURNITURE AND THINKING OF HOW I CAN MODEL IT.

What are some of your top LEGO tips?

I think it's important to just play with putting bricks together, not even building anything: two little pieces you put together can suddenly look a bit like something you've seen elsewhere and may give you a brilliant idea for a creation. Look for interesting ways to connect two pieces and find out what fits together. Another good idea is to look at a lot of pictures if you're going to build something in model or replica. Getting tricky bricks apart is much easier with two brick separators – that's an important tip for everyone!

What else do you enjoy making apart from houses/buildings?

I've started to build some small sculptures and useful items like LEGO bookends, a clock and a birdhouse. My first 3-D sculpture was a heart for Valentine's Day and I really enjoyed the challenge of forming the heart to get the curves just right.

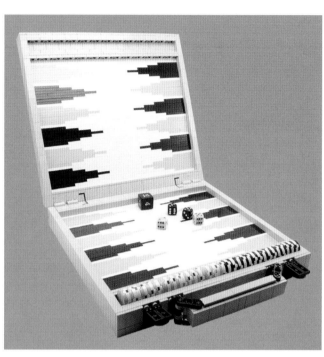

I was starting to build things that weren't houses and furniture so I thought I could start making useful things. I'd never seen a backgammon game made from LEGO pieces so I wanted it to be portable and playable, and it is.

How much time do you spend building?

When I'm in the middle of a project, full of ideas, I spend most evenings and weekends building, which is probably about 10–14 hours a week, sometimes more. At other times I don't build anything for weeks.

This model was built specially for this book. I looked carefully for pieces that could be the "hands" of the clock and I wanted the clock tower to look a little old-fashioned

Do you plan out your build? If so, how?

Only in my head! I think of one central feature of my new MOC (for example, the swimming pool, the main staircase or the roof line) and I'll build the rest of the model around it. I make up my mind as I go along. Sometimes, I'll quickly do a rough sketch of a small part of a building I've seen, then I think of other things I can add to that feature. Sometimes I take pictures to remind me of a nice staircase, porch or window I've seen that I'd like to try to replicate.

What is your favourite LEGO technique or technique you use the most?

I use a lot of hinges, especially the old finger hinges and I like to use LEGO Technic pieces to make interesting furniture. I also love to use a lot of SNOT (a LEGO fan term meaning Studs Not On Top).

What are you inspired by?

Mostly architecture and design – cool building ideas that I see in real life and I want to try to build in LEGO bricks. I like looking at very original furniture and thinking of how I can model it.

My LEGO club often has building challenges. So, for the Valentine's Day challenge I wanted to build something with dark red brick. I also wanted to try some 3-D shaping and a heart seemed a good shape to work with. I also wanted to add frilly lace and a way to curve the square edges so the tooth plates and hinges helped a lot.

This bookend is another useful MOC idea, something that anyone anywhere can enjoy and use. The "books" were fun to build and I printed the titles on clear sticker paper. The building has a little hiding spot for something special.

What is your favourite creation?

This changes all the time, especially after I've just finished a big creation. I think my most favourite will always be St Paul de Vence: I visited that town in France a long time ago. One day I decided to make some of the buildings there in LEGO bricks. There were about seven buildings and I built a walled platform for them, but because they were all separate, I could change the look just by moving the buildings around. Each separate building had a different challenge, which made it more fun to build.

How old were you when you started using LEGO bricks?

I was about seven or eight when I was first introduced to LEGO bricks. I stopped building, like many kids do, but I started again as an adult when I bought LEGO sets for my nieces and nephews. I really started buying and building for myself when I was 40. Then I found the online LEGO community, joined a local club for adults, and started to display publicly and post my work on the internet.

You're under attack! This spaceship seats a single minifigure and is great for engaging in fierce, close quarter space battles. (See p.82)

OUT OF THIS WORLD

Let's go intergalactic! But how will you get there?
You need a rocket, plus lots of cool spaceships,
moon buggies and other interplanetary vehicles.

STELLAR PIECES

To create spectacular space models, think about what sort of bricks you'll need. Curved pieces, moving parts, metallic details and antennas will give your models a sleek, space-age look. Here are some LEGO® pieces that may come in handy if you have them, but look through your own bricks and you're sure to find many more!

3x4 DOUBLE ANGLED PLATE

2x4 ANGLED PLATE

ALL ANGLES
Angled plates and slopes are great for building wings or giving your model a streamlined shape!

2x2 ROUND TILE

2x2 SLIDE PLATE

2x2 RADAR DISH

2x3 SLOPE

2x3 PLATE WITH WINGED END

1x2 JUMPER PLATE

1x2/2x2 ANGLE PLATE

STUDWAYS
Pieces with studs facing in more than one direction can help hold different sections of your model together.

1x2 INVERTED SLOPE

1x3 CURVED SLOPE

2x2 ROUND BRICK

2x2 ROUND TILE

LIGHTBULB

LIGHTSABER HILT

2x2 DETAILED CURVED SLOPE

1x4 BRICK WITH SIDE STUDS

1x3x2 CURVED HALF ARCH

2x2 CURVED BRICK WITH TOP STUDS

2x2 PRINTED SLOPE

1x2 PRINTED TILE

3x3x6 ENGINE

LEGO® TECHNIC PIN WITH BAR EXTENSION

1x1 CONE

1x1 TOOTH PLATE

1x1 HEADLIGHT BRICK

1x1 PLATE WITH SIDE RING

1x1 PLATE WITH VERTICAL CLIP

JOYSTICK

1x2 BRICK WITH 2 PINS

1x2 BRICK WITH SIDE STUDS AND STAND

LEGO TECHNIC BEAM WITH STICK

BIG BRICKS
A single large piece, such as this engine (above) can become the main body of a microbuild. (See Butterfly Shuttle, p.86)

ANTENNA

SMALL DETAILS
Add detail to your spaceship cockpit control panel with small parts.

2x2 TURNTABLE

HINGED PLATES

1x1 PLATE WITH HORIZONTAL CLIP

1x2 PLATE WITH HANDLED BAR

LOUDHAILER

1x1 SLOPE

BALL JOINT SOCKET

2x2 BRICK WITH BALL JOINT

STEERING WHEEL

ROBOT ARM

HANDLEBARS

1x1 SLOPE

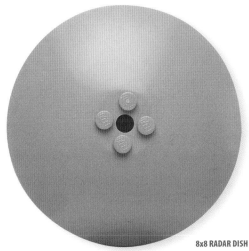

8x8 RADAR DISH

1x4 TILE

NEW IDEAS
If a piece makes you think of an idea for a specific vehicle, get building! This orange radar dish makes a great flying saucer. (See Flying Saucer, p.87)

WING-SHAPING
Mix long and short plates until your wings are the exact shape you want.

6x10x2 WINDSCREEN

3x12 ANGLED PLATE

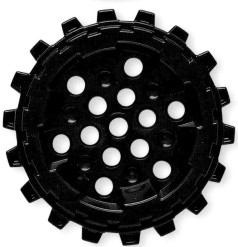

SPIKED WHEEL

2x4 PLATE WITH SIDE VENTS

1x2x3 WALL ELEMENT

CHOOSE AN UNUSUAL WINDSCREEN FOR YOUR COCKPIT AS A STARTING POINT

6x4x2 COCKPIT

INSPIRING PARTS
Large or unusually shaped pieces, like a spiked wheel (above) or curved arch brick (below), can help you come up with a design for your model. (See Rocket, pp.96–97)

GOING GREEN
Once you've chosen a windscreen, you could build the rest of the model to match. (See Nova Nemesis, p.85)

FLAG

1x4 HANDLE

1x2 GRILLE SLOPE

1x2 GRILLE

1x2 GRILLE

1x2 GRILLE

1x2 PLATE

AERIAL

1x2x2 LADDER

2x2 RUDDER

INNOVATION
Some pieces are obviously perfect for spaceships, such as turbines, antennas or aerials, but many other pieces can be adapted and work just as well!

8x8x2 CURVED ARCH BRICK

1x2 PLATE WITH JET ENGINE

2x2 PLATE WITH TURBINE

HOVER SCOOTER

When exploring alien worlds, your minifigure might need a small vehicle. But before you get building, ask yourself some simple questions. How will your vehicle travel? Does it roll on wheels, blast around with boosters or zoom along on jet-powered sleds? What do you want your vehicle to do? It could explore space, build a space base...or even deliver pizza to a hungry rocket crew. Anything is possible!

BUILDING BRIEF
Objective: Create space vehicles
Use: Exploration, transportation
Features: Must be able to hover
Extras: Radar, other comm devices

KEEPIN' IT SMOOTH
If you have any curved pieces, try using them to give the front of your vehicle a sleek, aerodynamic profile. Contrasting colours look space-age and striking, especially red and black!

Transparent radar dish could be swapped for a flag or a lightbulb

Thrusters mounted on the underside – you could replace with wheels, or leave the underside flat

I WONDER IF I SHOULD HAVE ADDED SEAT BELTS!

FRONT VIEW

Grille piece creates a hi-tech look. Can be swapped for a tile

OFF THE GROUND

This single-person hover scooter has an open cockpit at the front and a rear boot for storage. The two sections are made separately, then slotted together. You may not have curved pieces for the front, but think of it like the front of a car and get creative!

Joystick allows minifigure pilot to steer the vehicle

SAFE STORAGE

Hinges are very useful pieces. On vehicles, you can use them to allow doors to open, wings to tilt upwards or downwards or, as here, a trunk to open. Now just add your intergalactic cargo!

Don't have LEGO pizzas? Fill the trunk with tools, spare parts or moon rocks

GUARANTEED DELIVERY IN 30 LIGHT-YEARS OR LESS!

Small rocket booster – or you could use this piece as a clip for wings

Red lights made from round transparent plates. Or you could use 1x1 cones or plates

NO STUDS IN SPACE

Using bricks with side studs or angle plates, you can build a section like this red side panel. Attach it sideways so none of the brick studs stick out.

You don't have to use a space-themed minifigure. Alien planets could have breathable atmospheres like Earth

REAR VIEW

SPACE WALKERS

Once you've arrived on a distant planet, your minifigures will want to explore! A walker is the perfect vehicle to scale alien terrain. Remember to build a stable, balanced walker: make sure the cockpit is not too big and heavy for the legs to support it.

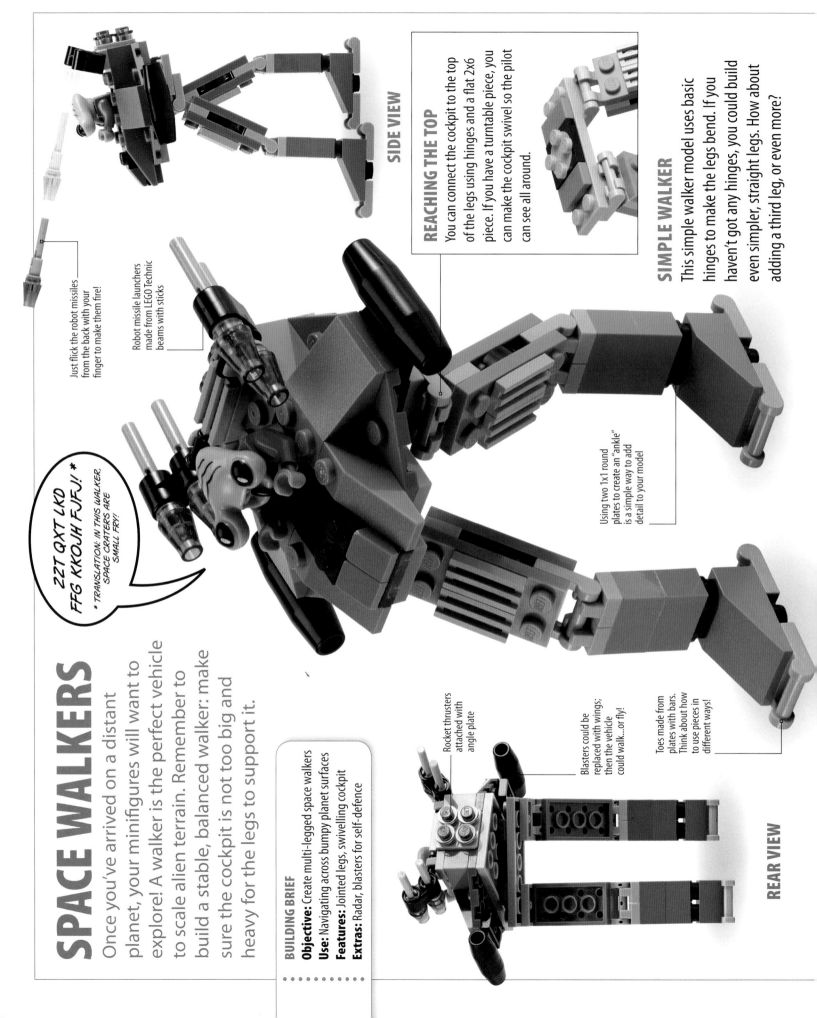

*ZZT QXT LKD FFG KKOJH FJFJ! *

* TRANSLATION: IN THIS WALKER, SPACE CRATERS ARE SMALL FRY!

Just flick the robot missiles from the back with your finger to make them fire!

Robot missile launchers made from LEGO Technic beams with sticks

SIDE VIEW

REACHING THE TOP

You can connect the cockpit to the top of the legs using hinges and a flat 2x6 piece. If you have a turntable piece, you can make the cockpit swivel so the pilot can see all around.

SIMPLE WALKER

This simple walker model uses basic hinges to make the legs bend. If you haven't got any hinges, you could build even simpler, straight legs. How about adding a third leg, or even more?

Using two 1x1 round plates to create an "ankle" is a simple way to add detail to your model

BUILDING BRIEF

Objective: Create multi-legged space walkers
Use: Navigating across bumpy planet surfaces
Features: Jointed legs, swivelling cockpit
Extras: Radar, blasters for self-defence

Rocket thrusters attached with angle plate

Blasters could be replaced with wings; then the vehicle could walk...or fly!

Toes made from plates with bars. Think about how to use pieces in different ways!

REAR VIEW

ADVANCED WALKER

With more practise and pieces, you can build a walker with extra flexibility and details. Remember, the cockpit can be as simple or as complicated as you like, just so long as your minifigure can sit in it. Adding details, such as antennas, weapons, steering and control panels, is the really fun bit!

Antennas are useful. Be creative – these ones are made from harpoon guns!

RACE YOU TO THE NEAREST LUNAR COLONY!

Blaster tips built from green transparent cones. Or you could use 1x1 round transparent pieces, radar dishes or even loudhailer pieces!

Ball-and-socket joints help shape your walker's legs

Bars, antennas and even screwdrivers can become rockets and blasters

Control panel made with a printed tile. A plain tile would work well too

TOP VIEW

Some leg positions work better than others. See what's best for your model

REAR VIEW

Headlight brick

BEST FOOT FORWARD

Look how easily you can make a cool foot with toes (for extra stability on rocky planet surfaces). 1x1 slopes form the toes, and they clip onto headlight bricks.

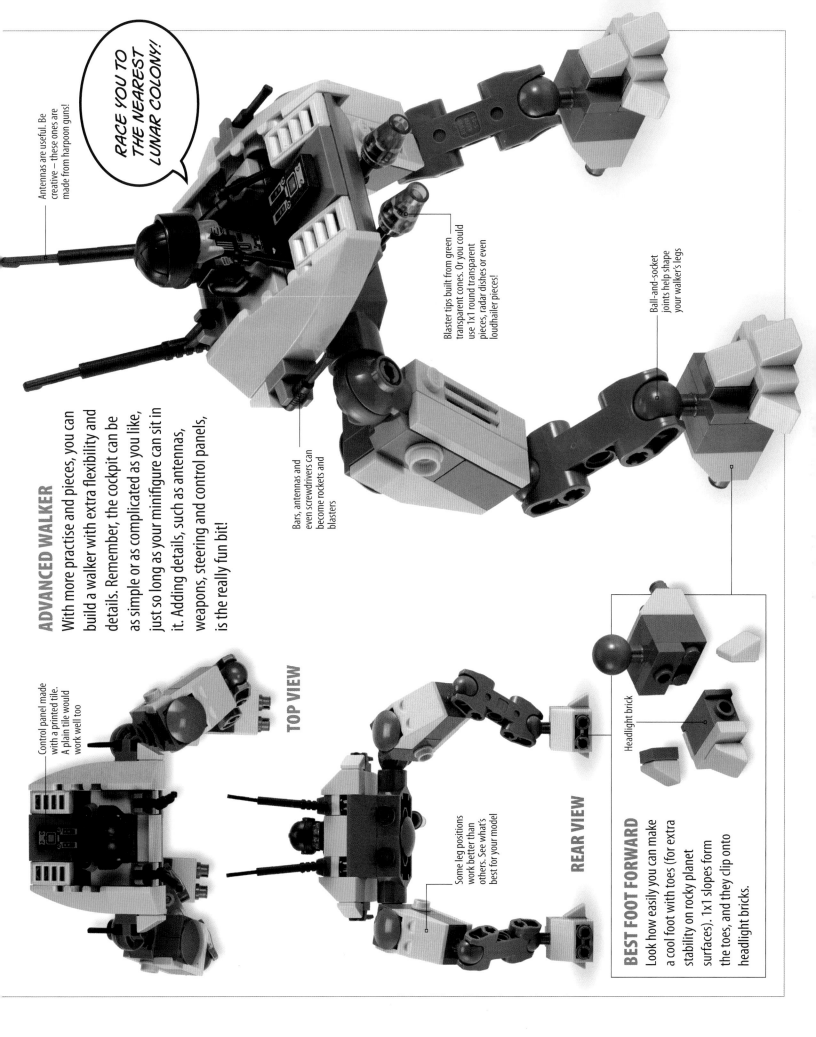

SPACEFIGHTER

When building a spacefighter, you could start with a single-minifigure cockpit, big pointed wings, multiple rear engines and big blasters pointing forward for high-speed space duels. Look to your favourite movies or TV shows for inspiration – but don't stop there! Use your imagination to make your model unique and inventive.

BUILDING BRIEF
Objective: Build spacefighters
Use: Intergalactic battles, chases
Features: Lightweight with plenty of speed and firepower
Extras: Force field generators, life-pods, hyperspeed engines

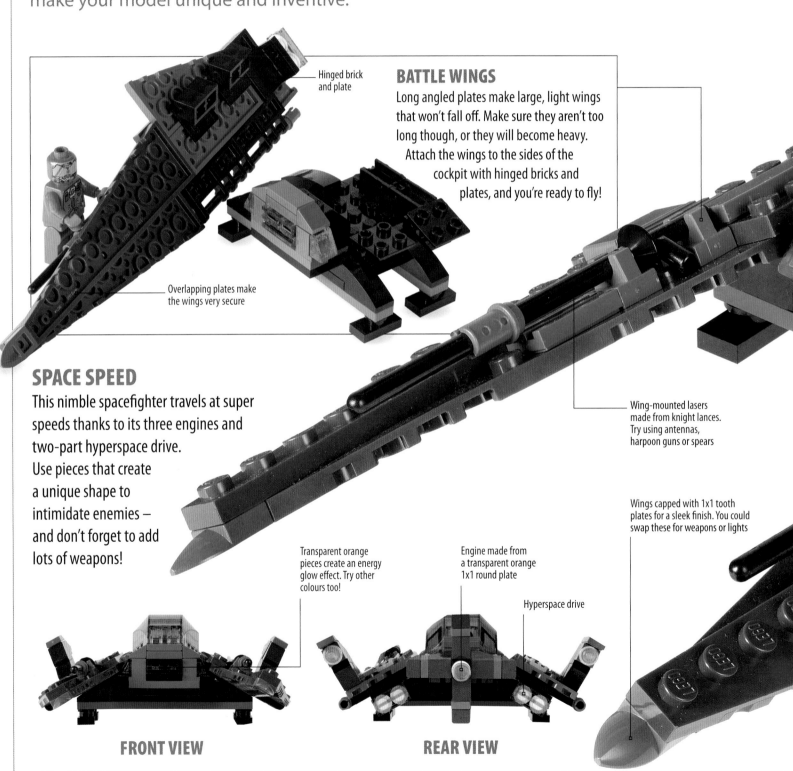

Hinged brick and plate

BATTLE WINGS

Long angled plates make large, light wings that won't fall off. Make sure they aren't too long though, or they will become heavy. Attach the wings to the sides of the cockpit with hinged bricks and plates, and you're ready to fly!

Overlapping plates make the wings very secure

SPACE SPEED

This nimble spacefighter travels at super speeds thanks to its three engines and two-part hyperspace drive. Use pieces that create a unique shape to intimidate enemies – and don't forget to add lots of weapons!

Wing-mounted lasers made from knight lances. Try using antennas, harpoon guns or spears

Wings capped with 1x1 tooth plates for a sleek finish. You could swap these for weapons or lights

Transparent orange pieces create an energy glow effect. Try other colours too!

Engine made from a transparent orange 1x1 round plate

Hyperspace drive

FRONT VIEW

REAR VIEW

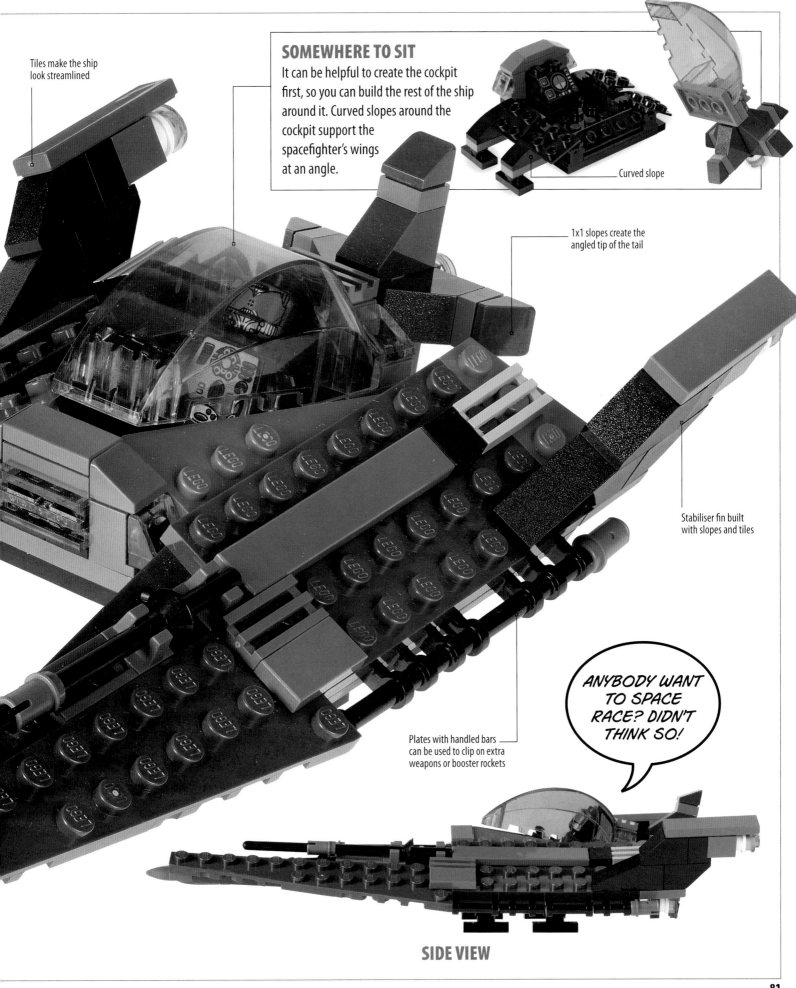

Tiles make the ship
look streamlined

SOMEWHERE TO SIT

It can be helpful to create the cockpit
first, so you can build the rest of the ship
around it. Curved slopes around the
cockpit support the
spacefighter's wings
at an angle.

Curved slope

1x1 slopes create the
angled tip of the tail

Stabiliser fin built
with slopes and tiles

Plates with handled bars
can be used to clip on extra
weapons or booster rockets

*ANYBODY WANT
TO SPACE
RACE? DIDN'T
THINK SO!*

SIDE VIEW

81

SMALL SPACESHIPS

All you need is a cockpit, some wings and an engine or two, and you can build a small spaceship that's the perfect size for some serious outer-space adventure. Try to find pieces with unusual shapes to complete your build – and remember, there are no rules about what a spaceship should look like! Here are some ideas to get you started.

BUILDING BRIEF
Objective: Create small spaceships
Use: Space travel, adventure
Features: Lasers, tailfins, pilot controls
Types: Spacefighters, scouts, escape pods, racing ships

ADMIRAL'S INTERCEPTOR

The admiral flies his sleek interceptor into a space battle. The base of the ship is built with the studs facing upward, but the wings are built sideways, with the studs concealed. Landing skids, weapons and a control pad add detail to the ship.

Choose a piece with an unusual shape to make a fancy tailfin

Curved slopes at the front lend a sleek and speedy look

Angled plates make the spaceship's outline look streamlined

You could add extra pieces to the tip to make a more powerful laser

Racing stripes made by placing plates between bricks of a contrasting colour

ALTERNATIVE INTERCEPTOR

This simpler version of the interceptor has wings built with the studs facing up.

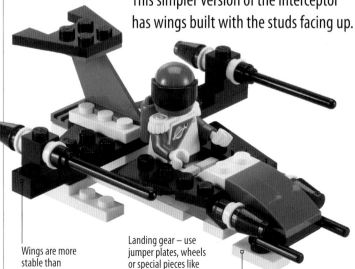

Wings are more stable than sideways-built wings

Landing gear – use jumper plates, wheels or special pieces like minifigure skis

WINGING IT

To create smooth-looking wings, build two small stacks and turn them on their sides. Attach them to the core of the ship with angle plates. Use sloped or curved bricks to give your wings an exciting shape!

1x2/1x4 angle plate

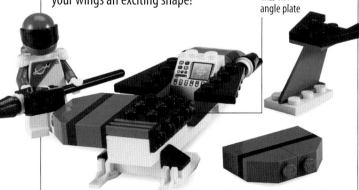

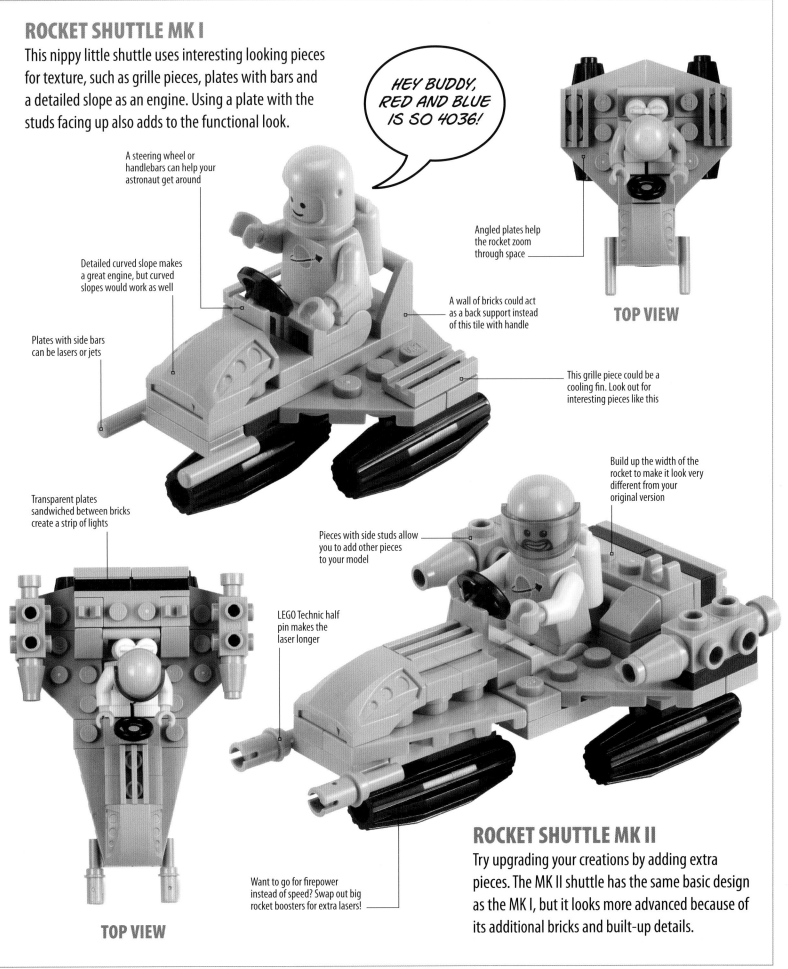

ROCKET SHUTTLE MK I

This nippy little shuttle uses interesting looking pieces for texture, such as grille pieces, plates with bars and a detailed slope as an engine. Using a plate with the studs facing up also adds to the functional look.

HEY BUDDY, RED AND BLUE IS SO 4036!

A steering wheel or handlebars can help your astronaut get around

Detailed curved slope makes a great engine, but curved slopes would work as well

Plates with side bars can be lasers or jets

Angled plates help the rocket zoom through space

TOP VIEW

A wall of bricks could act as a back support instead of this tile with handle

This grille piece could be a cooling fin. Look out for interesting pieces like this

Transparent plates sandwiched between bricks create a strip of lights

Build up the width of the rocket to make it look very different from your original version

Pieces with side studs allow you to add other pieces to your model

LEGO Technic half pin makes the laser longer

ROCKET SHUTTLE MK II

Try upgrading your creations by adding extra pieces. The MK II shuttle has the same basic design as the MK I, but it looks more advanced because of its additional bricks and built-up details.

Want to go for firepower instead of speed? Swap out big rocket boosters for extra lasers!

TOP VIEW

MORE SMALL SPACESHIPS

There are so many ways to build small space vehicles. You could try grabbing a random handful of pieces and seeing what you can make. You might be amazed! Or look around you at the shapes of everyday objects. They could inspire your creations. Now, get building!

Base made of plates

Headlight brick

SEPARATE SIDES

The sides are built separately and attached side-on to two headlight bricks on each side of the ship body.

> *I LOVE FEELING THE SOLAR WIND BLOWING MY TENTACLES!*

PURPLE PATROLLER

Guess what inspired this small patroller vehicle? A highlighter! The ship is built around a 2x8 plate with purple curved pieces for sides. The highlighter tip could be a sensor device – or maybe it emits a glowing beam!

These purple grilles make great engine cooling vents

1x2 brick with side studs

Front is made from black and green plates and slopes, and attached side-on to a brick with side studs

Even aliens need to get around!

Blue transparent piece peeps through the grille

Side details made from a 1x2 jumper plate and two black 1x1 round plates

Front lights created with a 2x3 curved plate with hole, behind which is a blue transparent piece

Joystick controls, but you could use a steering wheel or handlebars

Exhaust vent made from a transparent 1x2 grille attached side-on to two headlight bricks at the rear

REAR VIEW

SIDE VIEW

SIDE VIEW

NOVA NEMESIS

This sinister stealth ship is built around a really cool cockpit windscreen piece, with the cockpit and body of the ship designed to match. Use curved or sloping pieces to give your spaceship an interesting shape – and remember to leave enough room in the cockpit for a minifigure and the pilot controls!

Make sure the accessories you add are not too heavy either

SIDEWAYS ADVICE

If you're building a section that attaches sideways, don't make it too big or heavy. Without interlocking for extra stability, the link can't hold as much weight.

This 1x4 brick with side studs allows the wing section to be attached

Wing section

These wings are specialised pieces. Just hunt through your bricks for some cool pieces for wings

Windscreens come in many shapes, sizes and colours. Whichever one you choose will influence the ship you create!

For a sinister look, build your spaceship in dark tones like grey and black

Blaster focusing dish made from two radar dishes

Photon lasers made using transparent cones. They almost look like they are glowing!

Twin turbines propel the ship. These specialised pieces simply clip onto the top of the ship

Pins join the back section to the front

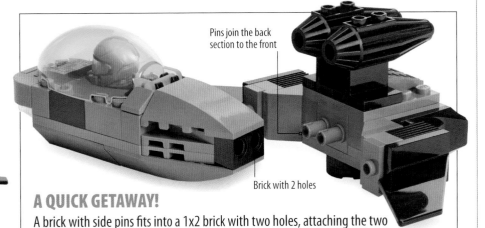

Brick with 2 holes

FRONT VIEW

A QUICK GETAWAY!

A brick with side pins fits into a 1x2 brick with two holes, attaching the two sections together. You could also use these pieces for detachable parts like escape pods!

MICROSHIPS

You may not have a lot of bricks to build with. Or perhaps the space model you want to make would be too complicated at minifigure scale. Or maybe you want a whole fleet of ships for a big space battle. Why not try microbuilding? It is exactly like regular minifigure-scale building but on a smaller scale, and you can assemble some of the coolest – and smallest – spaceships around!

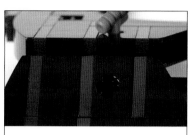

BUILDING WITH HOLES
You'll find that some pieces have holes in them, such as this 1x2 brick with cross axle hole. They are just the right size to grip blasters, antennas and other accessories.

BUILDING BRIEF
Objective: Build microscale spaceships
Use: Everything a big spaceship does...only smaller!
Features: Must have recognisable spaceship features
Extras: Escort fighters, motherships, space bases

Radio antennas built from accessories like harpoon guns or telescopes

Use antennas, lances or blasters as weapons

Hinged plates

Microcockpit – use transparent pieces, solid sloped pieces or even two contrasting 1x1 pieces

Laser weapons – neon transparent pieces look hi-tech

BUTTERFLY SHUTTLE
The wings and body of this microship were built separately, then attached together. The wings are connected to each other with hinged plates, allowing you to fold them at any angle you choose before clipping them onto the main body.

In microscale, a single engine piece can become an entire spaceship body

Lights match the cockpit windscreen here – but they can be any colour!

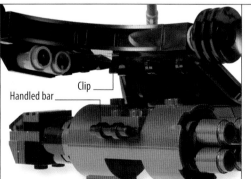

Handled bar

Clip

CLIP-ON WINGS
The wings are built with clips on the underside. These snap onto bars sticking out of the side of the ship's body. It can be tricky to attach the wings, but once they are in place they will look like they are floating!

SIDE VIEW

SPACE HAULER

This Space Hauler transports heavy freight across the galaxy. Round barrels full of cargo clip onto the main body of the hauler. The barrels have been unloaded and replaced so many times, it's no wonder they don't match!

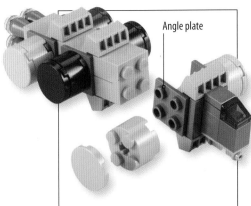

Angle plate

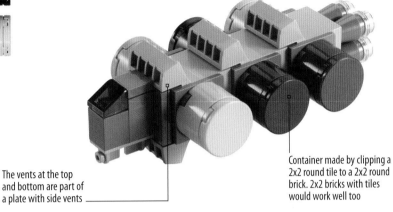

TOP VIEW

The vents at the top and bottom are part of a plate with side vents

Container made by clipping a 2x2 round tile to a 2x2 round brick. 2x2 bricks with tiles would work well too

CARGO COLUMN

The core of the Space Hauler is a simple column of bricks and plates turned on its side. Angle plates form attachment points for the cargo containers.

Brick with side studs

INNER WORKINGS

A simple exterior can conceal clever building techniques inside. Here, bricks with side studs support the white curved slopes, and LEGO Technic half pins hold the top and bottom dishes together.

A group of identical flying saucers with different-coloured parts could be a microscale invasion fleet!

FLYING SAUCER

Sometimes you have a piece that you just know would look great as part of a microship. The design of this classic UFO is inspired by a pair of big, orange radar dishes.

Flight wing made from two flag pieces. Rudder pieces would give a similar effect

Central ring, made of curved slopes attached together to form a circle

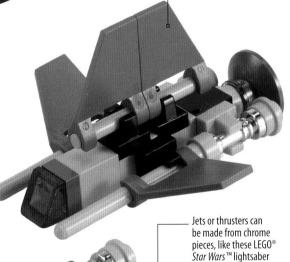

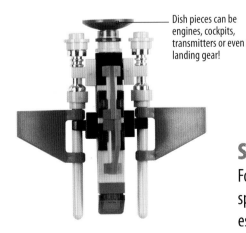

Dish pieces can be engines, cockpits, transmitters or even landing gear!

TOP VIEW

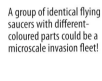

SHUTTLE AND ESCORTS

For an extra challenge, build a microscale spaceship and then make some even tinier escort vehicles with matching designs to protect it on its interstellar missions!

Jets or thrusters can be made from chrome pieces, like these LEGO® Star Wars™ lightsaber hilts

MORE MICROSHIPS

The design of your microship should say as much as possible about its purpose and function. Is your mission one of peaceful exploration? Galactic adventure? Combat and conquest? Think carefully about which pieces will best tell the story – because it only takes a few bricks to build a whole ship!

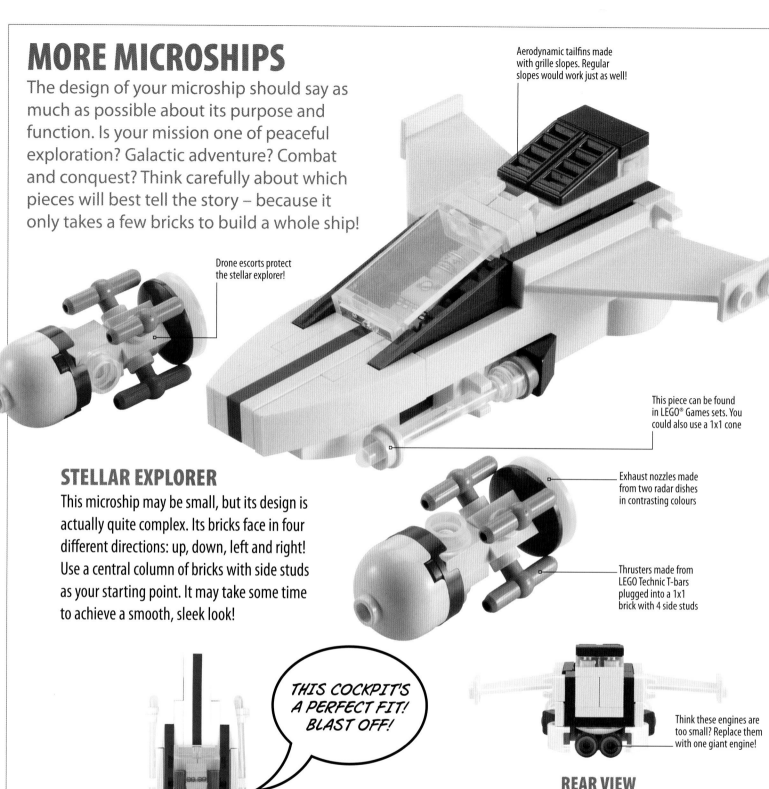

Aerodynamic tailfins made with grille slopes. Regular slopes would work just as well!

Drone escorts protect the stellar explorer!

This piece can be found in LEGO® Games sets. You could also use a 1x1 cone

STELLAR EXPLORER

This microship may be small, but its design is actually quite complex. Its bricks face in four different directions: up, down, left and right! Use a central column of bricks with side studs as your starting point. It may take some time to achieve a smooth, sleek look!

Exhaust nozzles made from two radar dishes in contrasting colours

Thrusters made from LEGO Technic T-bars plugged into a 1x1 brick with 4 side studs

THIS COCKPIT'S A PERFECT FIT! BLAST OFF!

Windscreen attached to the tail by a clip and bar hinge, so it can open and close

Rudder piece is a good size for a microship wing. You could also use flag pieces, or build wings of different shapes!

Think these engines are too small? Replace them with one giant engine!

REAR VIEW

Cockpit is a perfect fit for a microfigure from a LEGO Games set

TOP VIEW

FRONT VIEW

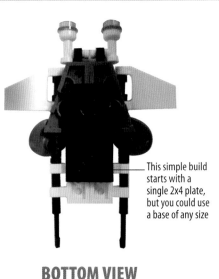

This simple build starts with a single 2x4 plate, but you could use a base of any size

BOTTOM VIEW

SIDE VIEW

APPROACHING TARGET FOR OPERATION MICRO!

STAR CARRIER

The Star Carrier is quite a basic build, but it transports troops and battle vehicles across the galaxy! Plates with horizontal clips hold weapons in place and tiles give a smooth finish.

Harpoon gun is a novel way to attach a radar dish

LEADING THE WAY

A slide plate forms a battering ram at the front – and hides the hollow bottom of the stack. Alternatively, you could use an inverted slope piece to give your cruiser a wedge-nosed shape.

1x1 round plate can be used to dock the microship onto a space station

Engine housings made from LEGO Technic beams with sticks. Swap the transparent pieces for flick-fire space torpedoes!

BATTLE CRUISER

This sturdy, menacing ship is on a mission to smash other microships to smithereens! The battle cruiser is built as a stack of bricks and then turned on its side.

Angled slope

Engine grille

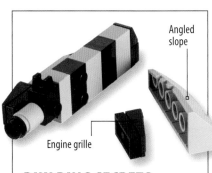

BUILDING SECRETS

Bricks with side studs hold the angled slopes and engine grilles in place. Transparent red pieces under the grille slopes make it look like energy is glowing through the vents.

SPACE AMBASSADOR

Friendly colours and curves, and the absence of weaponry, make this spaceship look like it belongs to a peaceful species. This microship is quite simple to build, but there are lots of areas where detail has been added.

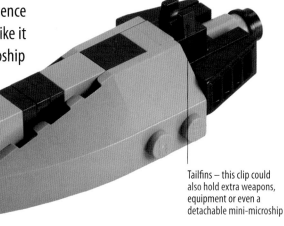

Microcockpit made with 1x1 slope. You could also use a 1x1 plate or a grille piece for an armoured cockpit!

Tailfins – this clip could also hold extra weapons, equipment or even a detachable mini-microship

SMALL TRANSPORTERS

Whether you're carrying supplies or crew, transporters will get your cargo wherever it needs to go. Before you build, think about what you want to transport, how big it is and what might be needed to hold it in place on the journey. There's a whole galaxy of space stuff out there, and someone's got to haul it all!

BUILDING BRIEF
Objective: Create small transporters
Use: Moving people and objects from one location to another
Features: Holds driver and cargo
Extras: Headlights, rocket boosters

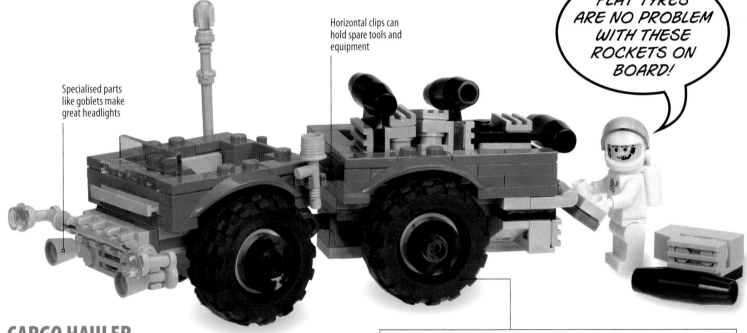

Specialised parts like goblets make great headlights

Horizontal clips can hold spare tools and equipment

FLAT TYRES ARE NO PROBLEM WITH THESE ROCKETS ON BOARD!

CARGO HAULER

The cargo hauler is built in two sections: the driver compartment and cargo trailer. For each section, start with a rectangle of bricks as a base and add wheel guards and other details. A ball-and-socket joint attaches the two sections together.

WHEELY FUN

Choose your wheels before building your wheel arches. There's nothing worse than wheels that don't fit!

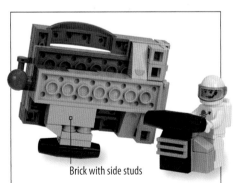

Brick with side studs

NO WHEELS, NO PROBLEM

Attach rockets to the hauler's base using bricks with side studs. Add details like grilles for a hi-tech look.

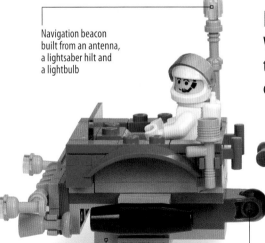

Navigation beacon built from an antenna, a lightsaber hilt and a lightbulb

ROCKET-POWERED HAULER

Wheels won't get you over every space terrain. That's why this version of the cargo hauler is powered by rockets!

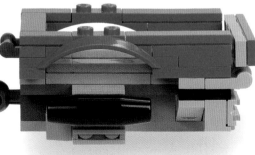

Ball-and-socket joint helps the hauler handle tight turns

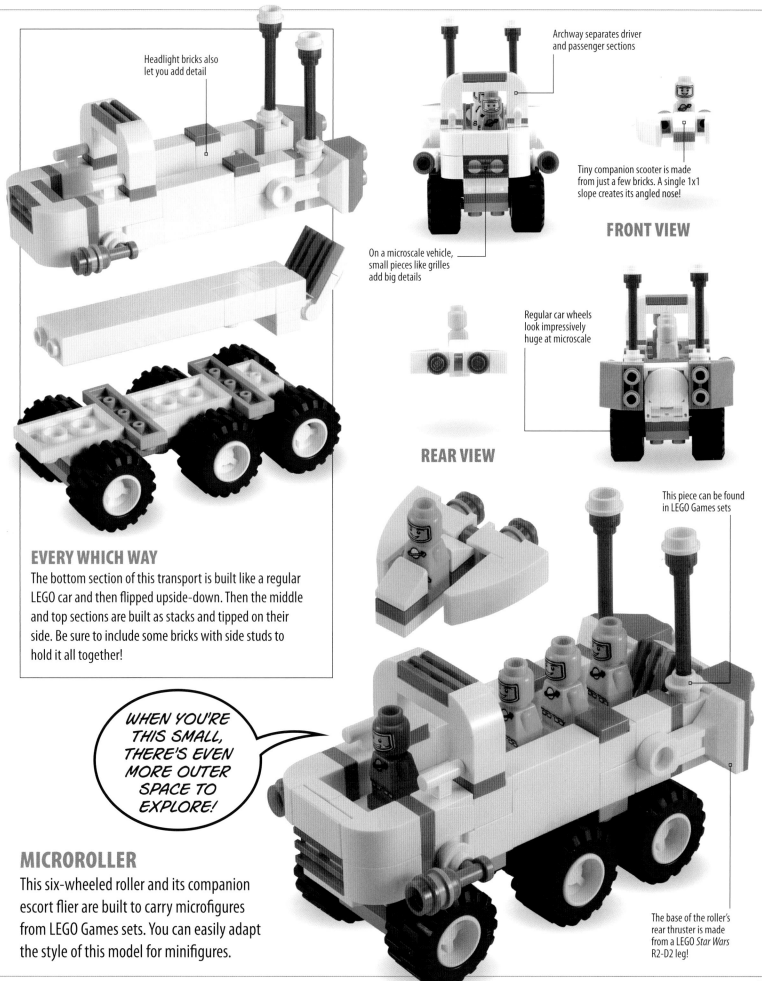

Headlight bricks also let you add detail

Archway separates driver and passenger sections

Tiny companion scooter is made from just a few bricks. A single 1x1 slope creates its angled nose!

FRONT VIEW

On a microscale vehicle, small pieces like grilles add big details

Regular car wheels look impressively huge at microscale

REAR VIEW

This piece can be found in LEGO Games sets

EVERY WHICH WAY

The bottom section of this transport is built like a regular LEGO car and then flipped upside-down. Then the middle and top sections are built as stacks and tipped on their side. Be sure to include some bricks with side studs to hold it all together!

WHEN YOU'RE THIS SMALL, THERE'S EVEN MORE OUTER SPACE TO EXPLORE!

MICROROLLER

This six-wheeled roller and its companion escort flier are built to carry microfigures from LEGO Games sets. You can easily adapt the style of this model for minifigures.

The base of the roller's rear thruster is made from a LEGO *Star Wars* R2-D2 leg!

MOON MINER

When you've got to build a new lunar colony or find valuable space rocks, big mining vehicles are just the thing. Once you've made your rugged mining machine, there are lots of small details to be added. Equip your miner with shovels, claws, saw blades, drills that spin or blast plasma and anything else it takes to get the job done!

BUILDING BRIEF
Objective: Build space mining vehicles
Use: Moving earth and rocks on other worlds
Features: Power, tools to dig through any surface
Extras: Scout vehicle, robot helpers, storage containers

Emergency beacon built from a telescope and transparent plates

HEY! I CAN SEE THE LUNAR OUTPOST FROM UP HERE!

TOP VIEW

The mining vehicle's base can hold ore containers or a small scout vehicle

Elevated control tower lets the driver keep an eye on the drill's work

Don't forget ladders and handles to help the crew climb to the top!

Laser drill

Oversized wheels are great for bumpy alien terrain. Use the biggest ones you can find for a really heavy-duty digger!

MACHINE WITH A VIEW

The Moon Miner is built in two parts: the base and the control tower. Make sure the base is big enough to fit the laser drill, and that the control tower is the right width so it can clip onto the back corners of the base.

Base platform – build it up higher to hold even more ore containers

A 2x2 brick with pin at each corner holds the wheels. They can also attach tank treads or even walker legs

Hinged lids provide easy access for loading and unloading freshly drilled space crystals

ORE CONTAINERS

Hinged lid pieces are great for building ore containers. You could also use a clip and bar hinge to attach a lid to a base, or even build a lid and base from scratch!

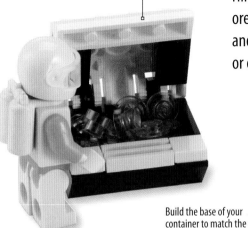

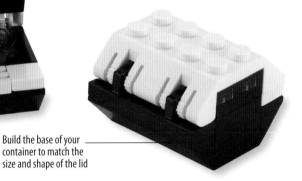

Build the base of your container to match the size and shape of the lid

WAIT, THAT'S NOT AN OUTPOST... THAT'S NEPTUNE!

Black slope

ROLL OF THE DICE

Proving that you really can find a use for any and every piece, the head of the laser drill is actually built around a LEGO Games die piece! You could also use two 2x2 bricks or a stack of plates.

MOON MINER WITH TREADS

Treads can be found on some LEGO construction vehicles. Each link is a separate piece, so you can build them as long or short as you want

Mining robots can be attached to the back of the control tower columns for transport

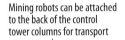

Miniature drills built using palm tree top pieces to match the Moon Miner's drill!

Green light for when crystals are detected underground. Swap it for a red one if your miners find something they don't want to dig up!

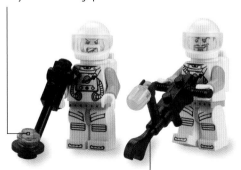

Hi-tech mining device built with a spanner. You could swap a screwdriver or a blaster, for different functions

READY, STEADY, DRILL!

LEGO Technic beam

An arm built from LEGO Technic parts holds the Moon Miner's laser drill. The arm pivots at two points, allowing the drill to be positioned accurately, or folded neatly away! It is supported by a pair of black 1x1 slopes on the support columns of the control tower.

ROBOTIC VEHICLES

Not all space vehicles need drivers! Just like the Mars missions of today, future interplanetary expeditions could make use of robots for exploration. This geological inspection rover is built around a simple stack of bricks, turned on its side and attached to four wheels. Detailed bricks and lots of tools give the rover a functional appearance!

No ice pick? Use another minifigure tool, like a magnifying glass, hammer or even a transparent chainsaw

Two antennas – the rover can receive and transmit information at the same time!

Visible mechanical systems – metallic pieces would look good here too!

Visible studs add to the industrial look

Mineral sensor built using a clip hinge and small radar dish. Several small antenna pieces would make a bank of sensors

TOP VIEW

Lights sit at different levels. To do this, build one into a socket and push the other forward on a 1x1 round plate

REAR VIEW

ROBOTIC ROVER

Unmanned rovers don't need driver controls or life-support systems, so build a shape that's basic and industrialised. Tools that fold out of the way and a low-to-the-ground profile will help prevent damage from wind and dust.

Cargo crate

ANATOMY OF A ROVER

The robotic rover is built in three sections, then joined together. Although the shape of the vehicle is quite simple, try using unusual pieces to add detail, like a cargo crate instead of regular bricks.

JETPACKS

What could be more fun than rocketing through space without any need of a spaceship? This is where jetpacks come in, from realistic to wildly inventive. Wings, rockets, jets, blasters – as long as the jetpack can attach to a minifigure, the rest is up to you!

BUILDING BRIEF
Objective: Build single-person jetpacks
Use: Travel and reconnaissance through atmosphere or outer space
Features: Small size, lightweight, high speed, manoeuvrable
Extras: Pilot controls, launch pad, blasters

CAVE RACER

This cavern-exploring vehicle has a core of a few bricks with side studs. A row of slopes on top and blade pieces on the wingtips complete its fierce design.

Handlebars connect minifigure to jetpack

Look for thin pieces like these wall pieces to make a jetpack's lightweight wings

ROCKET GLIDER

The specialised wing pieces on this jetpack can be found in sets like LEGO® Space Police and LEGO® Batman™. You could also use aeroplane wings or flag pieces to achieve the same shape.

Minifigure angle plate fits around minifigure's neck and allows jetpack to be clipped on

SPACEWALK PACK

To perform maintenance and repairs on the outside of a space station, you just need a box shape with some tools built into it. Make sure it is the right size for a minifigure!

I JUST NEED TO REMEMBER TO HOLD ON TIGHT!

These grey bars are just the right distance apart for minifigure hands to clip onto

Flames – LEGO sets with knights and castles are a good place to find these pieces! You can also use any fire-coloured transparent bricks

SIDE VIEW   **REAR VIEW**

ROCKET

3...2...1...BLAST OFF! This sleek, streamlined rocket launches straight up and then levels out to fly, so it has a big, flat-bottomed main engine, and a tailfin and wings as well. When building your own rocket models, think about where they will travel and what they will encounter on their outer space adventures!

BUILDING BRIEF

Objective: Build rockets

Use: Vertical blast-off into space

Features: Cone or needle shape with a flat engine underneath

Extras: Wings, detachable boosters, launchpad

Choose a windscreen to fit your design

Sensor built into sides to keep rocket's profile smooth and sleek

Grille pieces lock windscreen in place in case of bumpy asteroid fields

SPACE FRAME

The central body has a frame built from outwards-facing plates and bricks, held together at the corners by four 1x1 bricks with side studs.

Curved arch bricks give the central body a circular shape

1x1 brick with side studs

Bricks with holes

READY FOR LAUNCH

The front section of the rocket is built with curved wedge pieces and the back section has aeroplane features, giving the model a streamlined, tube-like shape that looks like it could blast right up into space.

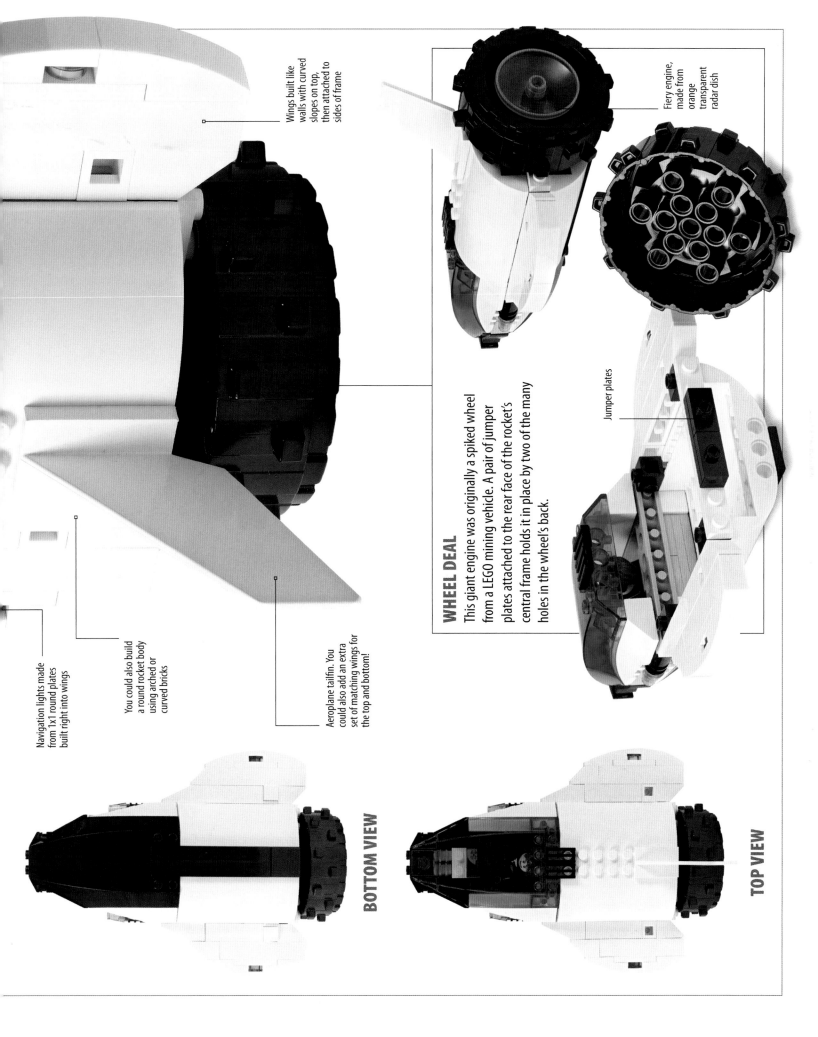

Wings built like walls with curved slopes on top, then attached to sides of frame

Fiery engine, made from orange transparent radar dish

WHEEL DEAL

This giant engine was originally a spiked wheel from a LEGO mining vehicle. A pair of jumper plates attached to the rear face of the rocket's central frame holds it in place by two of the many holes in the wheel's back.

Jumper plates

Navigation lights made from 1x1 round plates built right into wings

You could also build a round rocket body using arched or curved bricks

Aeroplane tailfin. You could also add an extra set of matching wings for the top and bottom!

BOTTOM VIEW

TOP VIEW

ALIENS

When it comes to building alien creatures, if you can imagine it, you can make it. Think about what kind of planet your alien lives on and how it should behave, and then start building your idea of life on the distant world. Try looking at real animals for inspiration and using the most unusual pieces you can find to make your creations look truly out of this world!

BUILDING BRIEF
Objective: Create alien creatures
Use: Friend or foe to space explorers
Features: Limbs for swimming, flying, hopping, climbing...you name it!
Extras: Claws, fangs, suckers, wings, tails, extra limbs

Creepy glowing eyes are red transparent plates. Glow-in-the-dark pieces would work well too, and some can be found in LEGO® Harry Potter™ sets

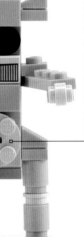

Round, scaly belly made from a 2x2 round plate in a contrasting colour

SWAMP HOPPER

Green frog-like skin, a long tail and webbed toes show that this alien comes from a watery world. A printed tile with a car grille pattern creates an extraterrestrial face with two mouths. Don't forget to position the arms and tail so it can balance while standing up!

FRONT VIEW

Don't have this flexible tail piece? Try a long, flat plate and add spikes and other details!

Webbed feet are flipper pieces. You could also use a 1x2 plate

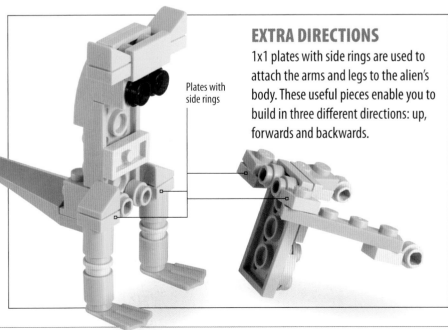

EXTRA DIRECTIONS

1x1 plates with side rings are used to attach the arms and legs to the alien's body. These useful pieces enable you to build in three different directions: up, forwards and backwards.

Plates with side rings

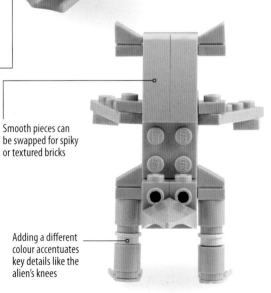

Smooth pieces can be swapped for spiky or textured bricks

Adding a different colour accentuates key details like the alien's knees

REAR VIEW

ASTEROID INSECTIPEDE

A segmented body and lots of legs make a creature look armoured and insect-like. Each of this alien's six limbs are attached to a jumper plate on its body by a single stud, so they can rotate and be posed to look like it's walking or running.

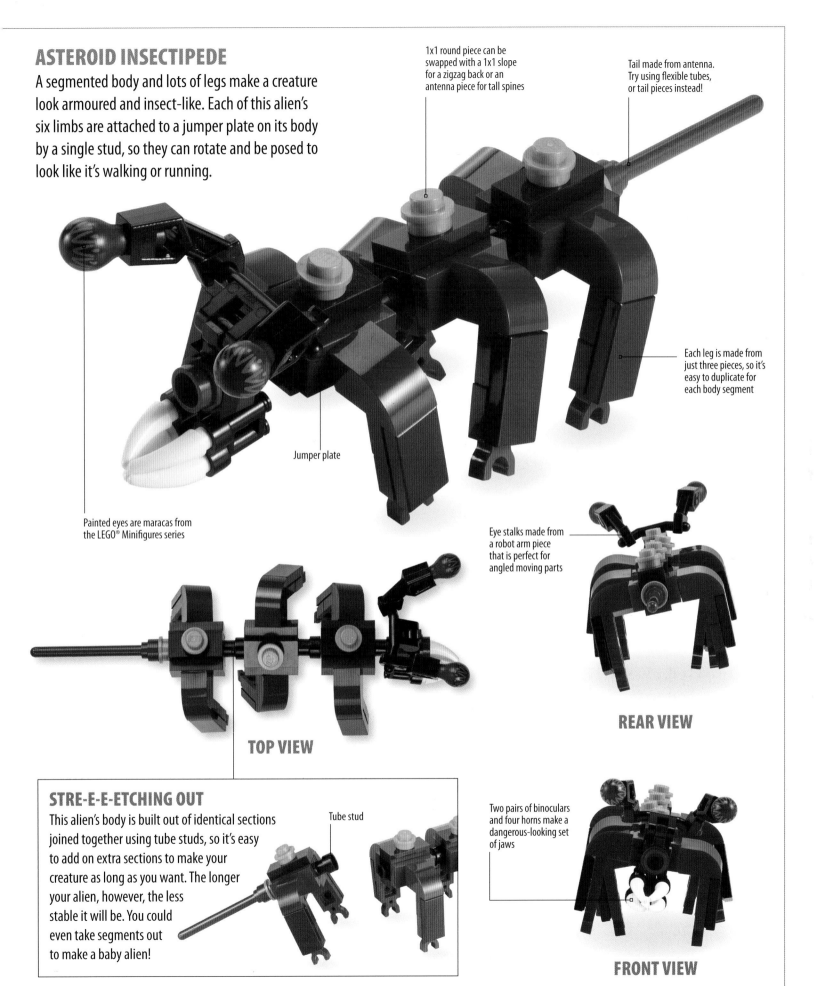

1x1 round piece can be swapped with a 1x1 slope for a zigzag back or an antenna piece for tall spines

Tail made from antenna. Try using flexible tubes, or tail pieces instead!

Each leg is made from just three pieces, so it's easy to duplicate for each body segment

Jumper plate

Painted eyes are maracas from the LEGO® Minifigures series

Eye stalks made from a robot arm piece that is perfect for angled moving parts

TOP VIEW

REAR VIEW

STRE-E-E-ETCHING OUT

This alien's body is built out of identical sections joined together using tube studs, so it's easy to add on extra sections to make your creature as long as you want. The longer your alien, however, the less stable it will be. You could even take segments out to make a baby alien!

Tube stud

Two pairs of binoculars and four horns make a dangerous-looking set of jaws

FRONT VIEW

MEET THE BUILDER

TIM GODDARD

Location: UK
Age: 34
LEGO Speciality: Microscale space

What are some of your top LEGO tips?

Use SNOT a lot! This is a term that LEGO fans use, it stands for Studs Not On Top and means that you don't just build with the brick studs pointing up. There are loads of interesting bricks that have studs on the side that can be used for this. Another tip is to sort out the bricks in your collection a bit. It may seem like it takes a lot of time, but it can save you time in the long run, as you know just where that brick you need is stored!

This shows the hangar area and part of a road system on a recently settled alien world. This is only part of a large display that was built as a collaboration with another LEGO builder, Peter Reid.

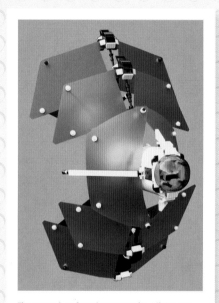

This research craft studies stars in far-off systems. It uses giant solar sails to power its scientific equipment and its engines.

This is the headquarters of the space police. It can communicate over vast distances and is used by commanders to meet up and discuss what the evil aliens have been up to.

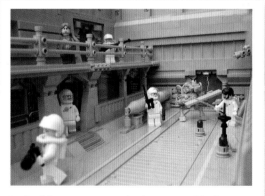

Inside a federation outpost a worker discovers one of the fibre optical cables has been damaged. Did it break or was it sabotage?

> THE BEST THING TO DO WITH LARGER MODELS IS PLAN AHEAD.

How much time do you spend building?

It probably averages out at about an hour a day. I don't always have time but I find late in the evening is the best time for inspiration, while playing my favourite music.

What things have gone wrong and how have you dealt with them?

Larger models, such as big spaceships, can be a bit unstable. This is especially a problem when I concentrate more on the detail and shape above the structure of the model. The best thing to do with larger models is plan ahead – build a nice solid frame then add the fancy stuff on top.

What is your favourite creation?

The one I'm working on at the moment! I do like the models that I've made to have a bit of character to them, such as a giraffe I've finished recently. Even robots can have a bit of character – building so you can tilt the head a bit to one side or have the arms in expressive positions is really satisfying.

Outside an alien nightclub the space police catch up with a wanted fugitive, but not before he has caused some chaos!

What is the biggest or most complex model you've made?

The largest things I have built have been a couple of small-scale *Star Wars* dioramas (scenes). I have built a couple about 12ft 11in by 2ft 6in (1.5m by 0.75m) filled with lots of small ships and walkers. The great thing about large scenes is you can gradually build and design the small craft and then make landscape, plants and buildings and gradually add to the whole display. When it is all put together you end up with a great, entirely LEGO environment.

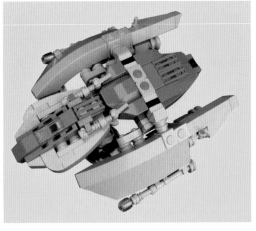

This spaceship is one of the fastest in the galaxy! The yellow and black markings are called bumblebee stripes.

This cargo hauler is specially adapted to travel over bumpy lunar terrain. It has room for one minifigure astronaut

How old were you when you started using LEGO bricks?

I've been building for as long as I can remember! I must have been four or five when I started building.

Do you plan out your build? If so, how?

It depends on what I'm building: I just tend to go for it with smaller models but larger models need a bit more planning. I sometimes sketch out the shape of a spaceship or the layout of a diorama but never in too much detail. I often have an idea of a particular little bit of design – like a wing shape – and just build what I think looks good with it. I carry on designing as I build, seeing what I think looks good as well as using the bricks I have available.

If you had all the LEGO bricks (and time!) in the world, what would you build?

A really big space display that has lots of minifigures and spaceships, with lots of moving parts and brick-built landscaping, and a large moon base with loads of internal detail. I would also like to build a what LEGO fans call a SHIP (Seriously Heavy Investment in Parts) of original design, maybe that could land at the moon base above! But these big ideas don't mean I don't enjoy building little models that can fit in your hand.

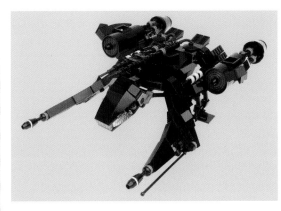

This powerful ship uses a neutralising weapon to catch unsuspecting transport spaceships.

A small submarine discovers some underwater ruins. Could this be the remains of the lost city of Atlantis?

This green space walker, with coordinating green alien minifigure, would be hard to spot on a jungle planet!

How many LEGO bricks do you have?

I have no idea! Lots and lots, but I never seem to have the bit that I'm looking for!

What are you inspired by?

All sorts of things: sci-fi films and TV programmes, buildings and scenery I see when I am driving around, old LEGO® Space sets. But the thing that inspires me to build interesting things more than anything else is seeing other people's LEGO creations.

What is your favourite LEGO technique or the technique you use the most?

SNOT is a real favourite and I use it all the time. I also enjoy combining pieces with clips and bars – it's great for making robots!

What types of models do you enjoy making, apart from space?

I enjoy building everything and anything in LEGO bricks! I like building animals – I've built a giraffe and some hippos. I also like town buildings and anything that involves minifigures. I think the more different things and areas you build in, the better you get as you discover new techniques.

At the robotics development facility the professor of robotics introduces his latest creation to the senior spacemen. The new robot will help around the base, carrying out various maintenance duties.

This trio of aliens are ready to take on the space police. Aliens of all shapes and sizes are welcome here, as long as they are bad!

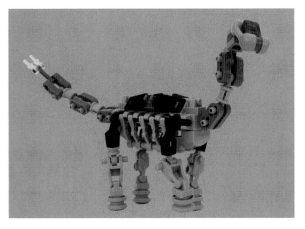

This dinosaur-style mechanical transport is used to traverse treacherous, unexplored planets. It has room for one minifigure pilot to sit in the head section.

What is your favourite LEGO brick or piece?

The standard 2x4 LEGO brick is a real classic, but I think the piece I use the most is a 1x1 plate with side ring. You can do so many things with it!

Which model were you most proud of as a young LEGO builder?

As I was growing up I had a lot of the LEGO Space sets. I made my bedroom into a giant alien planet and had different settlements around the room, one on a shelf and one on a chest of drawers, and had spaceships hanging from the ceiling flying between them. So I suppose the answer is not just one model but a whole series that made up my own world!

I'VE BEEN BUILDING FOR AS LONG AS I CAN REMEMBER!

103

IN DAYS OF OLD

Let's travel back in time! Fire-breathing dragons roam this land, brave knights battle for honour and the way to get around is by horse-drawn wagon. What will you build? A mighty stone castle or a dangerous trap? A fearsome catapult or a gigantic battering ram?

Who goes there? This drawbridge can be pulled up to make the castle safe from invaders. (See p.110)

HARNESS

FLAME

HORN

SHIELD

BAT

ROBOT ARM

2x4 WINCH

READY TO BUILD
Specialised pieces like harnesses, winches and horses are great for building your medieval world. But if you don't have them, you can also make your own. (See Horse of Bricks, p.119)

FLAG WITH 2 CLIPS

MEDIUM WAGON WHEEL

BIONICLE® SHIELD

TUBE

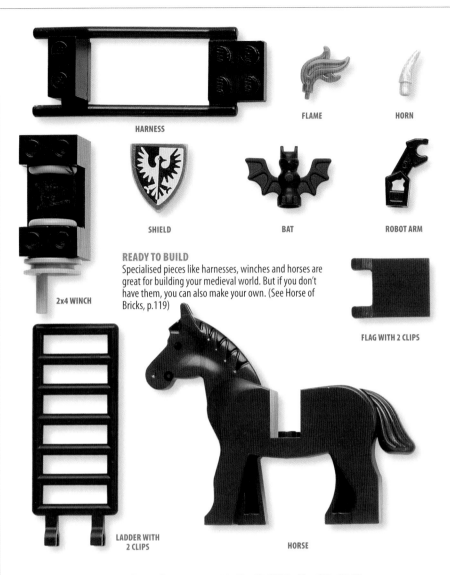

LADDER WITH 2 CLIPS

HORSE

MIX AND MATCH
Use pieces from all your LEGO sets to build your medieval scenes – don't just stick to LEGO® Castle sets!

PLANT

STREAMER

LONG CHAIN

SEAT

PIECES OF HISTORY

Who needs a time machine when you can build your own medieval models? Search your LEGO® collection for wheels, weapons and chains. Brown and grey pieces make good wooden or stone structures, while LEGO® Technic parts can help create working mechanisms. Here are some pieces that might come in useful – what else can you find?

4x6x3 ROLLCAGE

TAIL

TORCH

SWORD

SPEAR

LANCE

4x8 DOOR

MEDIEVAL WEAPONRY
Your minifigures can wield weapons – or you could incorporate them into your models as traps or defensive features. (See Siege Tower, p.127)

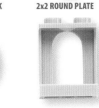 2x2 ROUND BRICK

2x2 ROUND PLATE

 SMALL NARROW RIMS AND 2x2 AXLE PLATE WITH 2 PINS

 1x1 ROUND PLATE

1x1 ROUND BRICK

1x2 TILE WITH TOP BAR

 LEGO TECHNIC CROSS AXLE 8

CRANK

LEGO TECHNIC RIGHT ANGLE AXLE CONNECTOR

LEGO TECHNIC LIFT ARM

2x2 DOMED BRICK

 1x2x2 ARCHED WINDOW

1x1 SLOPE

1x1 CONE

LEGO TECHNIC
LEGO Technic pieces can make wheels turn, cannons tilt and drawbridges drop. (See Crank Drawbridge, p.110)

LEGO TECHNIC AXLE CONNECTOR

1x2 TEXTURED BRICK

1x2 JUMPER PLATE

1x4 PANEL

2x4 RIDGED ROOF SLOPE

COMPLETE CASTLES
Roof pieces, cones and slopes can add the perfect finishing touch to your castles.

 2x2 PLATE WITH 2 RINGS UNDERNEATH

 1x6 TILE

2x2 TILE

1x1 BRICK WITH 4 SIDE STUDS

LEGO TECHNIC 12 TOOTH GEAR

1x1 BRICK WITH HOLE

 LEGO TECHNIC HALF PIN

 1x2 BRICK WITH HOLE

1x2 BRICK WITH CROSS AXLE HOLE

 1x1 PLATE WITH SIDE RING

 1x1x6 ROUND COLUMN

 1x2x3 SLOPE

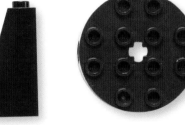 4x4 ROUND BRICK

 2x4 ANGLED PLATE

2x16 ANGLED SLOPE

2x2 CORNER PLATE

 2x2 TURNTABLE

 1x2/2x2 ANGLE PLATE

2x2 INVERTED SLOPE

1x2 PLATE WITH HANDLED BAR

 1x2 PLATE WITH CLICK HINGE

 1x1 HEADLIGHT BRICK

 4x4 PLATE

EVEN SIMPLE MODELS CAN HAVE MOVING PARTS AND LOTS OF DETAIL!

 1x3x2 HALF ARCH

 1x2 LOG BRICK

 1x1x5 BRICK

 1x3 ARCH BRICK

 1x4 HINGE PLATE AND 4x4 HINGE PLATE

MEDIEVAL ARCHES
Arches are a common feature in medieval architecture. Try to use them in your buildings.

 1x5x4 HALF ARCH

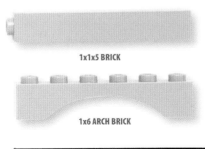 1x6 ARCH BRICK

1x4 BRICK WITH SIDE STUDS

1x12 PLATE

CASTLE

Medieval castles are huge, sturdy structures. Other than that, you can build your model however you want: grand, ornate, plain, strong, majestic, or crumbling. You could even build it as a combination of all these things! Look at pictures of ancient castles, or find inspiration in your favourite books and movies. Think about including details like flags, wall-mounted torches and knight minifigures to bring your creation to life.

CASTLE FORTRESS

Castles are built up over time as each king or queen adds what he or she needs. Start with an impressive doorway and a grand central building. Then add on sections to house sleeping quarters, viewing platforms, dining rooms, chapels, stores and anything else you can think of. They don't even have to match!

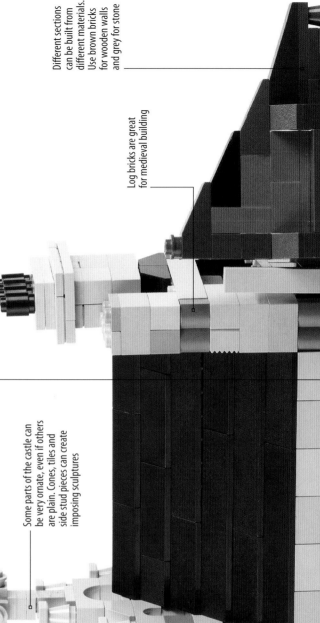

Different sections can be built from different materials. Use brown bricks for wooden walls and grey for stone

Log bricks are great for medieval building

ARCHITECTURE

An interesting architectural feature can really give your model a boost. Here, a smaller arch has been built in behind a larger arch, which adds depth and detail to the chapel walls. Cones, round bricks and round plates are stacked to make decorative columns. Be inventive!

Some parts of the castle can be very ornate, even if others are plain. Cones, tiles and side stud pieces can create imposing sculptures

CURVED BATTLEMENTS

Rounded battlements can help your knights keep a lookout in all directions. Use hinged plates to connect several sections of wall together. Then angle the walls into a circle, semicircle or whatever shape you want.

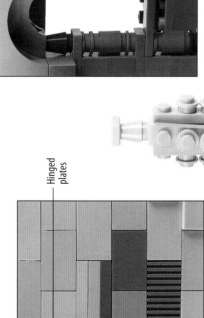

Hinged plates

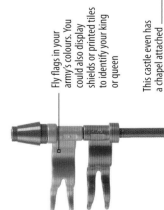

Fly flags in your army's colours. You could also display shields or printed tiles to identify your king or queen

This castle even has a chapel attached

Arched windows. If you haven't got arched bricks, use half arches or inverted slopes

Arrow slits made from bricks with cross axle holes

A green brick here and there looks like a moss-covered stone!

Bricks in different shades of grey, textured bricks and log bricks help break up large stone walls

Green baseplate is a good starting point, but why don't you try building your castle on a hill, or on an island in the middle of a lake?

Scattered plates and tiles look like fallen ruins

Overgrown foliage suggests an old castle. You could build a well-tended garden instead

Imposing entrance. You could also add a gatehouse with a way to keep invaders out! (See pp.110–113)

Wooden structures with lattice windows look really medieval!

DRAWBRIDGES

Every castle needs protection from invading armies. First build a simple gatehouse as an imposing front to your fortification. Then, think about how best you want to defend your castle and design a mechanism to suit. You could create a portcullis, a heavy stone door or a drawbridge. Here are two clever ways to build a drawbridge!

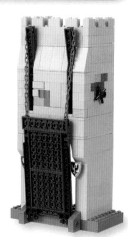

Crank controls drawbridge

OPEN   **CLOSED**

GATEHOUSE

A simple gatehouse can be the first point of protection for your castle. Grey bricks and LEGO Technic half pins on either side of the door attach the drawbridge.

Make sure the doorway is high enough for a knight to ride through on horseback!

LEGO Technic half pin allows drawbridge to pivot

Push lever to release gears and send drawbridge crashing down!

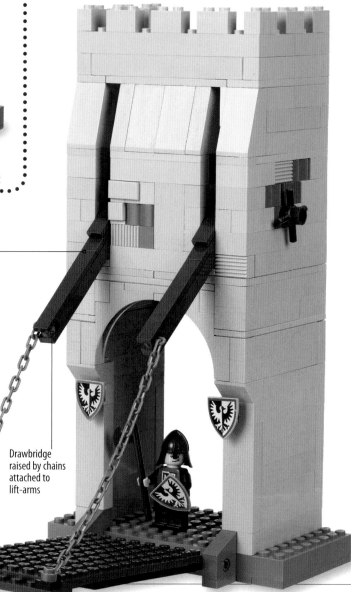

MEDIEVAL MECHANISM

LEGO Technic gears turn to raise the lift-arms. These pull the chains, raising the drawbridge. A lever secures the drawbridge in place by locking an axle connector against the gears.

CRANK DRAWBRIDGE

A crank system is a simple way to raise and lower a drawbridge. This mechanism is housed in a stone battlement that connects to the top of the gatehouse. It uses LEGO Technic bricks, axles and gears that allow you to operate the drawbridge using a crank on the side of the building.

Make drawbridge wide enough to cover entrance when raised

Drawbridge raised by chains attached to lift-arms

CABLE DRAWBRIDGE

There's more than one way to raise a bridge! This version of the gatehouse uses a spool and string cable system instead of chains and lift-arms. The mechanism is housed in a rustic-style gatehouse room.

CLIPPING THE CABLES

Use plates with handled bars to secure your drawbridge's cables. Thread the cable through both handles before clipping them to the underside of the drawbridge.

Winch

Not enough grey bricks? Build the top of your gatehouse using wood colours instead!

Hand-cranked winch is not as fast as a gear system, but it gets the job done!

SPOOL SYSTEM

The cables are attached to a winch inside the gatehouse, which is turned by a handle on the outside. This system takes up little space, which leaves room in the gatehouse for guards and ammunition.

Use a brick with cross axle hole in it to feed the cables through

Winch

CLOSED

OPEN

Don't have LEGO Technic parts? Use hinged bricks or plates to build a movable drawbridge

Plate with handled bar

PORTCULLIS

A portcullis is a heavy gate that can be raised and lowered on a pulley system. It is another great way to let friends into your castle – and keep enemies out! Start with a simple gatehouse like the one on the previous page, and adjust it to house your portcullis.

AW. THANKS TO THAT PORTCULLIS, WE NEVER GET TO BATTLE ANYBODY ANYMORE!

Put knights and soldiers on top to defend gatehouse

One-brick-wide channel between two layers of the front wall

Tall gatehouse tower leaves room for portcullis to slide all the way up

Decorative windows built with 1x1 round bricks, plates and small arches

GATE GAP

Build two layers into the front wall of the gatehouse, leaving a narrow channel between them. Drop the portcullis into this gap before building the roof, so it is trapped inside the gatehouse, but able to slide up and down freely.

Display your castle's coat of arms on the gatehouse walls. You could also fly flags or hang weapons!

PORTCULLIS

This portcullis is built from crisscrossed long, thin plates, with no special pieces needed. A string attached to a plate with handled bar at the top raises it through a channel created by the space between the two layers of the front walls.

NO ONE GETS IN UNLESS THEY KNOW THE PASSWORD!

BRICKS IN THE WALL

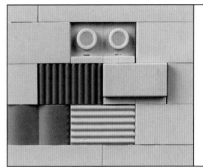

To add realistic textures to a stone wall, include textured bricks and log bricks among regular bricks, or attach 1x2 tiles to pairs of headlight bricks so they protrude from the wall.

When portcullis is closed, brick at end of drawstring sits on top of the tower

Plate with handled bar attaches string to door

To raise gate, pull brick down and attach it to top of archway, holding portcullis in place

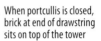

REALLY? OK... THE PASSWORD IS "LET ME IN OR ELSE"!

PORTCULLIS LOWERED

You could also put a portcullis behind your castle's front door!

Portcullis moves smoothly because nothing blocks its way

PORTCULLIS RAISED

CASTLE DOORS

When building a door for your castle, think about what it's for. Royal processions and grand entrances? Then make it really big and fancy! To keep out unwanted guests, make it sturdy and strong with a way to lock it from inside. Or perhaps you'd like a secret door to protect a room full of treasure? It's all up to you!

BUILDING BRIEF
Objective: Build doors for your castle
Use: Letting people in, or keeping people out!
Features: Must be able to open and close
Extras: Locks, traps, signs, secret panels

DOOR OF DANGER

The door to a villain's castle should say "keep out!" to any heroes who approach. This simple door is made from standard bricks and tiles and attaches to the frame with clips and handled bars.

UNHINGED

Build the doors of this creepy entrance first. Next, construct the doorframe around them so you can position the clip pieces correctly.

A bat or a flaming torch would look just as scary here!

Rattling chain hints at the spooky danger waiting inside

Use pieces with unusual or dramatic shapes to make creepy decorations

Horn pieces warn intruders to keep out. You could also use tooth plates or tools

Locking mechanism – a LEGO Technic cross axle slides through a brick with a hole through it to lock the door

No welcome mat here!

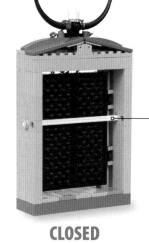

OPEN   **CLOSED**

SECRET DOOR

The trick to building a secret door is to make it blend in with the castle's wall. First build an arched doorway with two clip plates at the back. Then design your door to match!

You could add a clip to the front of your doorway to hold a sword, shield or torch that could double up as a secret lever

Old stone walls, built with grey bricks of different shapes and shades

Textured bricks look old and crumbling. Great for a haunted castle!

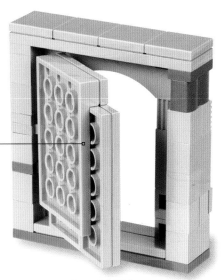

With just a push, the secret passage is revealed

REAR – OPEN

FRONT – CLOSED **FRONT – OPEN**

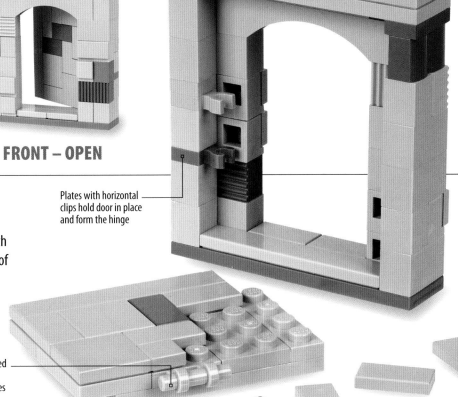

Plates with horizontal clips hold door in place and form the hinge

DOOR DESIGN

Just a few basic plates form the foundation of the door. Cover them with tiles that match the colour and design of the tiles around the doorframe. Now your door will be camouflaged! Make sure there's enough space around the door for it to swing open smoothly.

Plate with handled bar secured with overlapping pieces

TRAPS

To build up your medieval scene, why not add some extra detail to your castle? Perhaps your castle has hidden treasure, which needs protecting from thieves. Or maybe you'd rather design a clever way to trap your enemies. Design some sneaky traps to keep your secrets safe! Adding moving parts to your models really brings them to life!

BUILDING BRIEF
Objective: Build medieval traps
Use: Fun with moving parts
Features: Spinning, dropping or chopping mechanisms
Extras: Mazes, dungeons

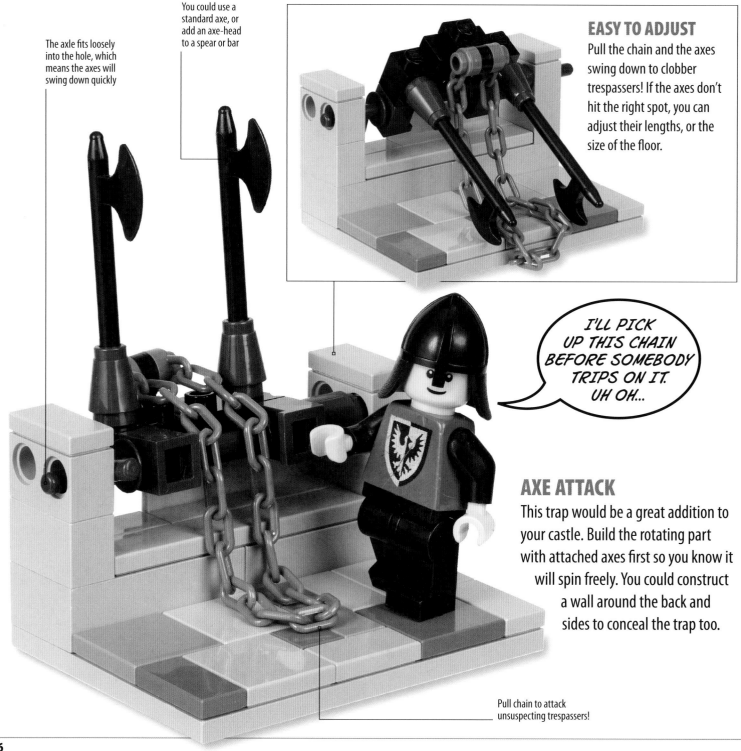

You could use a standard axe, or add an axe-head to a spear or bar

The axle fits loosely into the hole, which means the axes will swing down quickly

EASY TO ADJUST

Pull the chain and the axes swing down to clobber trespassers! If the axes don't hit the right spot, you can adjust their lengths, or the size of the floor.

I'LL PICK UP THIS CHAIN BEFORE SOMEBODY TRIPS ON IT. UH OH...

AXE ATTACK

This trap would be a great addition to your castle. Build the rotating part with attached axes first so you know it will spin freely. You could construct a wall around the back and sides to conceal the trap too.

Pull chain to attack unsuspecting trespassers!

TRAPDOOR

A trapdoor needs to swing down to drop people out of sight, so build it up high. The door should match the rest of the floor (whether wooden or stone) so it's a huge surprise for unsuspecting minifigures!

WHAT A GREAT VIEW. NOW, HOW DO I GET DOWN?

POLES APART
Two lance pieces support the door. One acts as a hinge, while the other can be pulled out to send the door swinging down.

Railing – you could also add stairs

Stopper keeps trap door from swinging too far

Build this platform into your castle's floor to include it in your medieval scene!

Trapdoor built separately from the rest of the platform

Extra piece on end of trap-release pole for better grip

Lance fits loosely in holes so the trap swings open easily

A minifigure who fell through the trap...a long time ago!

KNIGHTLY STEEDS

What's a knight without his faithful horse? On foot, that's what! Many LEGO Castle sets include horses, but you can also build your own. It's simple to give each horse its own individual character! Build and customise special saddles and horse armour, also known as barding. You can even build your knight's armour to match!

BUILDING BRIEF
Objective: Make horses worthy of a knight!
Use: Riding forth for deeds of derring-do
Features: Must be interesting and colourful
Extras: Coat of arms, plumes, pennants, weapon and shield clips

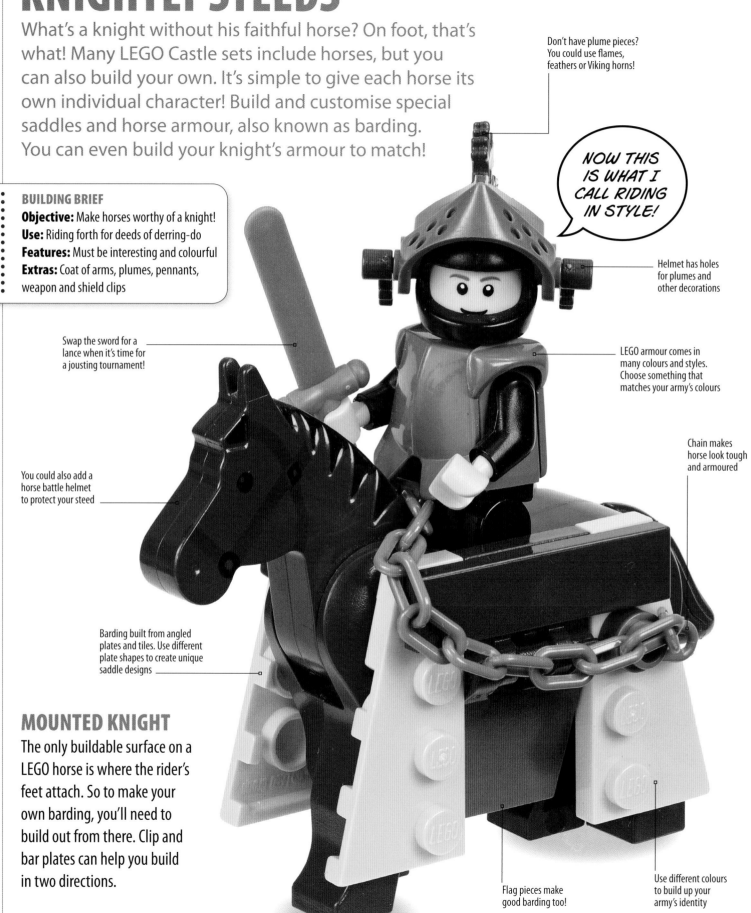

Don't have plume pieces? You could use flames, feathers or Viking horns!

NOW THIS IS WHAT I CALL RIDING IN STYLE!

Helmet has holes for plumes and other decorations

Swap the sword for a lance when it's time for a jousting tournament!

LEGO armour comes in many colours and styles. Choose something that matches your army's colours

You could also add a horse battle helmet to protect your steed

Chain makes horse look tough and armoured

Barding built from angled plates and tiles. Use different plate shapes to create unique saddle designs

MOUNTED KNIGHT

The only buildable surface on a LEGO horse is where the rider's feet attach. So to make your own barding, you'll need to build out from there. Clip and bar plates can help you build in two directions.

Flag pieces make good barding too!

Use different colours to build up your army's identity

You can use a LEGO saddle or build your own!

MY HORSE IS TOTALLY OFF THE CHAIN!

1x1 plate with horizontal clip

This clips to 1x1 plate with horizontal clip on saddle

A tile locks the plates together without adding too much bulk

Two-toned coat, created by mixing classic and modern brown bricks. Create your own patterns!

Ears made from cone pieces

HORSE OF BRICKS

If you don't have a horse for your knight, try building one! This brick-built horse has a gap to fit a minifigure. Its body is built from simple bricks and plates, with a few slopes and inverted slopes.

You could make the bricks around the gap a different colour to resemble a saddle

Hooves made from round black bricks

WAGONS & CARTS

Every medieval villager needs a trusty horse-drawn wagon to get them to the market. Before building your cart or wagon, think about what you want it to carry: food, equipment, passengers? You could even make an armoured battle-wagon with lots of spears and spikes!

BUILDING BRIEF
Objective: Create carts and wagons
Use: Travel, transportation
Features: Pulled by horse, carry supplies
Extras: Lanterns, repair tools, horse food

WOODEN WAGON

This wagon has plenty of room for carrying supplies from town to town. Build the part that attaches to the horse first to ensure everything is the right height and all four wheels touch the ground to roll evenly.

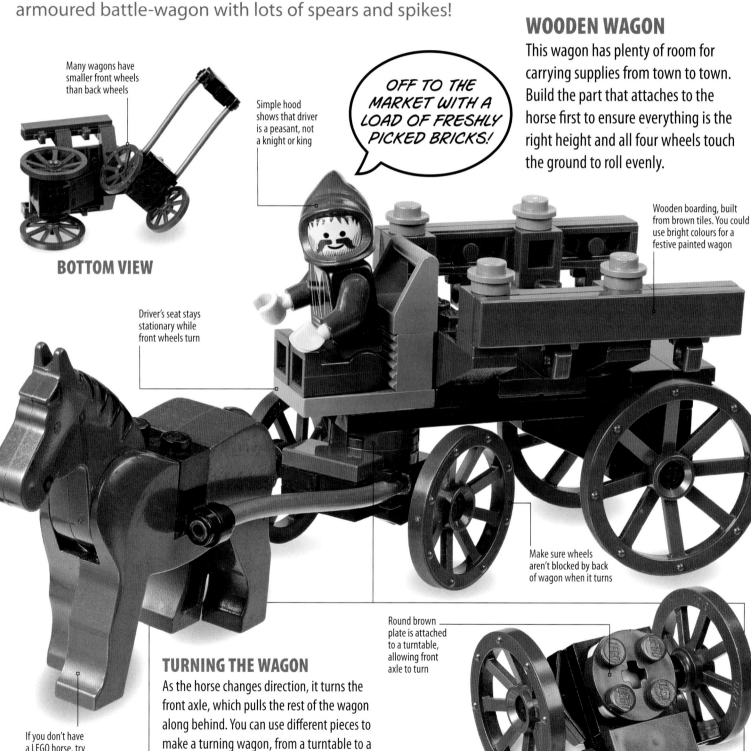

Many wagons have smaller front wheels than back wheels

Simple hood shows that driver is a peasant, not a knight or king

OFF TO THE MARKET WITH A LOAD OF FRESHLY PICKED BRICKS!

BOTTOM VIEW

Driver's seat stays stationary while front wheels turn

Wooden boarding, built from brown tiles. You could use bright colours for a festive painted wagon

Make sure wheels aren't blocked by back of wagon when it turns

Round brown plate is attached to a turntable, allowing front axle to turn

TURNING THE WAGON

As the horse changes direction, it turns the front axle, which pulls the rest of the wagon along behind. You can use different pieces to make a turning wagon, from a turntable to a LEGO Technic pin.

If you don't have a LEGO horse, try building your own! (See p.119 and p.143)

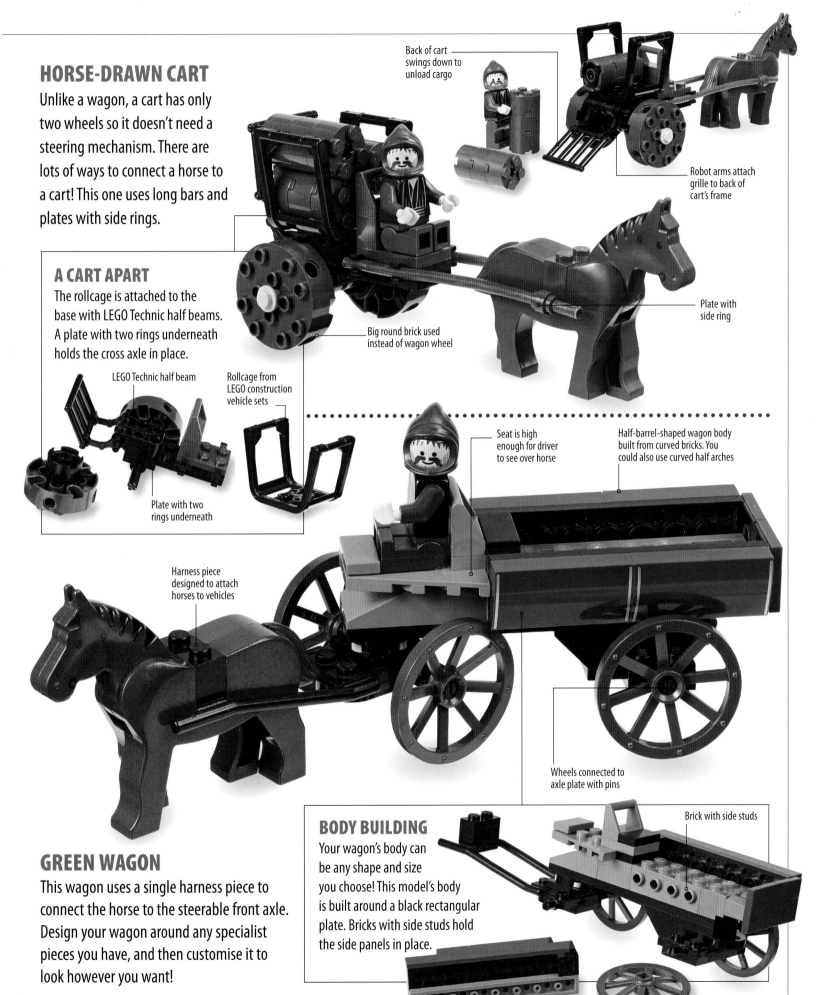

HORSE-DRAWN CART

Unlike a wagon, a cart has only two wheels so it doesn't need a steering mechanism. There are lots of ways to connect a horse to a cart! This one uses long bars and plates with side rings.

Back of cart swings down to unload cargo

Robot arms attach grille to back of cart's frame

A CART APART

The rollcage is attached to the base with LEGO Technic half beams. A plate with two rings underneath holds the cross axle in place.

LEGO Technic half beam

Rollcage from LEGO construction vehicle sets

Plate with two rings underneath

Plate with side ring

Big round brick used instead of wagon wheel

Harness piece designed to attach horses to vehicles

Seat is high enough for driver to see over horse

Half-barrel-shaped wagon body built from curved bricks. You could also use curved half arches

GREEN WAGON

This wagon uses a single harness piece to connect the horse to the steerable front axle. Design your wagon around any specialist pieces you have, and then customise it to look however you want!

Wheels connected to axle plate with pins

BODY BUILDING

Your wagon's body can be any shape and size you choose! This model's body is built around a black rectangular plate. Bricks with side studs hold the side panels in place.

Brick with side studs

DRAGONS

No medieval world is complete without a fierce, fire-breathing dragon. Dragons are mythical creatures, so there are no rules about what they should look like. Give yours spikes, fangs, horns, tails, chains, curves and as many wings as you like! What else can you think of?

FLYING SERPENT

This lean, agile dragon has a twisted body built from lots of LEGO Technic parts. Its back is shaped and held together with ball-and-socket joints, while axles and LEGO Technic half beams make up the front arms.

Don't have these horn pieces? Use screwdrivers, daggers or bars – anything long or pointy will do!

Horns face backwards so dragon is streamlined when flying

Neck joint is not fixed in place so the head can be posed as you like

ALL IN HIS HEAD

The dragon's head is built in four different directions. The bottom part has studs facing up, the sloped sides are built outwards to the left and right, and the inside of the mouth has a jumper plate facing forwards, which holds the flame piece in place.

Printed angled slopes add detail

Angle plates allow sideways building

Jumper plate faces forwards

Use joints to create posable ankles and knees

Build the shape of your dragon using ball-and-socket joints

I MIGHT BE MADE OF HEAT-RESISTANT PLASTIC, BUT I'M STILL SCARED!

Can your minifigure tame the dragon?

Dragons don't have to have feet! Why not build some claws instead?

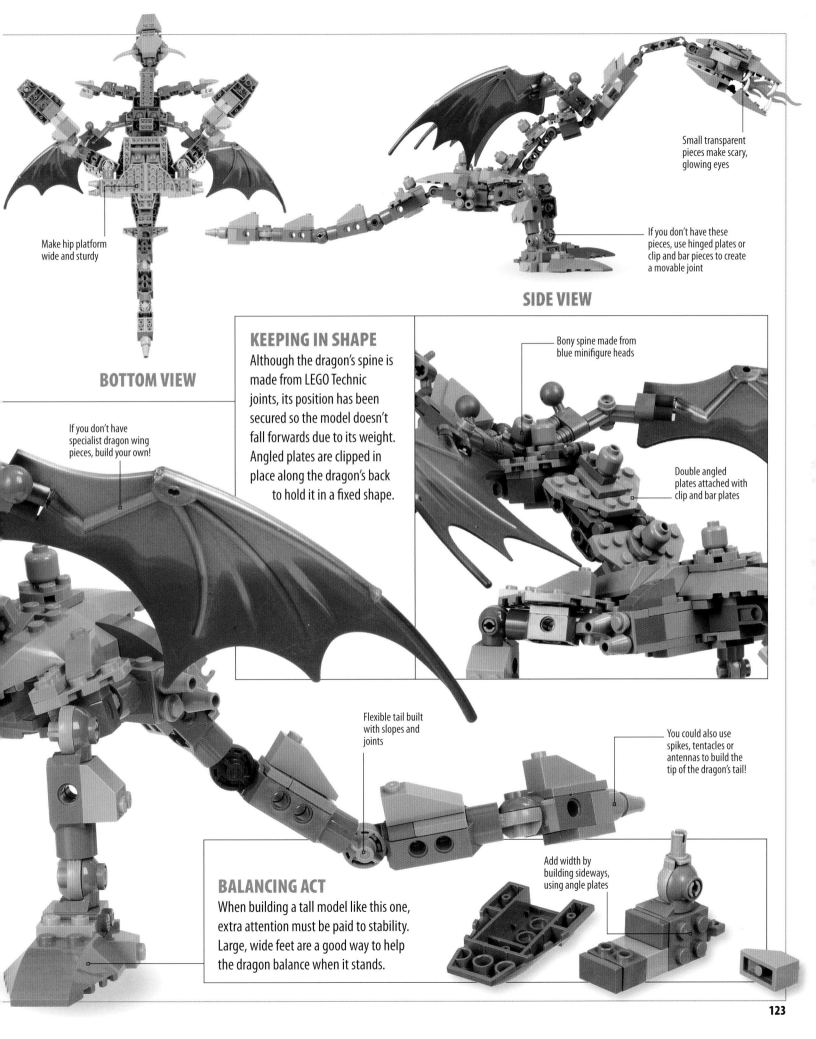

Make hip platform wide and sturdy

BOTTOM VIEW

Small transparent pieces make scary, glowing eyes

If you don't have these pieces, use hinged plates or clip and bar pieces to create a movable joint

SIDE VIEW

KEEPING IN SHAPE
Although the dragon's spine is made from LEGO Technic joints, its position has been secured so the model doesn't fall forwards due to its weight. Angled plates are clipped in place along the dragon's back to hold it in a fixed shape.

Bony spine made from blue minifigure heads

Double angled plates attached with clip and bar plates

If you don't have specialist dragon wing pieces, build your own!

Flexible tail built with slopes and joints

You could also use spikes, tentacles or antennas to build the tip of the dragon's tail!

Add width by building sideways, using angle plates

BALANCING ACT
When building a tall model like this one, extra attention must be paid to stability. Large, wide feet are a good way to help the dragon balance when it stands.

BATTERING RAMS

A battering ram is like a medieval tank: heavy, tough and almost unstoppable. It needs a sturdy frame and a strong, swinging ram that can smash through your enemy castle's best defences. It needs a set of wheels too, so your LEGO knights can move the huge contraption around!

BUILDING BRIEF
Objective: Build battering rams
Use: Breaking through the fortifications of enemy castles
Features: Strength, stability, swinging mechanism
Extras: Wheels, shields, armour plates, flags

SWING AND SMASH

A swinging mechanism is built into this ram's support frame. The castle's attackers stand behind the ram, pull it back as far as they can, and then let go. Gravity and momentum take care of the rest!

Axles at the top and bottom of the lift arms let the battering ram swing back and forth freely

Battering ram hangs from two pairs of LEGO Technic lift arms

You could also use wagon wheels for a lighter, faster battering ram

Swinging hinge made from LEGO Technic cross axle and bricks with holes

Make the frame as sturdy as you can with overlapping bricks

Angle plates attach sides to the base

I LOVE THE SOUND OF CASTLE GATES CRASHING DOWN IN THE MORNING!

Silver plates look like bolted metal to hold heavy loads

REAR SIDE VIEW

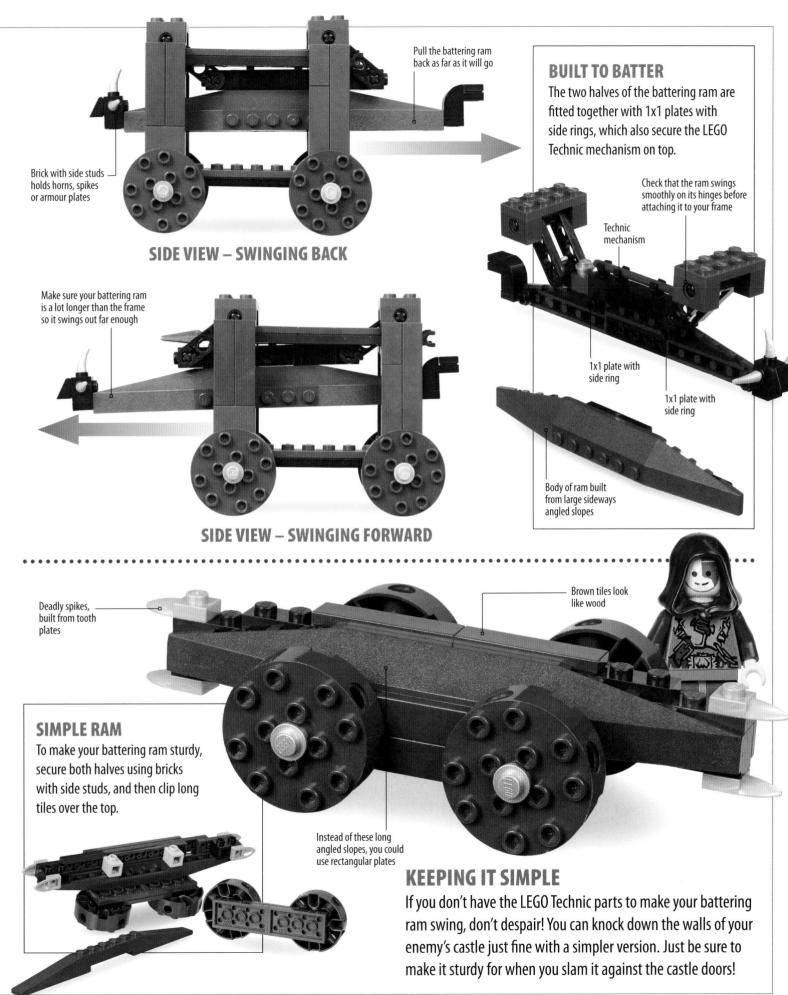

SIDE VIEW – SWINGING BACK

Pull the battering ram back as far as it will go

Brick with side studs holds horns, spikes or armour plates

Make sure your battering ram is a lot longer than the frame so it swings out far enough

SIDE VIEW – SWINGING FORWARD

BUILT TO BATTER
The two halves of the battering ram are fitted together with 1x1 plates with side rings, which also secure the LEGO Technic mechanism on top.

Check that the ram swings smoothly on its hinges before attaching it to your frame

Technic mechanism

1x1 plate with side ring

1x1 plate with side ring

Body of ram built from large sideways angled slopes

Deadly spikes, built from tooth plates

Brown tiles look like wood

SIMPLE RAM
To make your battering ram sturdy, secure both halves using bricks with side studs, and then clip long tiles over the top.

Instead of these long angled slopes, you could use rectangular plates

KEEPING IT SIMPLE
If you don't have the LEGO Technic parts to make your battering ram swing, don't despair! You can knock down the walls of your enemy's castle just fine with a simpler version. Just be sure to make it sturdy for when you slam it against the castle doors!

LAYING SIEGE

Laying siege to an enemy castle is no easy task! You can build all kinds of equipment for your army of knights. A portable shield will protect them from spears and arrows as they advance across the battlefield, while a tall siege tower will help them climb over the castle walls.

Use grey bricks to create a stone wall – but remember, a stone wall wouldn't be portable!

Cones at top create the look of wooden poles bound together

PORTABLE SHIELD

Offering protection for knights on the move, this shield wall is made by alternating 1x2 log bricks with 1x1 round bricks. This structure makes the wall flexible enough to bend into a curve.

IT'S LIKE A GAME OF HIDE AND SEEK...READY OR NOT, HERE WE COME!

Siege army is safe and sound behind the wall!

Plate with click hinge

Rolling wheel rims allow knights to push wall toward castle

ROLLING WALL

The portable shield rolls on small wheel rims without tyres. You can attach a horse to the click hinge at the front to tow the wall to the battlefield!

REAR VIEW

Wheel rim

SIEGE TOWER

A siege tower is like an armoured ladder for reaching the top of enemy walls. This one is built on a rectangular plate and has a drawbridge-like gangplank to deposit the knights onto castle walls.

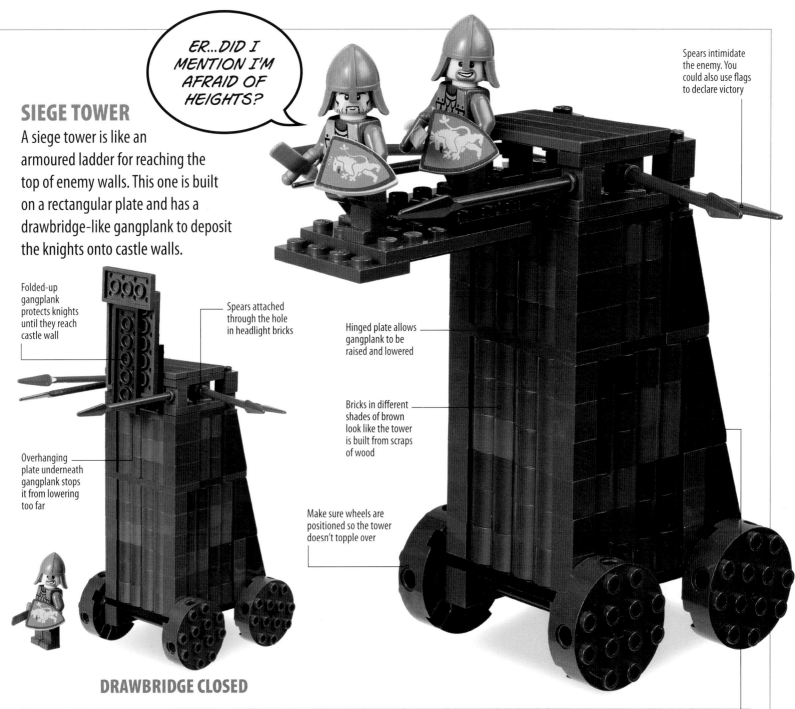

ER...DID I MENTION I'M AFRAID OF HEIGHTS?

Spears intimidate the enemy. You could also use flags to declare victory

Folded-up gangplank protects knights until they reach castle wall

Spears attached through the hole in headlight bricks

Hinged plate allows gangplank to be raised and lowered

Bricks in different shades of brown look like the tower is built from scraps of wood

Overhanging plate underneath gangplank stops it from lowering too far

Make sure wheels are positioned so the tower doesn't topple over

DRAWBRIDGE CLOSED

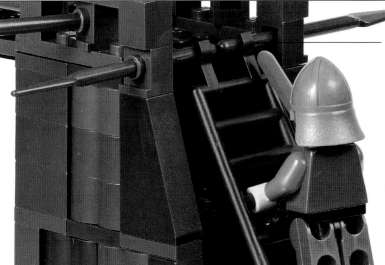

Knights climb up ladder or take shelter inside open back of tower

HOLLOW INSIDE

The back of the siege tower is left open so that the knights can hide inside. A ladder is clipped on to two of the side spears. It can be folded out to allow the knights to climb up it.

REAR VIEW

CANNONS & CATAPULTS

Siege weapons are designed to throw objects at or over a castle's walls. Beyond that, the only limit is your imagination! So be creative and keep an eye out for parts that would work as catapult buckets or cannon barrels. And remember – don't aim anything at your eyes!

BUILDING BRIEF

Objective: Build siege weapons

Use: Attacking castle walls and towers

Features: Ability to throw, fling or launch projectiles

Extras: Wheels, guards, spare ammo wagons

TILT TO AIM

This cannon can be tilted up and down thanks to a few LEGO Technic pieces. The barrel is built around two bricks with holes, through which is fitted a cross axle.

Axle allows cannon to tilt

Brick with a hole

Barrel made from 2x2 round bricks with a domed brick at the back

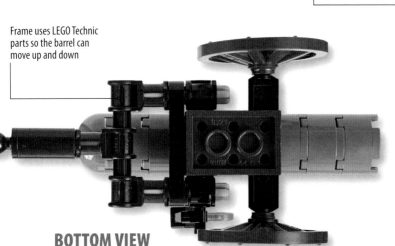

Frame uses LEGO Technic parts so the barrel can move up and down

BOTTOM VIEW

Wagon wheels make a heavy cannon more portable

MICROCATAPULT

The basic components of a catapult are a bucket attached to an arm and a sturdy base to support them. With a rotation point in the middle of the throwing arm, this catapult works like a see-saw.

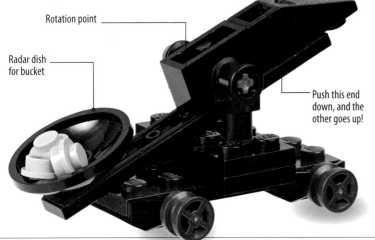

Rotation point

Radar dish for bucket

Push this end down, and the other goes up!

MICROCANNON

For a siege on a smaller scale, you can make a microcannon. This model is built out of two LEGO Technic tubes, supported by headlight bricks.

ASSEMBLE YOUR WEAPONS!

The LEGO Technic tubes are connected by a plate with horizontal clip, which attaches to the headlight bricks with 1x1 round plates.

1x1 round plate

Plate with horizontal clip

Torch made from a flame piece and robot arm

THIS CANNON IS SURE TO GO WITH A BANG!

CANNON

Official LEGO cannons can be found in many ship sets. If you don't have one, though, just build your own! You need a long barrel, a base and some wheels if you want to make it mobile.

MICROMEDIEVAL

Have you ever wanted to build a really big castle, but didn't have enough bricks? Try shrinking it down! Build it at a smaller-than-minifigure scale to make huge structures from just a few bricks. Your LEGO knights might not fit inside, but with the right pieces and some imagination, you can create churches, houses, animals – even a whole micromedieval world!

BUILDING BRIEF
Objective: Build microscale castles and other microcreations
Use: Building up a medieval world
Features: Tiny but easily identifiable
Extras: A whole surrounding kingdom

FANTASY CASTLE

This magical castle may be small, but it has plenty of interest. A small arch is used to top the front gate, a tile can be a drawbridge and round 1x1 bricks make the towers. The roofs are covered in 1x1 dark grey slopes, cones and tiles to complement the sand-coloured walls.

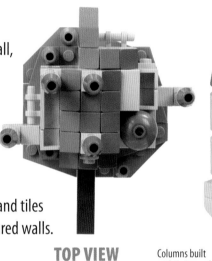

TOP VIEW

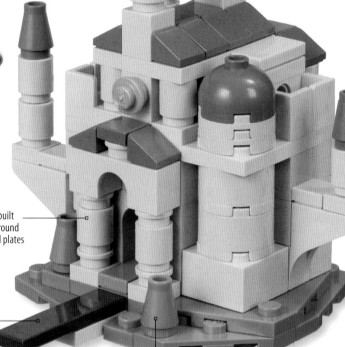

Make your castle as elaborate as you want!

Columns built with 1x1 round bricks and plates

Drawbridge is a single tile supported by plates

A 1x1 cone makes a great tree at microscale!

Square windows are actually the backs of headlight bricks

Castle roof made from ridged roof slopes

Arched window

STONE CASTLE

For a traditional-looking castle, start with a few plates to make a base. Next, add the corner towers and then build the rest of the castle between them. Pointy roofs, arched doors and thin walls complete the look!

Tree made from 1x1 round brick

TOP SIDE VIEW

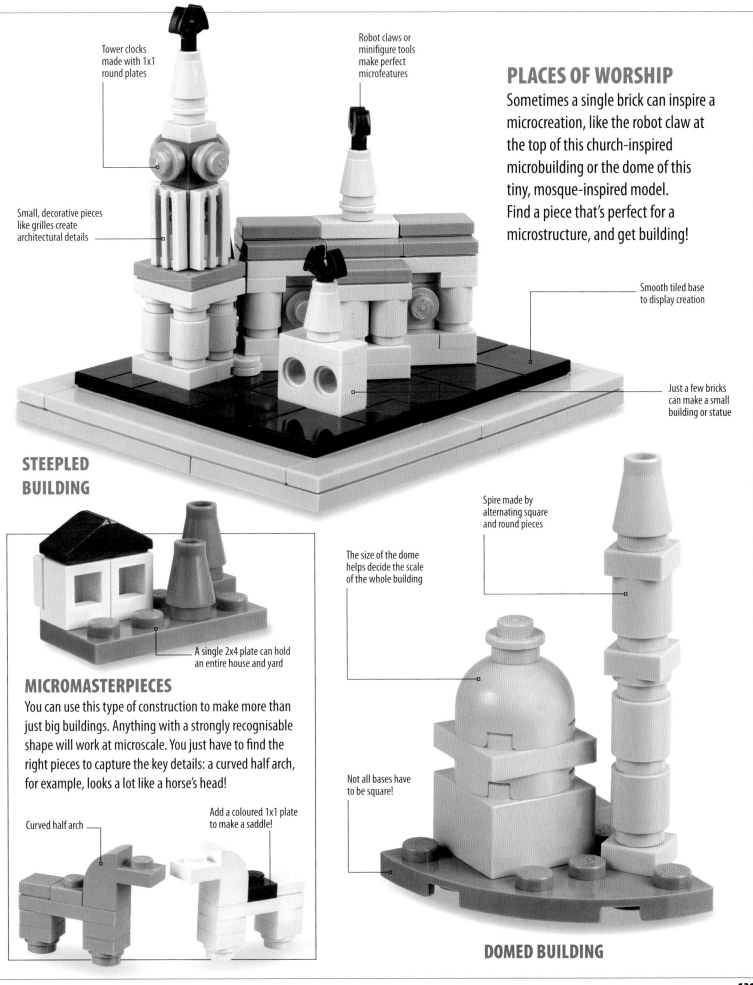

Tower clocks made with 1x1 round plates

Robot claws or minifigure tools make perfect microfeatures

PLACES OF WORSHIP

Sometimes a single brick can inspire a microcreation, like the robot claw at the top of this church-inspired microbuilding or the dome of this tiny, mosque-inspired model. Find a piece that's perfect for a microstructure, and get building!

Small, decorative pieces like grilles create architectural details

Smooth tiled base to display creation

Just a few bricks can make a small building or statue

STEEPLED BUILDING

A single 2x4 plate can hold an entire house and yard

Spire made by alternating square and round pieces

The size of the dome helps decide the scale of the whole building

MICROMASTERPIECES

You can use this type of construction to make more than just big buildings. Anything with a strongly recognisable shape will work at microscale. You just have to find the right pieces to capture the key details: a curved half arch, for example, looks a lot like a horse's head!

Not all bases have to be square!

Curved half arch

Add a coloured 1x1 plate to make a saddle!

DOMED BUILDING

MEET THE BUILDER

SEBASTIAAN ARTS

Location: The Netherlands
Age: 27
LEGO Speciality: Castles and other medieval buildings

What are you inspired by?

I mostly make buildings, so I often get inspiration just walking around town. Whenever I watch documentaries or read articles about castles and medieval buildings, my fingers really itch to build! I also get a lot of inspiration from movies – I pay particular attention to the background buildings and scenery. Seeing LEGO creations by other builders is also a great source of inspiration: sometimes I'll see a clever building technique or part of a creation that makes me think, so I can't stop myself from sitting down and building.

Placing part of your building at an unusual angle can really make your castle a lot more interesting looking.

It's not all about castles! You can also build churches, houses and farms in a medieval setting. This model is based on the church of Scherpenheuvel in Belgium.

To the walls! Siege towers like this were used very widely in the Middle Ages. Invaders could approach their enemy's castle walls protected in their siege tower and then use the height of the tower to climb up and over the castle walls.

NOTHING IS IMPOSSIBLE WITH LEGO BRICKS!

If you had all the LEGO bricks (and time!) in the world, what would you build?

This is a subject that has come up in conversations with other fans many times before, and for me that's an easy answer. There's a castle on a rocky island in the north of France named Mont Saint-Michel. I would love to build that whole castle in full minifigure scale. That would be my dream creation.

What is your favourite creation?

The "Abbey of Saint Rumare", a fictional fortified church built on a rock. It's big, complex and full of different techniques and building styles – the landscape alone combines water with landscaping, rocky surfaces and vegetation. The main structure has a huge church in tan, grey fortifications and lots of different buildings inside in different colours and styles, to create that messy, thrown-together look that you would often find in medieval castles.

What things have gone wrong and how have you dealt with them?

My first response to any question like this would be that nothing is impossible with LEGO bricks! If you're building something that doesn't quite fit, there's always a different combination of parts that will fit. If you can't figure it out, step back for a bit, do something else and go back to your "problem" later – you'll often suddenly see a solution.

What is the biggest or most complex model you've made?

The biggest model I've made is the "Abbey of Saint Rumare". This model was also quite complex, because everything is built at different angles. My most complex model by far was a star-shaped fort, which I named "Herenbosch". The star shape created a series of odd angles linked together, which then had to fit snugly with the buildings inside the castle. This took a lot of work – mostly trial and error – to find exactly the right angles for every part of the castle.

Height can add another dimension to your creation. A tall castle can look a lot more impressive than a bigger, more spread out one. This is my favourite creation, the Abbey of Saint Rumare.

How old were you when you started using LEGO bricks?

On my fourth birthday I received my first LEGO sets, and it all started there: I got hooked straightaway. For every birthday that followed, all I wanted was more LEGO sets. From an early age, I always enjoyed building my own creations.

A drawbridge can also be used as an effective door. However, you need to make it big enough to cover the gate when raised

What are some of your top LEGO tips?

When building a castle, don't limit yourself to just one or two colours. Real castles often took a long time to build, and sometimes bits were added later with a different material. You should also be open to building in different directions: Don't have enough bricks to build a wall? A plate with tiles on its side makes a perfect wall. Don't have enough tiles to make a smooth floor? Try building a wall and placing it on its side to make the floor.

Do you plan out your build? If so, how?

Yes, definitely. Whenever I have a building in mind, I draw a plan of it first, to determine how big each part of the castle should be compared to the other parts around it. I really love building at odd angles, so this requires quite a bit of measuring before I can even start building. I always get the plan on paper before I start building, that way when I do start building, I know exactly where to begin. Of course, I leave enough room for improvisation – if something doesn't quite fit as planned, or if I suddenly come up with a better idea when I actually have the bricks in my hands. So, even if I have drawn a plan to begin from, I usually change it and improvise while building.

Star-shaped forts such as my "Herenbosch" model were very common in the late Middle Ages, after the invention of gunpowder and cannons. The angle of the walls makes it more difficult for cannonballs to punch straight through them.

Adding detailed and uneven terrain around your castle looks more realistic and also more dynamic.

What else do you enjoy making, apart from castles?

I really love everything that I can make with LEGO bricks! I'm mostly into buildings – not just medieval buildings but also more modern town buildings or even science-fiction laboratories or spaceship hangars. Apart from that I also enjoy building cars, spaceships, pirate ships and heavy machinery such as bulldozers or excavators. It really depends what I'm in the mood to build.

Which model were you most proud of as a young LEGO builder?

I was always into castles as a kid too, so my most fond memories are of the biggest castles I could build. I would use as many of my LEGO pieces as I could to build the biggest possible castle. One castle I can particularly remember being proud of was one that had a big dragon's head as a gate – that was very tricky to make and I thought it looked very real and menacing.

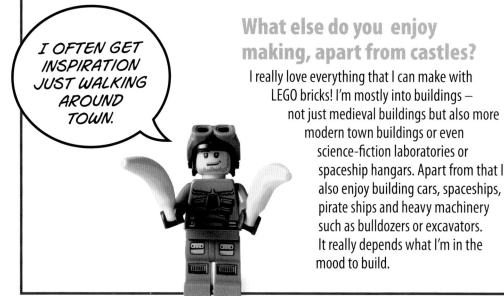

I OFTEN GET INSPIRATION JUST WALKING AROUND TOWN.

What is your favourite LEGO technique or technique you use the most?

I always love finding new ways to make the same thing, and I love using as many different techniques in the same creation as I can, while still keeping it coherent. What I use the most is the technique of using different-coloured and different-shaped bricks to break up an otherwise boring grey wall. Other than that, I love building at all sorts of odd angles to make any building look more interesting. There are many ways to place things at an angle, and there's really no right or wrong way to do it, as long as your chosen technique achieves the correct angle.

What is your favourite LEGO brick or piece?

That's an easy choice for me: the headlight brick.

How much time do you spend building?

This really depends on how inspired I am. Sometimes, I don't build at all for a few weeks. But sometimes, when I have an idea in my head I just can't stop building, and I build from the moment I get home from work until the moment I get so tired that I just have to go to bed.

Don't have enough bricks of the same colour? You can always combine different colours. In this case I used grey for stone and red for clay bricks.

How many LEGO bricks do you have?

I don't know the exact number, because I buy bricks in bulk and trade bricks with other LEGO fans. However, based on other people's collections and logical guesswork, I estimate my collection at about 700,000-750,000 pieces.

If you build a trapdoor, make sure it looks just like the rest of the floor, so it's not easy to spot

A WORLD OF ADVENTURE

Where will your imagination take you? Will you become a treasure-seeking pirate? Will you sail the seven seas in a Viking longship? Will you explore dangerous jungles? Or will you invent a super cool robot? Go ahead, it's your LEGO® fantasy!

Ahoy there matey! Keep an eye out for enemy ships from this pirate hideout. Who knows what other treasures may be hidden on the island... (See pp.146–147)

BRICKS FOR ADVENTURE

In your world of adventure, anything is possible. Swinging vines, towering ships and hi-tech robots all have a place in your LEGO world. Here are some bricks that might be useful when building your fantastic adventures, but search your own collection for cool pieces, and use them! What else can you build?

PLANT

VINE/WHIP

CARROT TOP

TELESCOPE

FLAME

LEGO® TECHNIC DISK

SKELETON HEAD

ANTENNA

PALM TREE LEAF

TURKEY

HORN

LIGHTBULB

1x1 TOOTH PLATE

1x1 ROUND PLATE

THAT FINAL TOUCH
Keep an eye out for small pieces that will add detail to your adventure scene. A flaming candlestick can bring a Viking celebration to life! (See Feasting Table, pp.150–151)

1x1 ROUND PLATE

FLOWER WITH OPEN STUD

1x1 CONE

2x2 PRINTED SLOPE

SMALL WAGON WHEELS AND 1x4 AXLE PLATE

LONG BONE

2x2 PALM TREE BASE

TAIL

2x2 BARREL

PALM TREE TOP

1x2x3 CURVED WINDOW FRAME AND LATTICE WINDOW

1x2 GRILLE

1x1 ROUND BRICK

1x1 ROUND BRICK

1x2 PRINTED TILE

VERSATILE PIECES
Long pieces like aerials and antennas are very versatile. They can be used for anything, from a flagpole to a bowsprit. (See Pirate Ship, pp.140–141)

MUSKET

1x4x2 BARRED FENCE

AERIAL

OAR

1x4 PRINTED TILE

STRING WITH STUDS

HINGED PLATES

SHORT CHAIN

1x1 PLATE WITH HORIZONTAL CLIP

1x1 PLATE WITH VERTICAL CLIP

LEGO TECHNIC PIN

1x2 INVERTED SLOPE

1x2 PLATE WITH CLICK HINGE

1x2 JUMPER PLATE

1x1 BRICK WITH VERTICAL BAR

LEGO TECHNIC HALF BEAM

1x2 PLATE WITH HANDLED BAR

HINGE CYLINDER

HINGE CYLINDER WITH PIN

1x2 PLATE WITH VERTICAL BAR

HOOKS AND HOLES
Pieces with clips, bars, hooks and holes can help turn a good model into a great model!

6x6 ANGLED PLATE

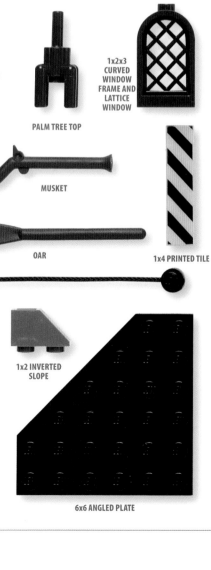

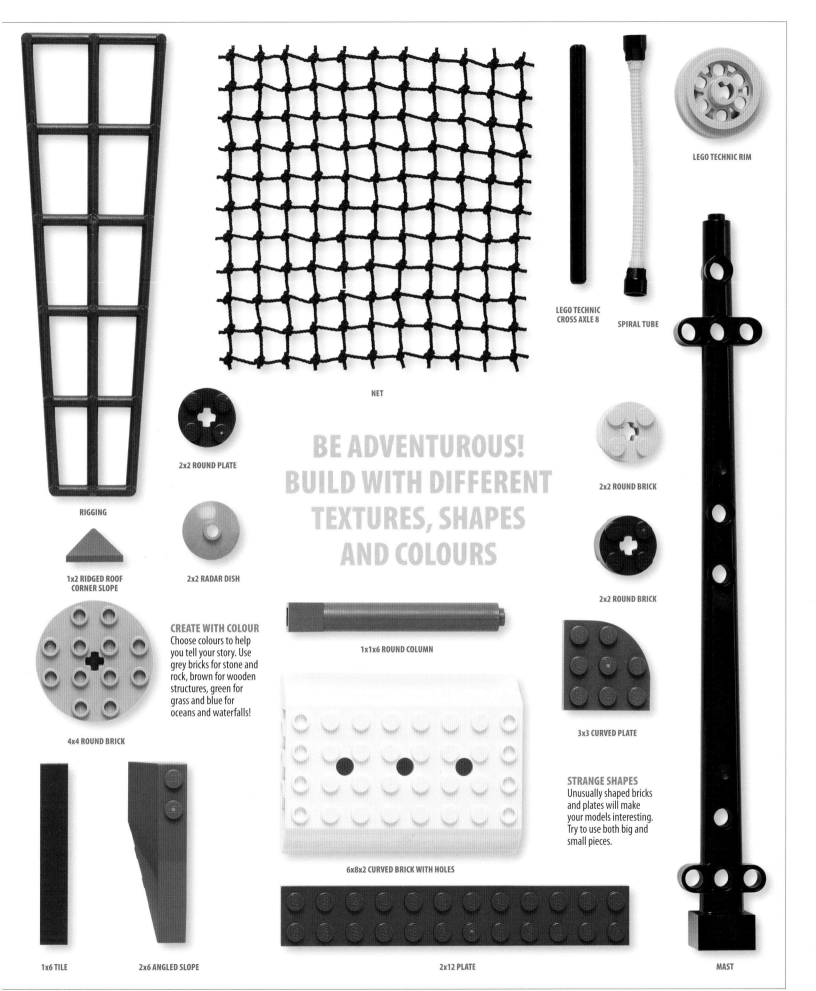

RIGGING

NET

LEGO TECHNIC CROSS AXLE 8

SPIRAL TUBE

LEGO TECHNIC RIM

2x2 ROUND PLATE

2x2 ROUND BRICK

1x2 RIDGED ROOF CORNER SLOPE

2x2 RADAR DISH

2x2 ROUND BRICK

**BE ADVENTUROUS!
BUILD WITH DIFFERENT
TEXTURES, SHAPES
AND COLOURS**

CREATE WITH COLOUR
Choose colours to help you tell your story. Use grey bricks for stone and rock, brown for wooden structures, green for grass and blue for oceans and waterfalls!

4x4 ROUND BRICK

1x1x6 ROUND COLUMN

3x3 CURVED PLATE

STRANGE SHAPES
Unusually shaped bricks and plates will make your models interesting. Try to use both big and small pieces.

6x8x2 CURVED BRICK WITH HOLES

1x6 TILE

2x6 ANGLED SLOPE

2x12 PLATE

MAST

PIRATE SHIP

Ready to set sail for plunder and adventure, me hearties? Build yourself a mighty pirate ship! You'll need a tall mast with a sail and a fearsome skull and crossbones, a treasure hold for all your loot, a plank to make the landlubbers walk, a cannon or three and, of course, a scurvy gang of buccaneers as crew!

BUILDING BRIEF

Objective: Make pirate ships

Use: Sailing the seven seas in search of treasure

Features: Masts, sails, pirate flags, cannons, planks, steering wheel

Extras: Figureheads, treasure chests, crew quarters, rigging

A BOATLOAD OF BRICKS

There are all kinds of specialist pieces that you can use to build a pirate ship, from hulls to cannons to bowsprits, but here's a way to make one using mostly standard bricks and pieces.

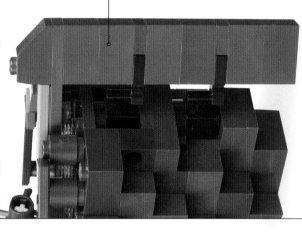

Rudder is important for steering the ship

STEER CLEAR

The movable rudder is built from 1x2 bricks and 1x1 plates. Two clip plates attach it to bricks with vertical bars on the ship's squared-off back end.

Railings built from tiles and supported by 1x1 round bricks

Skull and crossbones pirate flag made from a skeleton minifigure head and bone accessories

REAR SIDE VIEW

CAPTAIN'S CABIN

A small ship like this one doesn't have a lot of room below deck, but if you leave a hollow space under the rear top deck, you can make a cabin for your pirate captain. Give it a door and fill it with weapons, secret maps or looted treasure!

Sail built from angled plates and attached to mast with LEGO Technic beams

PIRATE'S PROW

To build a pointy front end, build columns of overlapping staircases that get narrower as you move towards the front of the boat.

Use a LEGO mast piece or stack 2x2 round bricks, running an axle up the centre for strength

Pirate weapons stored in barrels on deck

NOW TELL US WHERE THE PLUNDER BE OR YOU'LL WALK THE PLANK!

Tiles make for a slippery plank. Use a piece with exposed studs to stand a minifigure on the end

Bowsprit made from an aerial. You could also use an antenna, or even a fishing pole

A PIRATE'S WORLD

There is more to being a pirate than just sailing around in a ship! You can create an entire world for your bold buccaneers full of buried treasure, rival bands of pirates, cannon battles and daring captures and rescues. There's plenty of swashbuckling action to be had!

BUILDING BRIEF
Objective: Add to your pirate world
Use: Expanding stories, adventures and play ideas
Features: Places, vehicles, treasures, creatures
Extras: Pirate prison island, treasure cave

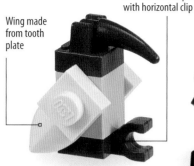

Wing made from tooth plate

Feet made from plate with horizontal clip

Beak made from horn

PARROTS
Every bad pirate should have a parrot! Start with a body of a 1x1 brick with side studs and clip on feet, wings and a beak to create a colourful bird. You could use a 1x1 tile and feather pieces to add plumage.

Build a giant box to store your own valuables (see pp.180–181)

Lock made from plate with handled bar

ALL THAT GLITTERS
Create treasure using transparent and metallic pieces for gems, coins and gold. Make sure your treasure chest is big enough to hold it all!

ARR, I'VE GOT THE TREASURE... NOW I JUST NEED A BIG HOLE TO BURY IT IN!

Plate with handled bar

Hinged brick and plate attaches lid to chest

PIRATE TREASURE
You could make a removable lid, but why not use hinged bricks and plates to allow your chest to open and close? You could even add a keyhole by using a brick with a hole.

TREASURE CHEST
Once you've found your treasure, you'll need somewhere to hide it away! You can build treasure chests in all shapes and sizes using plates and tiles that resemble wooden boards. Handles can be made using any piece a minifigure hand can clip onto.

PIRATE CANNON

Here's a cannon of a piratey variety. The flat platform and small wheel rims are ideal for rolling across the deck of a ship during a pitched sea battle.

READY... AIM... BUILD!

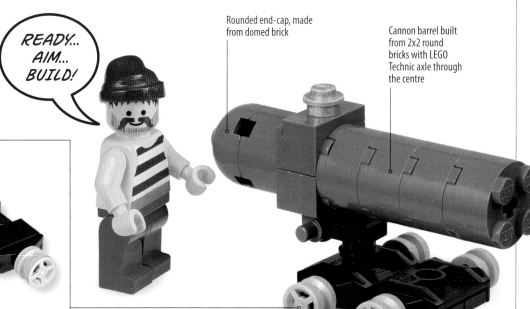

Rounded end-cap, made from domed brick

Cannon barrel built from 2x2 round bricks with LEGO Technic axle through the centre

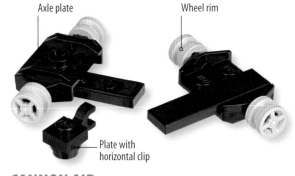

Axle plate

Wheel rim

Plate with horizontal clip

CANNON AID

For the cannon platform, attach wheel rims to upside-down axle plates held together by tiles. Then attach a clip to a handle on the cannon so it can tilt for aiming!

PRISON WAGON

Make a horse and wagon to whisk a captured pirate prisoner off to jail. For extra adventure, you could also build a secret hatch into the roof or floor for last-minute escapes!

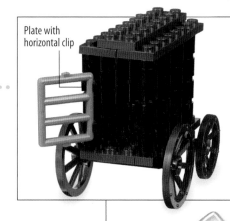

Plate with horizontal clip

LOCK-UP

A door hinge is created by building plates with horizontal clips into one of the bars of the cage. A single clip plate on the opposite bar makes a latch to close the door.

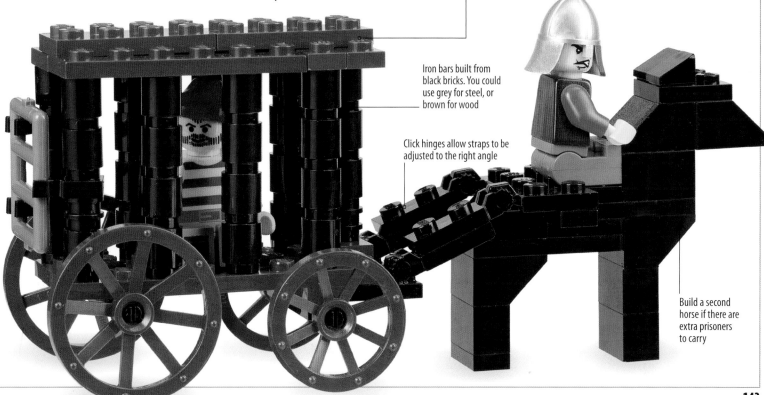

Iron bars built from black bricks. You could use grey for steel, or brown for wood

Click hinges allow straps to be adjusted to the right angle

Build a second horse if there are extra prisoners to carry

SHIPWRECK

Why not give your minifigures a pirate shipwreck scene to play in? You'll need a stormy sea, some ruinous rocks and a pirate ship smashed to smithereens! Think of what else you could add to the scene – perhaps some floating treasure or escaping prisoners? You could even build a rowboat to rescue any survivors!

BUILDING BRIEF
Objective: Build shipwreck scenes
Use: A scene to pose or play with your pirate crew
Features: Wrecked ship, rocks, water
Extras: Seagulls, waves, floating debris

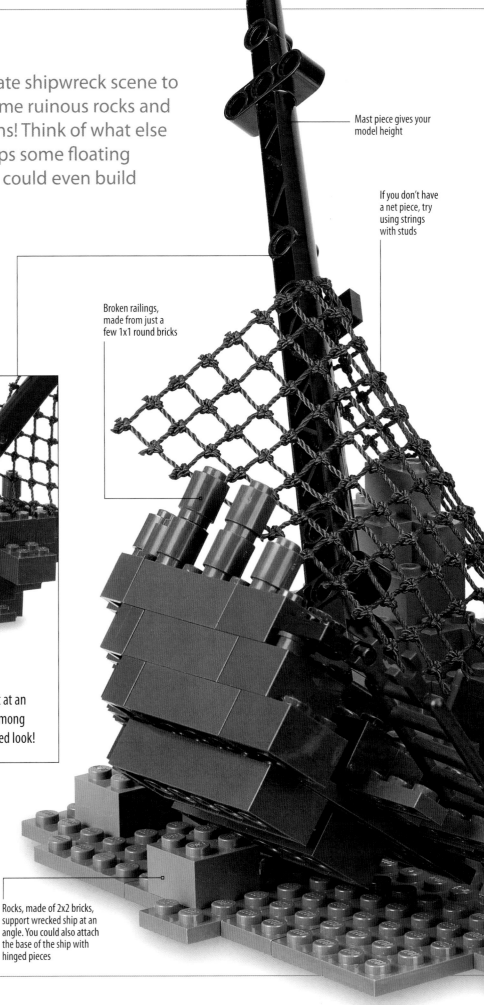

Mast piece gives your model height

If you don't have a net piece, try using strings with studs

Broken railings, made from just a few 1x1 round bricks

Ladder piece. You could also add other debris, like a seat or a ship's steering wheel!

Plate with click hinge

DECK DETAILS

Attach the mast with hinged plates so you can position it at an angle like it's been snapped at the base. A black ladder among the brown bricks adds interest and creates a really wrecked look!

HALF A SHIP

Once you know how to construct a ship, a wrecked one is easy – just build part of it! Make the edges of the hull uneven and add deck plates of different lengths so they look like boards smashed up by rocks in a storm.

Rocks, made of 2x2 bricks, support wrecked ship at an angle. You could also attach the base of the ship with hinged pieces

ROWBOAT

Build a rowboat just like you would make a pirate ship, but on a smaller scale. Use a rectangular brick or plate across two 1x2 bricks to make the pirate's seat.

Oars attached to clips that move back and forth

You could perch a parrot on the prow!

NOW THE TREASURE'S ALL...OOPS, I FORGOT TO TAKE THE TREASURE!

Flagpole, made from antenna. You could attach a small sail or pirate flag

TOP VIEW

You could use bricks in different colours for a patchwork boat made from salvaged materials!

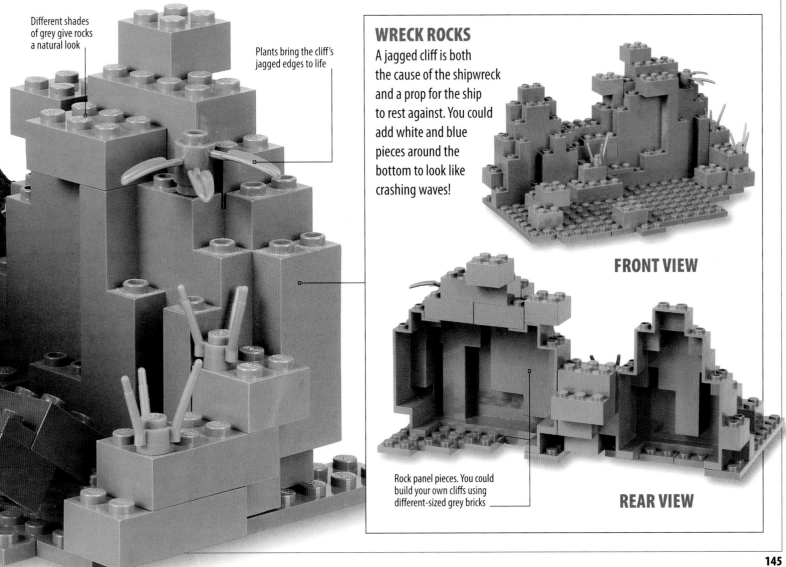

Different shades of grey give rocks a natural look

Plants bring the cliff's jagged edges to life

WRECK ROCKS

A jagged cliff is both the cause of the shipwreck and a prop for the ship to rest against. You could add white and blue pieces around the bottom to look like crashing waves!

FRONT VIEW

Rock panel pieces. You could build your own cliffs using different-sized grey bricks

REAR VIEW

PIRATE ISLAND

Even the most hardy sea dogs need somewhere to call home! Expand your pirate play with a pirate island. Imagine you're a pirate and think about what you might need in a hideout: how about a lookout for spotting enemy soldiers on the horizon? Or somewhere to moor your ship, or hide your treasure?

A pirate fort needs weapons to protect it. This huge cannon should scare away any soldiers!

NEVER MIND SOLDIERS. HAS ANYBODY SEEN MY PARROT?

BUILDING BRIEF
Objective: Build a base for your pirates
Use: Storing booty, battling soldiers
Features: Island, weapons, dock, lookout
Extras: Jail cell, treasure, hidden weapons, pirate flags

PIRATE PATCH

You could build a fancy fort or a humble home for your pirates. This hideout has a simple but interesting design, with two main levels and a lookout level, all built on a small patch of land anchored in the middle of the sea.

You don't need LEGO palm trees – make your own from brown 2x2 round bricks and leaf pieces

A base of blue sea gives way to yellow sand, then brown forest floor

Give your pirates a dock to moor their boats. Build it close to the fort for a quick getaway!

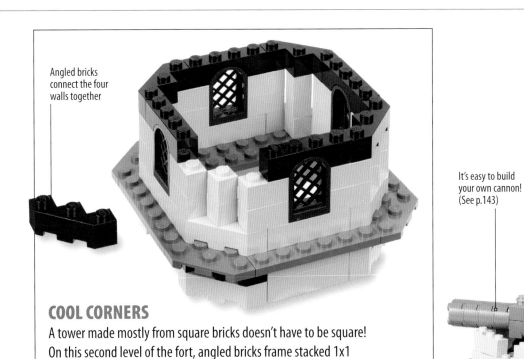

Angled bricks connect the four walls together

COOL CORNERS

A tower made mostly from square bricks doesn't have to be square! On this second level of the fort, angled bricks frame stacked 1x1 bricks to make the corners of the tower an interesting shape.

Add mast or hull pieces to your pirate base to make it look like it was built with salvaged parts from a shipwreck!

It's easy to build your own cannon! (See p.143)

Rigging attached to the lookout for the pirates to climb up

Plenty of plants bring your pirate island to life!

REAR VIEW

I'VE GOT A BOAT AND A COMPASS...NOW I'M OFF TO FIND TREASURE!

If you don't have a LEGO boat, turn back to p.145 to see how to make one

This lantern not only helps the pirates see at night – it can be moved sideways to lock the door!

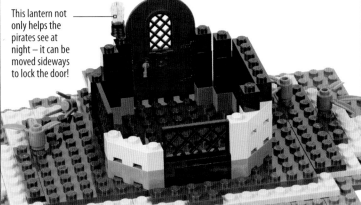

GROUND UP

The ground level features a large doorway and windows made from lattice fences. Dark tan bricks show where the tower has become dirty from the brown forest floor. Pirates aren't known for their cleanliness!

VIKING LONGSHIP

Are your minifigures ready to set sail and conquer the world? They'll need a longship for their Viking adventures. Viking longships have a distinctive look, with low walls and a tall bow and stern, but the rest of the details are up to you. How many oarsmen do you need? What figurehead will you build at the front of your model? You could even add a second level to your ship, or billowing sails!

BUILDING BRIEF
Objective: Create Viking ships
Use: Transportation, exploration, plunder
Features: Must hold a lot of oarsmen, stability, distinctive Viking appearance
Extras: Sails, additional levels, escort ships, enemy fleets

If you don't have a LEGO mast, you could build a stack of round 1x1 or 2x2 bricks

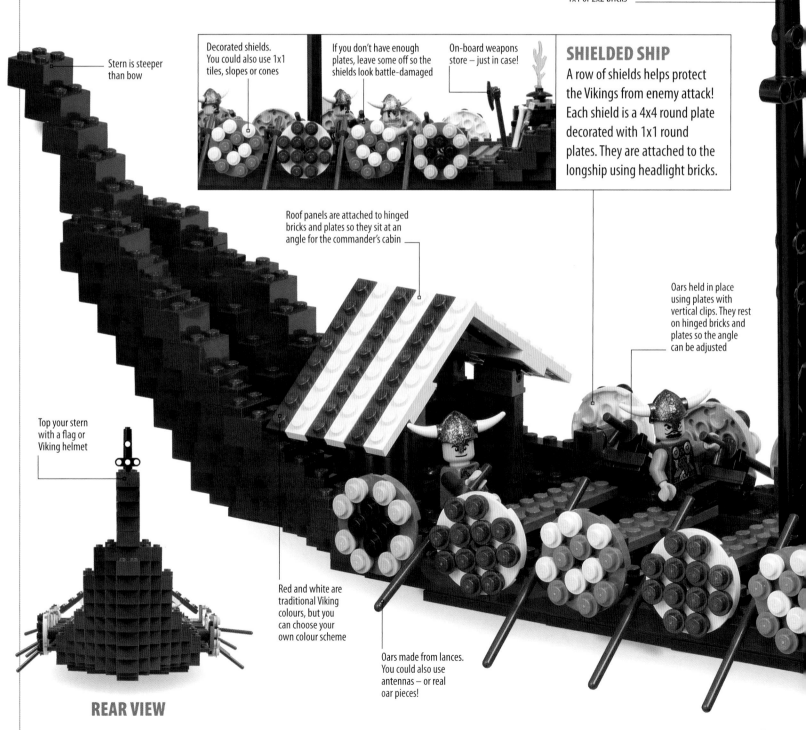

Stern is steeper than bow

Decorated shields. You could also use 1x1 tiles, slopes or cones

If you don't have enough plates, leave some off so the shields look battle-damaged

On-board weapons store – just in case!

SHIELDED SHIP

A row of shields helps protect the Vikings from enemy attack! Each shield is a 4x4 round plate decorated with 1x1 round plates. They are attached to the longship using headlight bricks.

Roof panels are attached to hinged bricks and plates so they sit at an angle for the commander's cabin

Oars held in place using plates with vertical clips. They rest on hinged bricks and plates so the angle can be adjusted

Top your stern with a flag or Viking helmet

Red and white are traditional Viking colours, but you can choose your own colour scheme

Oars made from lances. You could also use antennas – or real oar pieces!

REAR VIEW

MANPOWER

Viking ships are powered by a crew of strong oarsmen. Build a row of benches to seat the crew next to their oars. You could also add a furnace to provide light during the night.

This model is 16 studs wide. Decide how wide your longship will be. How many crew will it hold?

BOTTOM VIEW

Overlap plates to create a flat, sturdy base

A REALLY LONG SHIP

To get the shape of your longship right, start with a wide base of overlapping plates. Build the front and back sections separately using columns of stepped bricks that get narrower toward the bow and stern. Connect it all together at the base and secure with more plates if necessary.

Dragon head has white round plates for eyes and teeth

Flame held in place by a plate with vertical clip on top of a jumper plate

IF US DANES WANT TO CONQUER THE WORLD, WE SHOULD CONCENTRATE ON THE TOY MARKET.

Furnace built with log bricks, round bricks and a radar dish on top

Curved neck built from stepped 2x3 bricks

This style of building is also used for the Pirate Ship (see pp.140–141)

Don't have enough brown bricks? Use different colours for Viking war paint!

VIKING VILLAGE

Even the toughest Viking needs somewhere to come home to after a long sea voyage. Build him a village and fill it with everything you think a Viking clan would need, including hearty food, fresh water, a welcoming fire and a place to sleep. You could even build a wooden fence to protect the village from marauding enemies!

FEASTING TABLE

For a village feast, build long wooden tables and matching benches, then add as much food as you can find or build. Make it big enough for the whole clan to celebrate their Viking victories together!

SO WHAT ARE WE FEASTING ON THIS WEEK, GUYS?

THE FACT THAT WE FOUGHT THE BAD VIKINGS AND WON, REMEMBER?

Candlestick made from a telescope and a flame piece

If you don't have any Viking minifigures, combine armoured bodies with bearded faces

The longer your table, the more 1x1 round bricks you'll need to support it

UNDER THE TABLE

Long, narrow plates make good table planks, and 1x1 round bricks can be stacked to make legs. Small plates underneath hold the long plates together.

MESSY MEAL

Who needs table manners? If you have a piece that resembles food, stick it on the table. Bones and empty plates suggest the feasting has been going on for a while!

Don't forget goblets for toasts and quaffing!

I'M JUST PROUD THAT I BUILT THIS TABLE ALL BY MYSELF!

Knives, axes and swords come in handy at the dinner table, too!

Bench made in the same way as table, just with shorter legs

JUNGLE ROPE BRIDGE

You may never have been to a jungle, but everyone knows what they look like. Lots of green leaves, plants and vines. Ancient, twisted trees. Rivers and waterfalls. There are so many possibilities! And when you create the natural world in bricks, you can be as free form as you like – if you haven't got enough pieces to finish a tree, leave it as a stump!

BUILDING BRIEF

Objective: Create jungle scenes
Use: Exploration, adventure, discovery
Features: River, hanging bridge
Extras: Foliage, ladders, flowers

Vegetation placed on irregular tree surfaces for a natural effect

Only middle slat is doubled up to hold the string; string hangs loose elsewhere

This is a great piece to make a jungle vine, which only needs one stud. You could also build in clips into your tree to attach extra plants

ROPE BRIDGE

The coolest way to cross a jungle river is by rope bridge! This one is made from four lengths of string with studs on the ends. The slats are brown 1x4 plates. The trees are made from bricks, inverted slopes and plant leaves, arranged to look random and natural, with lumps and bumps all over.

Bumpy forest floor, created using brown and green plates arranged in an irregular pattern

Access to the bridge is via a ladder, attached to the tree with a plate with handled bar

FALLEN LOGS

Logs fall on the forest floor and plants grow around them. Side branches may also have leaves growing from them. These leaves grow in different directions, which is what this model is replicating.

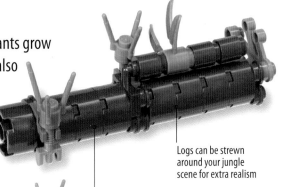

Logs can be strewn around your jungle scene for extra realism

1x1 round bricks form side branch

2x2 round brick

1x1 plate with horizontal clip

CLIP-ON LEAVES

The central trunk of the log is made from brown 2x2 round bricks. Then, a 1x1 plate with horizontal clip is fitted in so the plants can grow upwards from the trunk.

CAMP FIRE

Here's a camp fire for cooking or warmth — even the jungle can get cold at night. Brown 1x1 round bricks form the logs and robot arms and tube studs hold the flames.

If you don't have flames, you could create smouldering embers with any small red and orange pieces

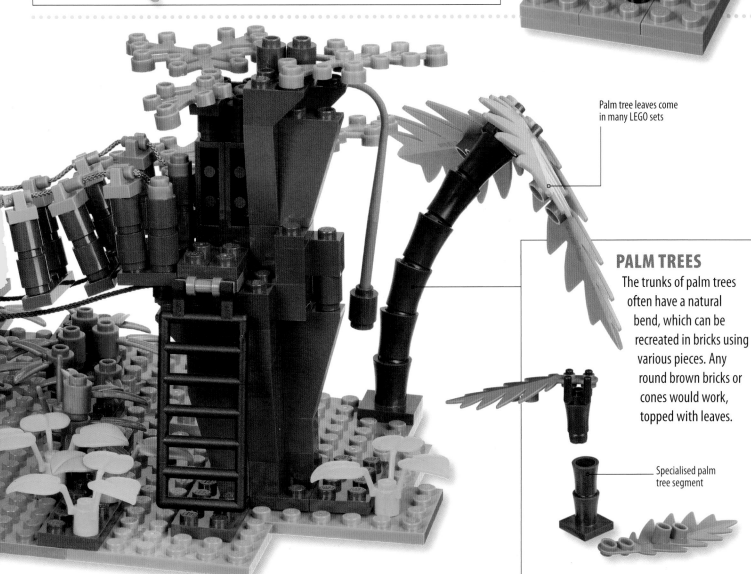

Palm tree leaves come in many LEGO sets

PALM TREES

The trunks of palm trees often have a natural bend, which can be recreated in bricks using various pieces. Any round brown bricks or cones would work, topped with leaves.

Specialised palm tree segment

INTO THE JUNGLE

Time to expand your jungle landscape! You can add mystery and adventure by building ancient ruins and long-lost forbidden temples. Not everything has to be man-made, either – how about a raging river full of snapping crocodiles or a rushing waterfall? Go wild with your creations!

BUILDING BRIEF

Objective: Expand your jungle
Use: New places to play and explore
Features: Crumbling ruins, waterfalls
Extras: Jungle animals, trees, mountains

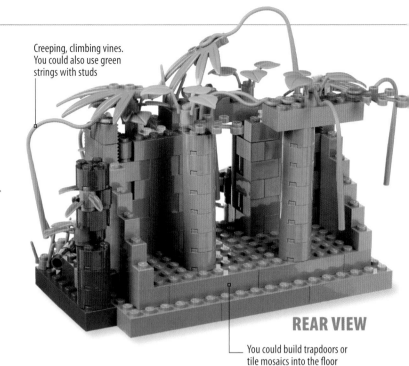

Creeping, climbing vines. You could also use green strings with studs

REAR VIEW

You could build trapdoors or tile mosaics into the floor

JUNGLE RUIN

To create an old, crumbling building, leave some of the walls incomplete so they look like they've fallen apart over the centuries. Creeping vines and other greenery show the jungle growing back over the ruins!

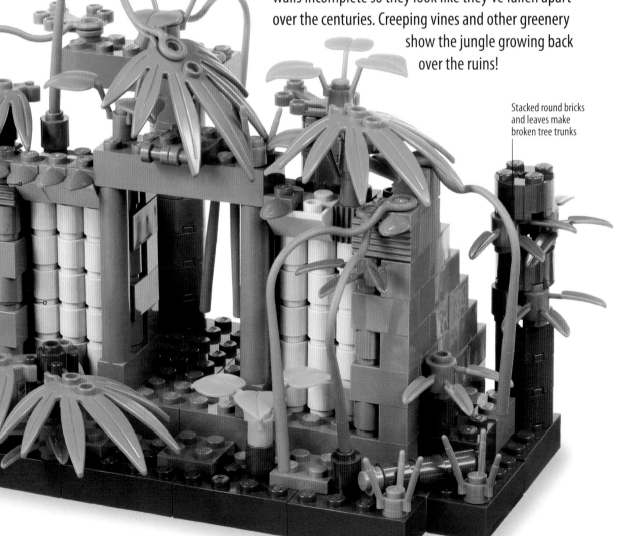

Mix different types of leaves and plants for an overgrown look

Grey pieces with unusual shapes or textures are good for old stone architecture

Contrasting colours create eye-catching details

Stacked round bricks and leaves make broken tree trunks

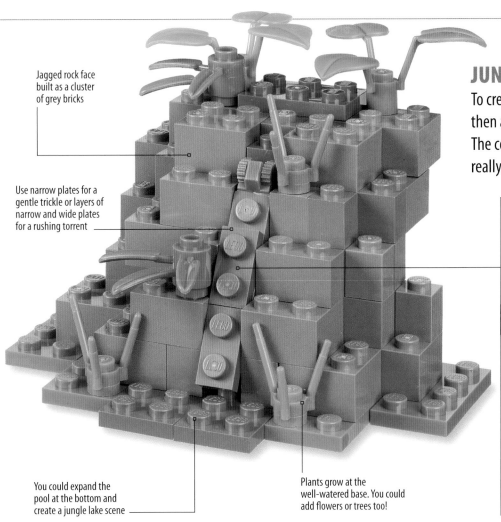

Jagged rock face built as a cluster of grey bricks

Use narrow plates for a gentle trickle or layers of narrow and wide plates for a rushing torrent

You could expand the pool at the bottom and create a jungle lake scene

Plants grow at the well-watered base. You could add flowers or trees too!

JUNGLE WATERFALL

To create a waterfall, first build a rocky base, then add blue bricks for running water. The coolest part is making it look like it's really flowing downhill.

FALLING WATER

The stream of this waterfall is made with one-stud-wide blue plates built onto plates with click hinges. Hinges allow the waterfall to be angled so it flows down the rocks. If you don't have hinges, try building the blue pieces directly onto the rock face.

GRAND ENTRANCE

The temple gate is built from a barred fence turned sideways. It is clipped to an antenna that is secured in the doorway. Use a plate with handled bar for the door handle.

Plate with handled bar

You can build the temple as large as you want!

You could completely cover your temple with vegetation and vines so it looks lost and forgotten

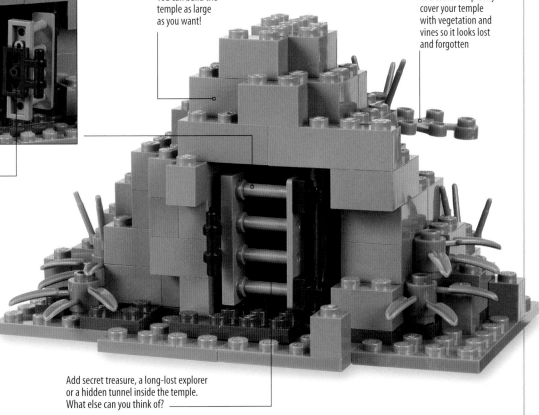

LOST TEMPLE

Even a small jungle building can make a big impact. This secret temple may look like an ordinary pile of rocks, but the barred gate hints that something important is hidden inside. What that is...is up to you!

Add secret treasure, a long-lost explorer or a hidden tunnel inside the temple. What else can you think of?

WILD ANIMALS

Fill your jungles, plains and savannas with wild animals of all species! Identify the shapes, proportions and patterns of your chosen animal and try to stick as close to the real thing as you can! The more you can show what makes the animal unique, the better your model will be!

Eyes, ears and horns attach to bricks with side studs

GIRAFFE

A giraffe's most recognisable feature is its long neck. Use a variety of bricks and slopes to get the body shape and markings just right. You could build a bigger head so you have more room for facial features.

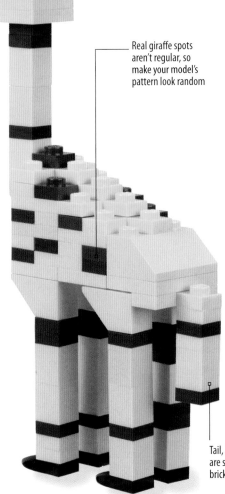

You could build a longer neck, but remember, the longer it is, the less stable it will be!

Real giraffe spots aren't regular, so make your model's pattern look random

Inverted slope creates natural shapes at base of neck and top of legs

Tail, legs and neck are stacks of 1x1 bricks and plates

Pointy hooves, made from tooth plates. You could use round plates for small hooves

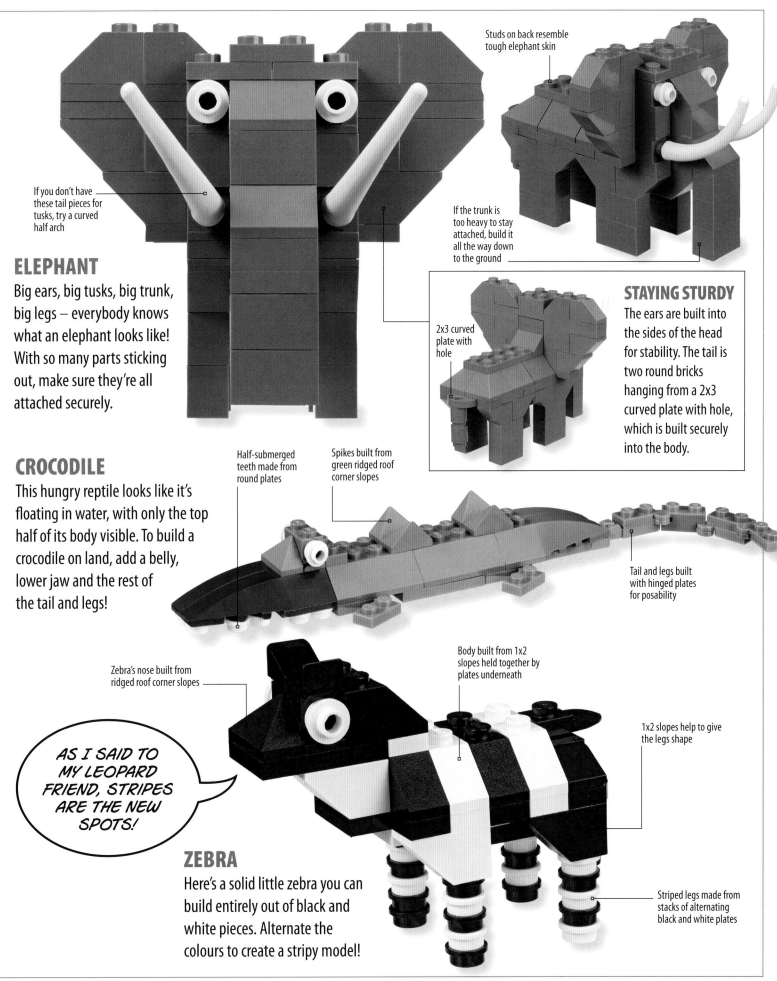

Studs on back resemble tough elephant skin

ELEPHANT

Big ears, big tusks, big trunk, big legs – everybody knows what an elephant looks like! With so many parts sticking out, make sure they're all attached securely.

If you don't have these tail pieces for tusks, try a curved half arch

If the trunk is too heavy to stay attached, build it all the way down to the ground

2x3 curved plate with hole

STAYING STURDY

The ears are built into the sides of the head for stability. The tail is two round bricks hanging from a 2x3 curved plate with hole, which is built securely into the body.

CROCODILE

This hungry reptile looks like it's floating in water, with only the top half of its body visible. To build a crocodile on land, add a belly, lower jaw and the rest of the tail and legs!

Half-submerged teeth made from round plates

Spikes built from green ridged roof corner slopes

Tail and legs built with hinged plates for posability

Zebra's nose built from ridged roof corner slopes

Body built from 1x2 slopes held together by plates underneath

1x2 slopes help to give the legs shape

AS I SAID TO MY LEOPARD FRIEND, STRIPES ARE THE NEW SPOTS!

ZEBRA

Here's a solid little zebra you can build entirely out of black and white pieces. Alternate the colours to create a stripy model!

Striped legs made from stacks of alternating black and white plates

ROBOTS

When building robots, anything goes! They can be simple or complicated, silly or cool. Who needs normal feet when you can roll around on wheels or clank across the floor with big stompers? Use hinges, joints and turntables to add posability, and try adding printed tiles, radar dishes and LEGO Technic pieces for mechanical details!

BUILDING BRIEF
Objective: Build robots of all shapes and sizes
Use: Heavy lifting, major computation, battle
Features: Movable sections, tools
Extras: Swappable parts, lights, motorised functions

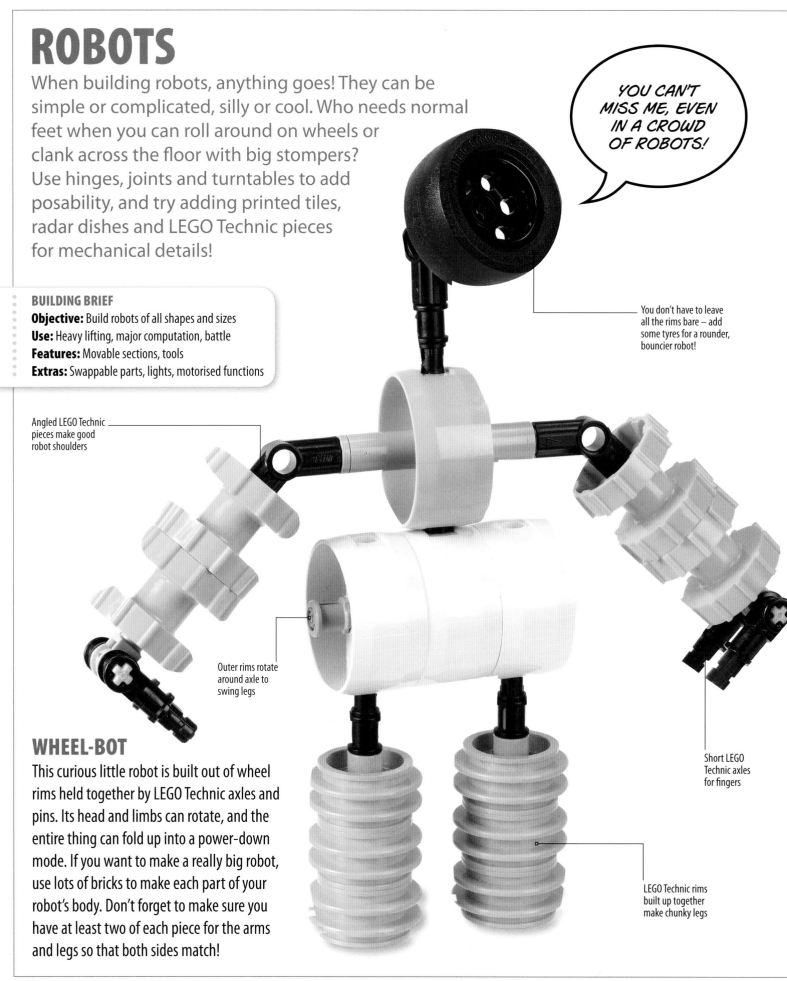

YOU CAN'T MISS ME, EVEN IN A CROWD OF ROBOTS!

You don't have to leave all the rims bare – add some tyres for a rounder, bouncier robot!

Angled LEGO Technic pieces make good robot shoulders

Outer rims rotate around axle to swing legs

Short LEGO Technic axles for fingers

LEGO Technic rims built up together make chunky legs

WHEEL-BOT

This curious little robot is built out of wheel rims held together by LEGO Technic axles and pins. Its head and limbs can rotate, and the entire thing can fold up into a power-down mode. If you want to make a really big robot, use lots of bricks to make each part of your robot's body. Don't forget to make sure you have at least two of each piece for the arms and legs so that both sides match!

ROBO-MOTION

The digger-bot's arms rotate on a LEGO Technic cross axle running through its body, so it can swivel each tool into place as and when needed!

Axle holds big wheel rims together back-to-back

DIGGER-BOT

It may not be the most mobile of robots, but put the digger-bot near a mine cave wall and watch it go! Minifigure tools, LEGO Technic gears and a construction vehicle shovel give each arm its own special function.

Long-distance antenna for communication with surface

Use any printed tiles you want for a control screen

Use different tools for different jobs

Radar dish for a base, but you could add wheels or treads so it can move around

If you don't have these hemisphere-dome eyes, try building crazy eyes of your own!

Hand made from palm tree top plugged into hinge cylinder with a LEGO Technic pin end

BUG-EYED BOT

Here's a big-eyed bug-eyed robot! It uses the same base as the digger-bot, but you could try adding legs if you wanted. Its round body complements its domed eyes, while the hinged arms make it really posable.

Spherical body built from overlapping plates. Or build a body in any shape you like!

Claw lets robot grab and hold on to other robots!

CREATURE 'BOTS

Robots don't need to have arms, legs or even heads. They can be wide, skinny, tall, short, huge or tiny. They can resemble real-life creatures or look like nothing you've ever seen before! Use unusual pieces to create your creature 'bots – the crazier the better!

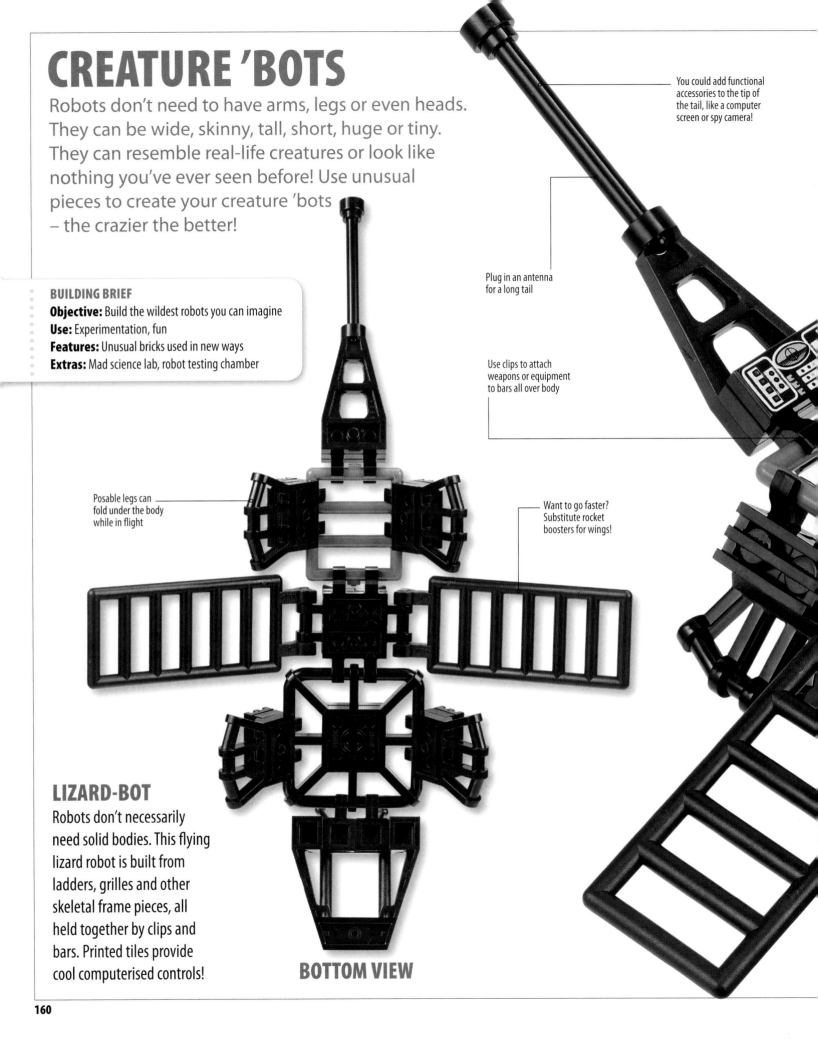

You could add functional accessories to the tip of the tail, like a computer screen or spy camera!

Plug in an antenna for a long tail

Use clips to attach weapons or equipment to bars all over body

Posable legs can fold under the body while in flight

Want to go faster? Substitute rocket boosters for wings!

LIZARD-BOT

Robots don't necessarily need solid bodies. This flying lizard robot is built from ladders, grilles and other skeletal frame pieces, all held together by clips and bars. Printed tiles provide cool computerised controls!

BOTTOM VIEW

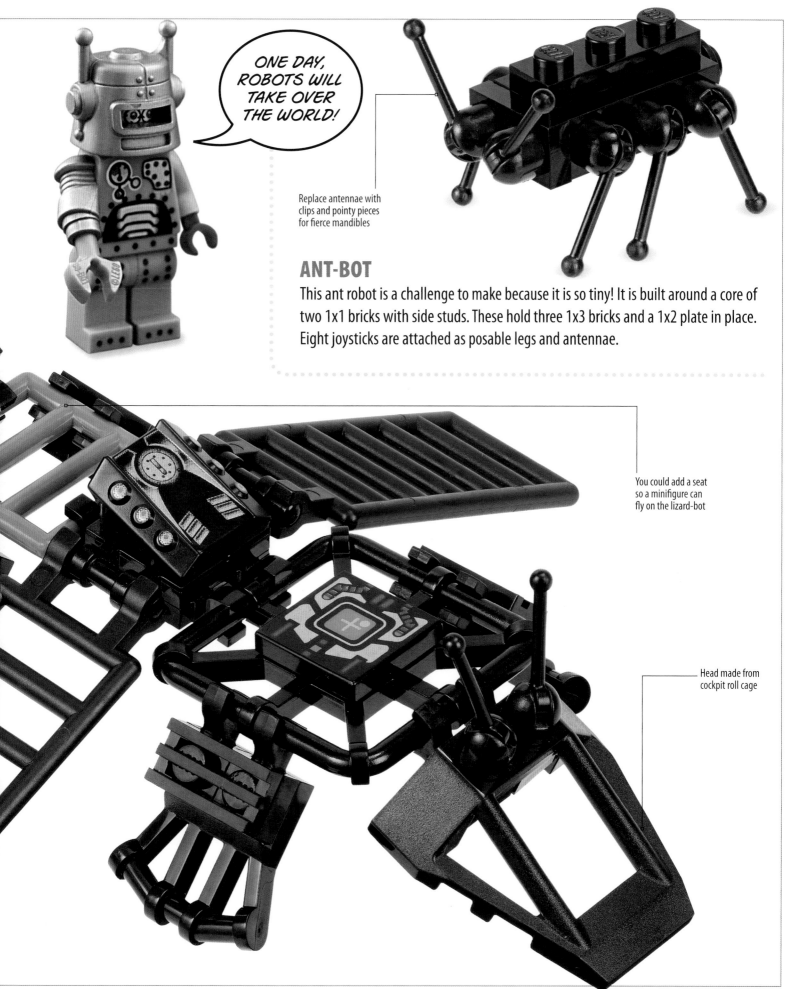

ONE DAY, ROBOTS WILL TAKE OVER THE WORLD!

Replace antennae with clips and pointy pieces for fierce mandibles

ANT-BOT

This ant robot is a challenge to make because it is so tiny! It is built around a core of two 1x1 bricks with side studs. These hold three 1x3 bricks and a 1x2 plate in place. Eight joysticks are attached as posable legs and antennae.

You could add a seat so a minifigure can fly on the lizard-bot

Head made from cockpit roll cage

REAL-WORLD ROBOTS

Robots aren't only from science fiction. They're all around us in the world today – assembling cars, working with dangerous objects, exploring the depths of the ocean and outer space and performing all kinds of other tasks that human beings can't safely do. When building a real-world robot, think about its function and what kind of design and tools it needs to do its work!

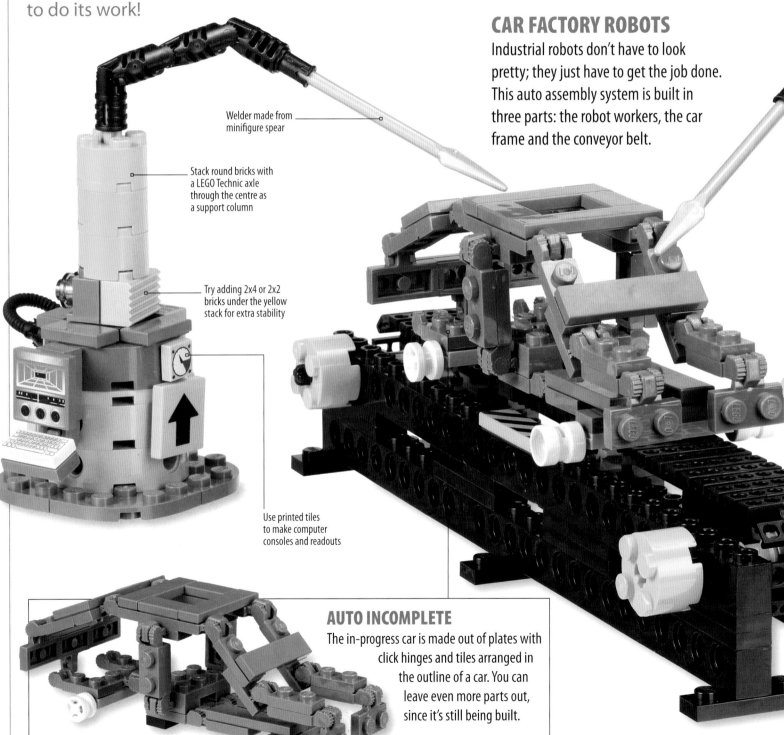

Welder made from minifigure spear

Stack round bricks with a LEGO Technic axle through the centre as a support column

Try adding 2x4 or 2x2 bricks under the yellow stack for extra stability

Use printed tiles to make computer consoles and readouts

CAR FACTORY ROBOTS

Industrial robots don't have to look pretty; they just have to get the job done. This auto assembly system is built in three parts: the robot workers, the car frame and the conveyor belt.

AUTO INCOMPLETE

The in-progress car is made out of plates with click hinges and tiles arranged in the outline of a car. You can leave even more parts out, since it's still being built.

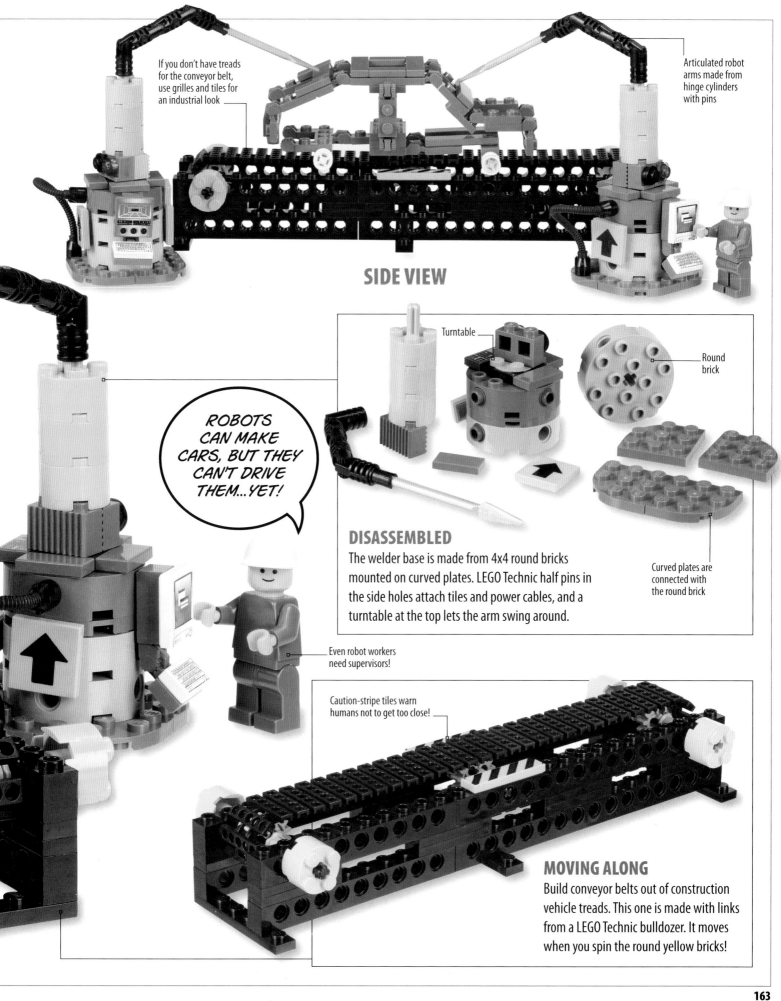

If you don't have treads for the conveyor belt, use grilles and tiles for an industrial look

Articulated robot arms made from hinge cylinders with pins

SIDE VIEW

ROBOTS CAN MAKE CARS, BUT THEY CAN'T DRIVE THEM...YET!

Turntable

Round brick

DISASSEMBLED

The welder base is made from 4x4 round bricks mounted on curved plates. LEGO Technic half pins in the side holes attach tiles and power cables, and a turntable at the top lets the arm swing around.

Curved plates are connected with the round brick

Even robot workers need supervisors!

Caution-stripe tiles warn humans not to get too close!

MOVING ALONG

Build conveyor belts out of construction vehicle treads. This one is made with links from a LEGO Technic bulldozer. It moves when you spin the round yellow bricks!

MEET THE BUILDER

DUNCAN TITMARSH

Location: UK
Age: 40
LEGO Speciality: Mosaics

What is the biggest or most complex model you've made?

I made a large version of LEGO set #375. It was the first castle the LEGO Group ever made and was in yellow. To make it bigger I built all the bricks six times bigger – some were easy but there were a few more difficult bricks to make, such as the hinges. I was then able to assemble the set from the original instructions and make a very large castle.

My wife likes the artist Banksy's pictures, so I built this LEGO mosaic version of it for her. It hangs in our hallway at home.

This is another of my mosaics. I wanted to see what a flower would look like so I picked a daisy and built it using 9,216 1x1 plates.

How much time do you spend building?

Every day. I have turned my hobby into a job and I am one of only 13 LEGO® Certified Professionals in the world. I build larger-than-life creations for companies who want to promote their products. I also build family pictures from 1x1 plates to form LEGO mosaics.

> I THINK I HAVE IN THE REGION OF 1,000,000 BRICKS!

What is your favourite LEGO brick or piece?

The 1x2 brick is my favourite brick because you can use it to build big walls. You don't even need any 1x1 bricks as you can turn the 1x2 on its side to fill the gap. When building with these it gives a great looking brick wall effect. If you want to make a curved wall, add some round 1x1 bricks between the 1x2 bricks.

What is your favourite creation?

I made a mosaic of one of the pieces of wall art by the artist Banksy. It took a couple of days to do but I think it looks great.

What are some of your top LEGO tips?

I always use a brick separator as it's made for the job and you don't break your fingernails or damage the bricks. If I have a LEGO Technic pin stuck in a beam, I use an axle to push from the other side.

What things have gone wrong and how have you dealt with them?

You can be working close up on a model and it seems alright, but when you stand back it's not quite right or you have missed some detail that could look better. The only thing to do is to take some of the model apart and rebuild it. You always feel better in the end, even though it takes longer.

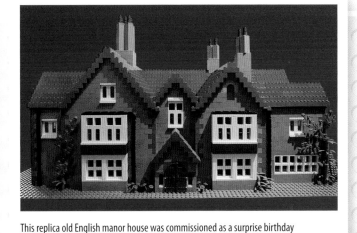

This replica old English manor house was commissioned as a surprise birthday present. Using only photographs for reference, it took me less than a day to build. The actual house is in Surrey, England.

The LEGO Group make specific boat hull pieces, but not everyone has them in their collection. I wanted to show you can make a boat just from regular bricks and this is my small pirate ship. I have added a gang plank and a pirate with a telescope. I made the skull and crossbones from new LEGO bone pieces

What are you inspired by?

I really enjoy building items that people see and use. The London underground map is a good example. I was on the Tube and the idea came to me, then I worked out what LEGO colours to use and it grew from there.

Do you plan out your build? If so, how?

I plan some builds using graph paper. I draw the outline of the model first then draw a square around it. This helps as a starting point for the shape of the model.

Which model were you most proud of as a young LEGO builder?

I built a town and the aim was to use all the LEGO bricks I had. I had lots of wheels so rather than build lots of cars I built a shop that sold wheels. This build helped me be creative with the bricks I had at the time.

How many LEGO bricks do you have?

I have not counted them all, but I think I have in the region of 1,000,000 bricks!

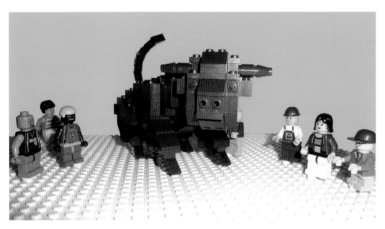

I was commissioned to make a model of the famous Bullring shopping centre in Birmingham, UK. This was the first section I built.

I wanted to build some furniture that actually worked. I built this chest of drawers for my daughter and it now stands proudly in her bedroom.

When building from real life you need to think of the key features to make your model recognisable. In this case, it's the giraffe's markings and long neck!

If you had all the LEGO bricks (and time!) in the world, what would you build?

If I had that much time I would really like to build a full-size town with all the shops and cars in it. I don't think it would be very practical, but it would be good fun to build!

What is your favourite LEGO technique or technique you use the most?

Using the bricks with side studs, which come as 1x4 and 1x1 bricks. The side-on build allows you to give a lot more detail to a model. For example, you can add lettering to the side of a building without having to build it in the wall by building the detail on a plate and then attaching it to the side studs.

How old were you when you started using LEGO bricks?

I was about four years old when I had my first LEGO set, but I was about 34 when I started building really big creations. Later, I met with some other fans of LEGO and the models got bigger and better!

What else do you enjoy making apart from adventure themes?

I really enjoy making pictures: it's like drawing but with bricks. Also, if you go wrong it is easy to change. My daughter likes to do them as well so it allows us to spend time together.

I REALLY ENJOY MAKING PICTURES: IT'S LIKE DRAWING BUT WITH BRICKS.

I really enjoy making pictures so I built this fat sheep in a field just for a bit of fun. I have also made a giraffe and elephant in this style.

I enjoy creative challenges. I built this pirate fort from a mixture of parts, using pieces from different LEGO sets

MAKE & KEEP

Here's an idea! Why don't you create some models that are so useful you won't ever want to break them up? LEGO® board games, pictures and small household items not only look great, they can have practical functions too.

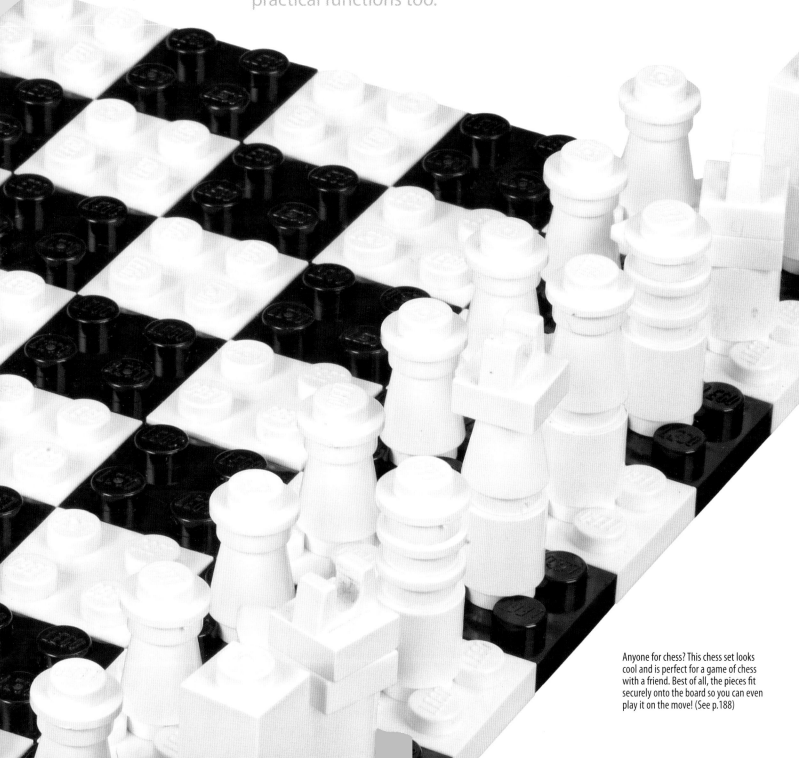

Anyone for chess? This chess set looks cool and is perfect for a game of chess with a friend. Best of all, the pieces fit securely onto the board so you can even play it on the move! (See p.188)

2x6x2 WINDSCREEN

1x2 BRICK

1x2x2 BRICK

2x2x3 BRICK

2x2x3 SLOPE

USEFUL PIECES

When building practical models, stability is key. Use lots of square or rectangular bricks to build a solid base before adding fancy and decorative pieces. To make your models exciting, build them up with different types of pieces, including bricks, plates, slopes, dishes, arches and cones. Here are some useful pieces to keep in your tool kit!

1x2 SLOPE

1x2x3 SLOPE

1x2 PLATE WITH HANDLED BAR

1x2 PLATE WITH BAR

2x8 PLATE

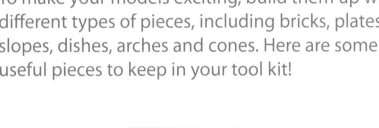

1x6 TILE

1x6 BRICK

1x2 BRICK

1x2 BRICK

1x1 BRICK

1x1 BRICK

1x6 PLATE

HINGES

Clip and bar plates are an easy way to build a hinge. Hinges are great for adding moving parts, like a lid that opens and shuts. (See Pirate Treasure Chest, pp.180–181)

1x4 BRICK

2x2 PLATE

1x2 TILE

1x2 TEXTURED BRICK

COOL COLOURS

Choose your colours carefully. Do you want your model to match something in your house or room?

2x3 BRICK

2x2 CURVED BRICK

2x2 BRICK

2x2 INVERTED SLOPE

2x4 ANGLED PLATE

2x4 DOUBLE ANGLED PLATE

4x4 CURVED PLATE

2x2 FLOWER

2x2 FLOWER

1x1 ROUND BRICK

1x1 PLATE WITH
VERTICAL CLIP

1x1 TOOTH PLATE

1x1 HEADLIGHT BRICK

2x2 CURVED BRICK

BAMBOO PLANT

1x1 ROUND PLATE

1x1 SLOPE

1x1 CONE

1x1 TOOTH PLATE

CLEAN CURVES
Curved pieces will help build
models with rounded edges.

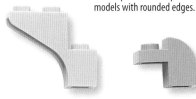

1x3x2 HALF ARCH

1x2 CURVED
HALF ARCH

VEGETATION DECORATION
Small pieces, such as flowers,
plants or transparent plates,
can decorate simple builds
like a picture frame. (See
Flower Power, p.183)

LEGO TECHNIC
T-BAR

THINK ABOUT WHAT
YOU WANT TO MAKE,
SELECT YOUR BRICKS
AND GET BUILDING!

1x3x2 CURVED
HALF ARCH

2x2 ANGLED
CORNER BRICK

SMALL PLANT LEAVES

2x2 ROUND BRICK

1x3 CAR DOOR

2x2 BRICK WITH WHEEL ARCH

WIDE RIM, WIDE TYRE AND
2x2 AXLE PLATE WITH 1 PIN

2x2 ROUND PLATE

2x2 RADAR DISH

LEGO® TECHNIC
CROSS AXLE 4

1x2 HINGED BRICK AND
2x2 HINGED PLATE

SPECIAL PIECES
If you have an unusual piece in your
collection, invent a model to include it
in! This white girder (below) works well
in a space-age display stand. (See Space
Station Display, p.177)

2x2 ROUND BRICK

2x2 DOMED BRICK

CONNECTING PIECES
Pieces that have holes and extra studs are a
great way to connect different sections of
your model together — and provide places
to attach decorative pieces.

4x4 ROUND PLATE

1x6 CURVED BAR WITH STUDS

4x4x2 CONE

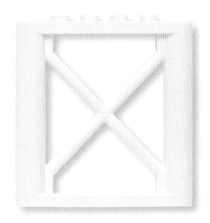

1x6x5 GIRDER

DESK TIDIES

Sort out your stationery with a LEGO desk tidy! Before you start, think about what you want to keep in your desk tidy: Pens, rulers, erasers? Do you need drawers? How big should it be? A desk tidy should be practical and sturdy, but it can also brighten up a workspace, so add decoration in your favourite theme or colour scheme!

BUILDING BRIEF
Objective: Make desk tidies
Use: Workspace organisation, decoration
Features: Drawers, shelves, dividers
Extras: Secret compartments

CASTLE DESK TIDY

This cool desk tidy has boxes for your pens and pencils, a drawer for smaller stationery – and it looks like a miniature castle! Start with the drawer and make sure it is big enough to fit whatever you want to store inside.

STEP-BY-STEP

After you've built the drawer, make a box that fits neatly around it. Once the box is high enough to cover the drawer, top it off with some plates, adding decoration and open boxes.

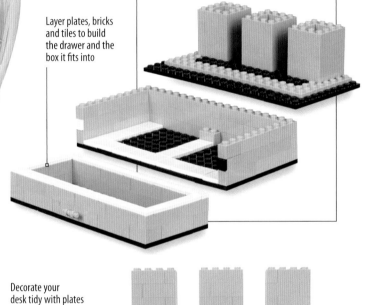

Layer plates, bricks and tiles to build the drawer and the box it fits into

Need even more room for your stationery collection? Build boxes in various widths and heights

Simple, square open-topped boxes hold pencils and pens

Decorate your desk tidy with plates in contrasting colours

FRONT VIEW

Grey, white and black bricks are good for a castle theme, but you can use any colours you want!

You could use a large plate to build the base of the drawer, but several small plates work if you reinforce them

Build a plate with handled bar into the drawer front so you can open it

SEA MONSTER

Scare away stationery stealers with a sea monster desk tidy! Begin with a basic box shape, build in dividers, then add the features that make a monster of the deep. Can you think of other creatures that could keep your stationery safe? Have a go at making those too!

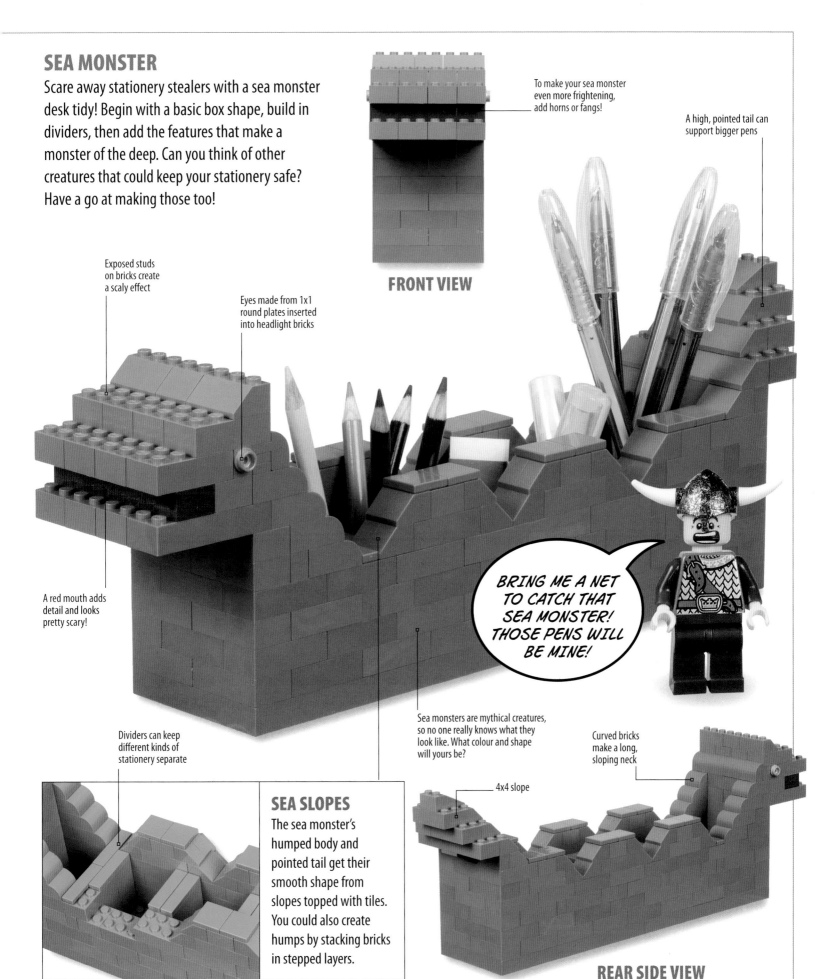

To make your sea monster even more frightening, add horns or fangs!

FRONT VIEW

A high, pointed tail can support bigger pens

Exposed studs on bricks create a scaly effect

Eyes made from 1x1 round plates inserted into headlight bricks

A red mouth adds detail and looks pretty scary!

BRING ME A NET TO CATCH THAT SEA MONSTER! THOSE PENS WILL BE MINE!

Dividers can keep different kinds of stationery separate

Sea monsters are mythical creatures, so no one really knows what they look like. What colour and shape will yours be?

Curved bricks make a long, sloping neck

SEA SLOPES

The sea monster's humped body and pointed tail get their smooth shape from slopes topped with tiles. You could also create humps by stacking bricks in stepped layers.

4x4 slope

REAR SIDE VIEW

TRUCK TIDY

Your desk tidy can look like anything you like. Why not take inspiration from everyday objects as with this colourful truck? It can deliver a truckload of stationery straight to your desk! What are your favourite things? What kind of shapes would make a good desk tidy? Try building one based on a car, an animal or a spaceship. Go ahead – it's your workspace!

Add lots of contrasting colours to brighten up your workspace!

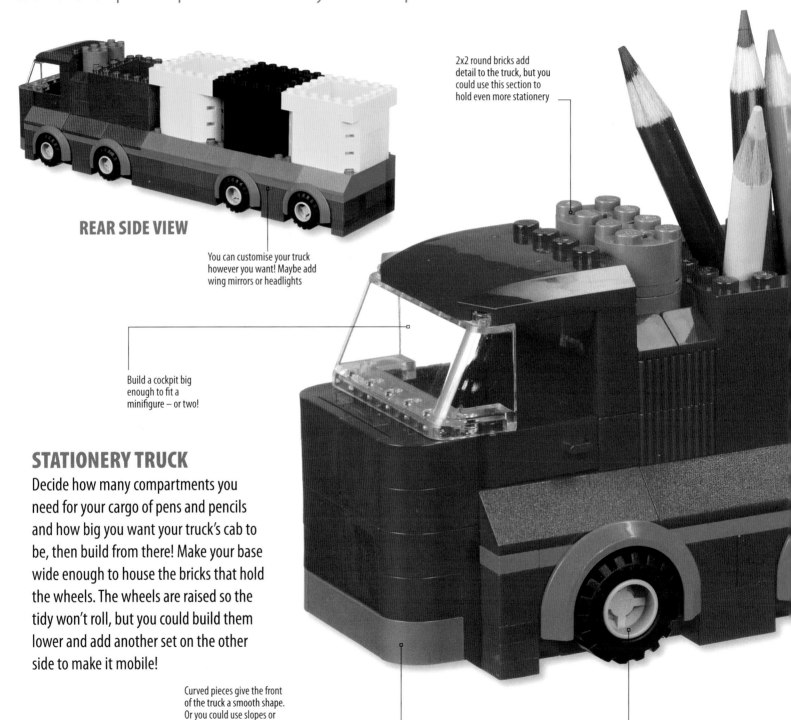

REAR SIDE VIEW

2x2 round bricks add detail to the truck, but you could use this section to hold even more stationery

You can customise your truck however you want! Maybe add wing mirrors or headlights

Build a cockpit big enough to fit a minifigure – or two!

STATIONERY TRUCK

Decide how many compartments you need for your cargo of pens and pencils and how big you want your truck's cab to be, then build from there! Make your base wide enough to house the bricks that hold the wheels. The wheels are raised so the tidy won't roll, but you could build them lower and add another set on the other side to make it mobile!

Curved pieces give the front of the truck a smooth shape. Or you could use slopes or angled plates

2x2 wheels fit into 2x2 bricks with wheel arches

SIDE VIEW

A brick separator could come in handy when you're building your desk tidy!

Compartments can be varying sizes, depending on what you want to store in them

Large buckets look like a real truck's cargo!

HANG ON... IF I'M IN HERE, WHO'S DRIVING THIS THING?!

Try using curved bricks instead of angular bricks to give your compartments a different look

This side sticks out from the cab so it can accommodate the wheels

TOP VIEW

MINIFIGURE DISPLAY

Be proud of your minifigures! Show off your building skills by making a display stand to house your growing collection. You can add to your stand every time you get a new minifigure. You can even build stands in different styles to display minifigures from different LEGO themes!

BUILDING BRIEF
Objective: Build display stands
Use: Storage, decoration
Features: Sturdy enough to hold minifigures
Extras: Doors, moving parts

DISPLAY STAND

You can make a display stand with simple bricks and plates. Build a basic structure that is stable and balanced. Then use special or interesting bricks to add detail. Choose exciting colours, or maybe use a colour that matches your bedroom. It's up to you!

REAR VIEW

NEW HEIGHTS
A height of five bricks is tall enough to fit most minifigures nicely, but if yours has a large hat or helmet you may need to make the level higher.

You will know straight away if one of your figures is missing!

A mix of minifigures makes your display stand interesting to look at

Use pieces like curved half arches if you have them

Unusual shapes built with half arches. Inverted slopes would work too

Use plates, not tiles, so your figures can't fall off

Headlight bricks could hold tiles that correspond to minifigures

NOW'S MY CHANCE TO MAKE A RUN FOR IT!

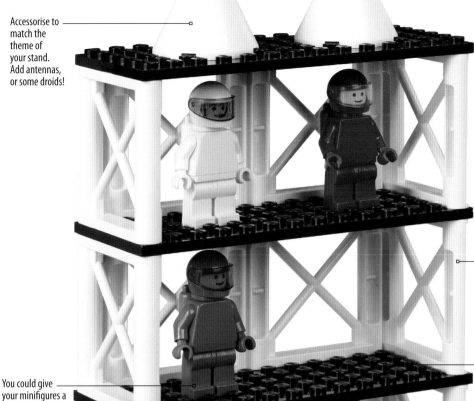

Accessorise to match the theme of your stand. Add antennas, or some droids!

You could give your minifigures a control panel or an escape pod!

SPACE STATION DISPLAY

This space station stand is out of this world! White girders make this display stand look like something from outer space. If you decide to use fun and unusual bricks for your walls, make sure they're tall enough to house your minifigures!

Build the stand as wide as you need to contain all your minifigures

If you don't have a big enough plate, overlap smaller plates to whatever size you want

5...4...3...2...1... BLAST OFF! WHOA, WAIT FOR ME!

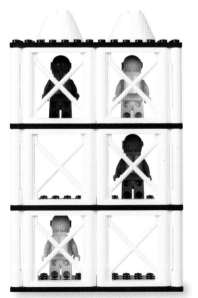

REAR VIEW

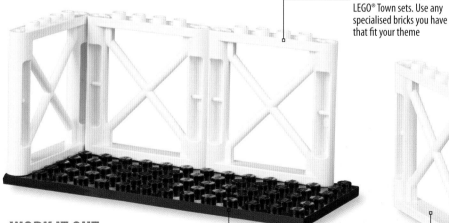

Girders come in a few LEGO® Town sets. Use any specialised bricks you have that fit your theme

WORK IT OUT

How many minifigures do you want to display in your stand? Once you know, build each layer accordingly using pieces that fit your theme. These white girders look really space-age.

Choose colours to match your theme. For an underwater theme, use blue and green. What else can you think of?

If you don't have these pieces, try building with transparent bricks like windows – they look great as part of a space theme!

BOXES

Are your LEGO pieces all over the place? Pencils scattered over your desk? These boxes are the answer. Think about what you will put in your box and how big it should be. It will need to be strong and stable to hold all your treasures. Choose a simple colour scheme and design – or just go crazy with your imagination. Don't feel boxed in!

BUILDING BRIEF
Objective: Make boxes to store your belongings
Use: Workspace organisation
Features: Hinges, drawers
Extras: Handles, dividers, secret drawers

FRONT SIDE VIEW

SHINY BOX

This box will brighten up any desk – and make it tidy too! The bottom is made of large plates, and the sides are built up with interlocking bricks and topped with tiles for a smooth finish. The lid is built as a wall that is slightly larger than the top of the box.

A row of shiny tiles finishes off the box lid

Choose your favourite colours for your box

You could increase the height of your box so you have more room inside

NOT SURE THESE COLOURS ARE THE BEST FOR A GOOD NIGHT'S SLEEP!

JOINTS THAT JOIN

The hinges are made from pairs of plates with bars and plates with horizontal clips. They are held in place by a row of tiles on top. To increase stability so you can use the box for longer, add more hinges.

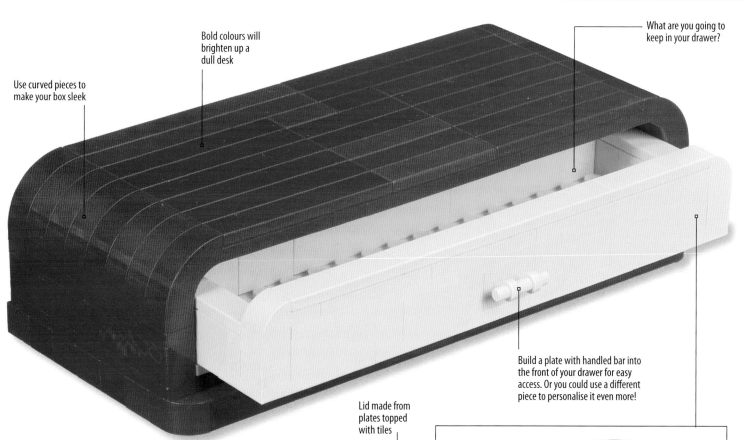

Use curved pieces to make your box sleek

Bold colours will brighten up a dull desk

What are you going to keep in your drawer?

Build a plate with handled bar into the front of your drawer for easy access. Or you could use a different piece to personalise it even more!

Lid made from plates topped with tiles

1x2 bricks stop drawer from sliding in too far

Layer of tiles

COOL CURVES

Boxes don't need to be boxy – they can be curvy too! Use curved pieces to create your desired shape. Make the drawer first, then build the box around it. Finally, create a base as a wall turned on its side. Use bricks with side studs to attach the base to the box.

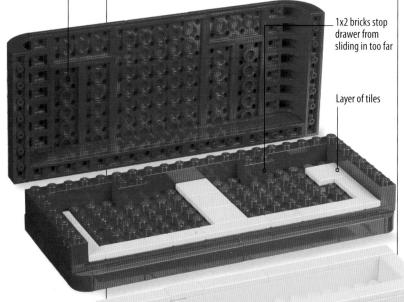

Curved half arch

FRONT VIEW

SLIDING DRAWERS

To help the drawer slide easily, fix some tiles to the base of the box. These will create a smooth layer so the drawer won't catch on the studs as it slides in and out.

TREASURE CHEST

You can make boxes in all shapes and sizes – and to match any theme you like! Maybe you want a medieval wooden trunk with big metal locks to store your knight minifigures. Or a hi-tech, zero-gravity space capsule for your astronauts and aliens. Use different colours to style your box, and remember, the lid doesn't have to be flat!

BUILDING BRIEF
Objective: Create fantasy boxes
Use: Storage, play
Features: Hinged lid, drawers
Extras: Secret compartments, decorations

PIRATE TREASURE CHEST

This treasure chest has a secret drawer at the bottom for hiding your most precious LEGO pieces (or any other treasures)! First, the lower half is built around the sliding drawer. Then the top half is constructed on top of that, with a hinged lid, built sideways. The more hinges you use, the more stable the lid will be!

A layer of plates divides the secret drawer from the chest above it

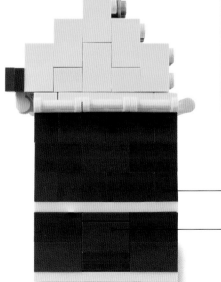

Overlap bricks for stability

Press on this secret brick and the drawer will slide out the other side!

Use different colours to theme your box – brown and yellow look like a pirate's treasure chest

SIDE VIEW

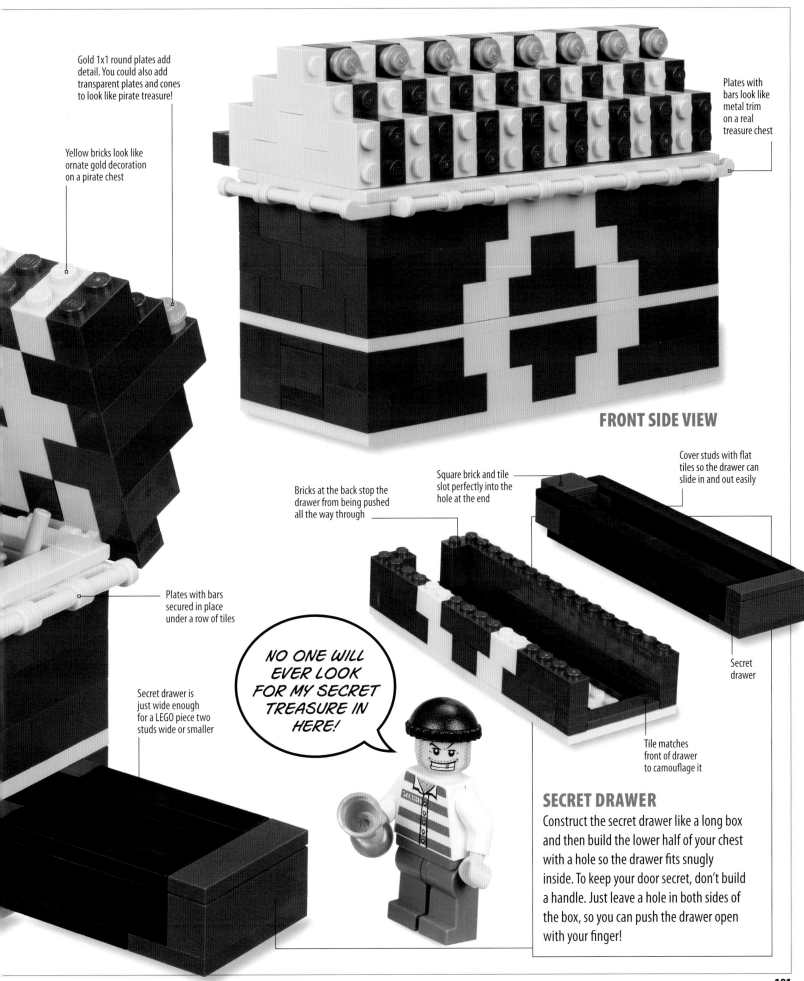

Gold 1x1 round plates add detail. You could also add transparent plates and cones to look like pirate treasure!

Yellow bricks look like ornate gold decoration on a pirate chest

Plates with bars look like metal trim on a real treasure chest

FRONT SIDE VIEW

Plates with bars secured in place under a row of tiles

Bricks at the back stop the drawer from being pushed all the way through

Square brick and tile slot perfectly into the hole at the end

Cover studs with flat tiles so the drawer can slide in and out easily

Secret drawer

NO ONE WILL EVER LOOK FOR MY SECRET TREASURE IN HERE!

Secret drawer is just wide enough for a LEGO piece two studs wide or smaller

Tile matches front of drawer to camouflage it

SECRET DRAWER

Construct the secret drawer like a long box and then build the lower half of your chest with a hole so the drawer fits snugly inside. To keep your door secret, don't build a handle. Just leave a hole in both sides of the box, so you can push the drawer open with your finger!

PICTURE FRAMES

Say cheese! How about building something to display your special pictures? You can use photos of your favourite LEGO models or treasured pictures of family and friends. Once you have a basic frame you can decorate it any way you want. You can even change the theme of your frame whenever you change the photo!

BUILDING BRIEF
Objective: Make frames for pictures
Use: Display your favourite pictures
Features: Sturdy frame, ability to stand
Extras: Multi-frames, themed frames, different shaped frames

BASIC FRAME

If you want your photo to be the main attraction, keep the frame simple. Use interlocking rows of plates to make two identical rectangles. A middle layer of one-stud-wide plates holds the two rectangles together and creates a gap to slide the photo in.

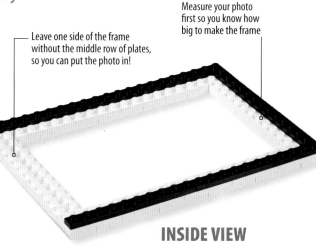

Measure your photo first so you know how big to make the frame

Leave one side of the frame without the middle row of plates, so you can put the photo in!

INSIDE VIEW

Add an angle plate to the top of the stand to make it more stable against the frame

REAR SIDE VIEW

Use a plate and a clip and bar hinge to build a stand

You could alternate the colours of the plates for a cool effect

SIDE VIEWS

I SURE MISS THE GANG FROM THE OLD NEIGHBOURHOOD!

FLOWER POWER

Now that you have the basic frame, you can get creative! Do you like flowers? Make them into a pattern to frame your pretty picture. You could also add some foliage or even a microbutterfly. Putting pieces at different angles creates an interesting pattern and helps fit more pieces on.

Use pieces that match your chosen theme

Use pretty flowers in your favourite colours

These radar dishes and transparent plates look really space-age

SPACE AGE

Why not decorate your frame to match your picture? This space frame has lots of translucent pieces and even a spaceman minifigure! To make the frame fit a portrait photo, simply move the position of the stands at the back of the frame.

Clip minifigures to bricks with side studs to add them to your frame!

Make extra pieces stick out to change the frame shape

Think of other pieces that would add to the jungle theme. Maybe a rope bridge or a mini waterfall?

JUNGLE FEVER

Add different coloured bricks to your frame to match your theme. Use brown pieces for a jungle theme and add lots of green foliage. You could even add animal figures. Go wild!

MOSAICS

Mosaics are the art of making pictures or patterns from small pieces of material, such as glass, stone...or LEGO bricks! First, plan how you want your mosaic to look. Will it lie flat or stand upright? Will it let through light? Will it be 3-D? You will have your own LEGO art gallery in no time!

BASEPLATE

A 16x16 baseplate supports these flag mosaics, but you can build your mosaic on any size base you like! You could also attach several plates together if you don't have the right size.

BUILDING BRIEF

Objective: Make mosaics

Use: Decoration, gifts

Features: Must be stable, especially if it stands upright

Extras: 3-D effect, recreate famous artworks, stands, frames

FUN FLAGS

Get patriotic and make your country's flag into a LEGO mosaic! These Union Jack designs are made from 1x1 bricks, with a few wider bricks where larger blocks of colour appear.

Use wider bricks for less detailed flags – it will save you some time!

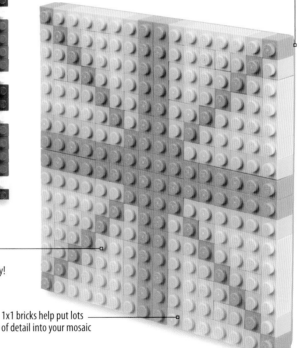

Your flag doesn't have to be in the traditional colours – go colour crazy!

1x1 bricks help put lots of detail into your mosaic

1x1 and 1x2 bricks are stacked like a wall to make this simple design

FLOWER ART

Say it with LEGO flowers! This flower mosaic stands upright to look like two flowers growing against a clear blue sky. Tall slopes form a stable base to hold the mosaic up.

WIDER BASE

Toward the bottom of the mosaic, an extra layer of bricks is built into the design to provide extra support for the base. The ledge is only visible on the back.

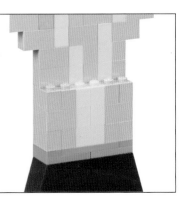

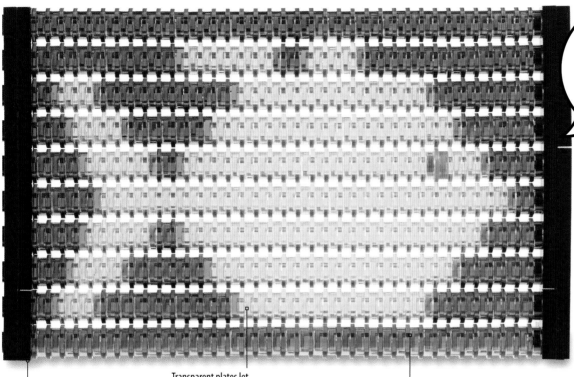

MARINE MOSAIC

This mosaic is entirely made from transparent 1x1 round plates. Ten rows have been carefully planned and assembled to make a floating yellow fish! Long black plates frame the rows.

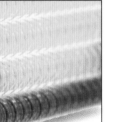

Transparent plates let light through, so the mosaic seems to glow!

CONSTRUCTION

The design of this mosaic takes careful planning. Transparent plates are stacked according to the pattern, then the stacks are attached on their sides to the end plates.

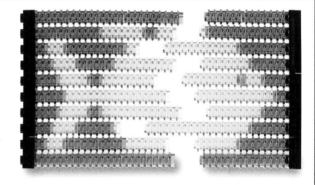

SUPPORT STAND

Add small plates at right angles to the end plate at both bottom corners. These allow the mosaic to stand up vertically, like a picture frame. If your mosaic is smaller, it will be even more stable.

ORANGE FISH

If you don't have enough transparent round plates to make an entire mosaic, it doesn't matter. You can mix and match! This orange aquatic artwork includes white round plates too. You can include 1x1 square plates as well!

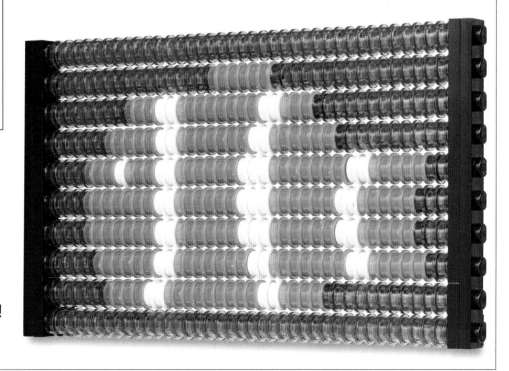

3-D MOSAICS

Mosaics don't always have to be flat. If you have bricks in different shapes and sizes, you could try adding 3-D elements to your LEGO mosaics to make them really stand out! First choose what picture you want to create, then decide which features will work best in 3-D. What do you want to draw the most attention to?

DID YOU REALLY HAVE TO DRAW EVEN MORE ATTENTION TO MY EARS?

Layer bricks at different heights to add perspective

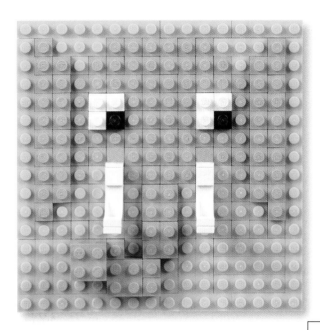

FRONT VIEW

White 1x1 tile covers the exposed stud on headlight brick

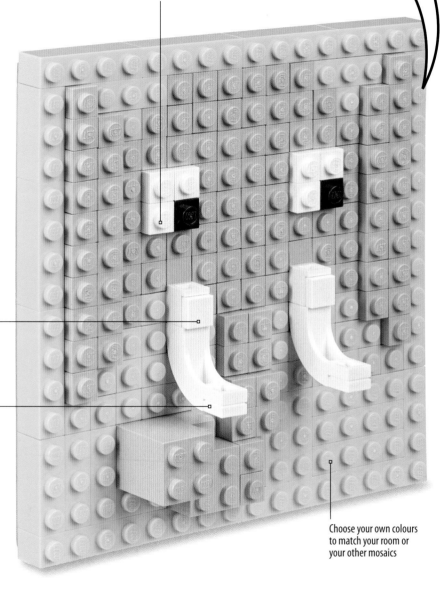

Choose your own colours to match your room or your other mosaics

TUSK TASK

The elephant's protruding tusks really bring the mosaic to life! They are made from curved half arches, which attach to the green background with white headlight bricks.

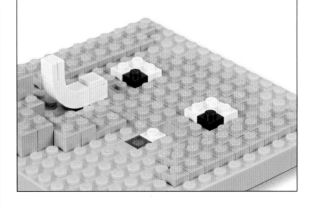

ELEPHANT

What is your favourite animal? Try making its likeness in 3-D! A 16x16 plate forms the base of this mosaic. The baseplate is completely covered in bricks, which form a green background and a basic grey elephant head shape. More bricks and plates are added to make the 3-D features.

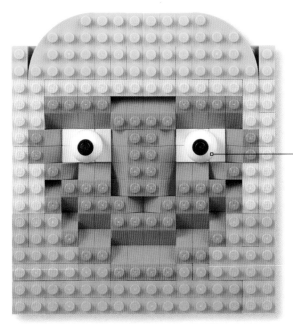

FRONT VIEW

FUNNY FACE

Don't restrict yourself to square bricks! Think about how you can form 3-D details with all different kinds of pieces. This girl's facial features are almost entirely formed from pink slopes! Used this way, the pieces create a cool, crazy-looking mosaic style.

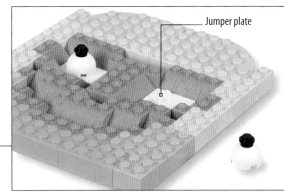

Jumper plate

EYE-POPPING

You don't have to stick to square bricks for your mosaics! Here, the eyes are made from domed bricks and black round plates. The domed bricks attach to white jumper plates.

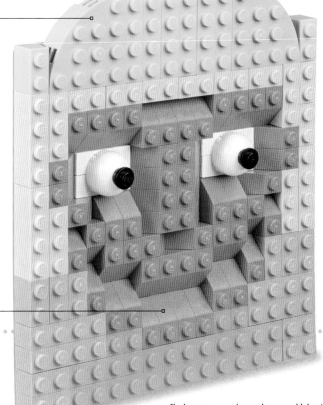

Curved plates form the rounded sides of the girl's green hat

Arrange opposite-facing slopes to make smiling lips

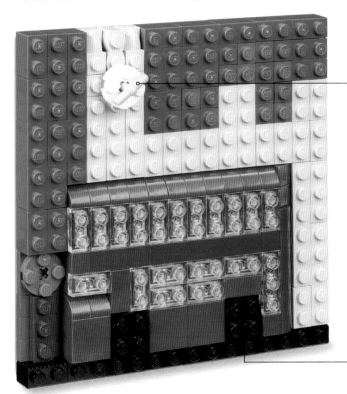

Big Ben's hands are a T-bar

CITYSCAPE

Lots of unusual bricks are used in this London cityscape. The clock tower, tree and red bus are all built using a variety of bricks. How inventive can you be?

Wheels are round plates

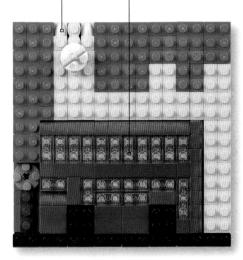

Clock tower built with tooth plates

Layer plates to add detail, like the transparent windows on this red bus

FRONT VIEW

CLASSIC BOARD GAMES

Classic board games can provide hours of fun. LEGO board games are no different – and they are ideal for long journeys because the pieces stay in place! All you need is a simple base and some game pieces. Don't know the rules? Ask your family or look online. You can even adapt the game to suit your favourite theme.

BUILDING BRIEF
Objective: Build board games
Use: Games to play with your friends
Features: Sturdy base, game pieces
Extras: Games table, bigger and more elaborate sets, dice

FINALLY, IT'S MY CHANCE TO CAPTURE THE KING!

Each side has eight pawns, two knights, two rooks, two bishops, one king and one queen

TOP VIEW

CHESS

A 16x16 base is a good size for lots of board games, including chess. If you don't have a baseplate, build one with overlapping plates to create a square. Then add eight rows of eight 2x2 plates in alternate colours to create a chessboard.

A standard chessboard has black and white squares, but you can use any colours you want!

CHECKMATE!

The chess pieces – pawns, knights, rooks, bishops, queens and kings –should be easy to distinguish. Will your queen have a big crown? Maybe your knight will have shining armour? Make sure the pieces are sturdy because they will be moved around a lot.

1x1 plate with vertical clip

Tooth plate for a horse's nose

Pawn	Bishop	Knight	King	Queen	Rook

Pawn	Bishop	Knight	King	Queen	Rook

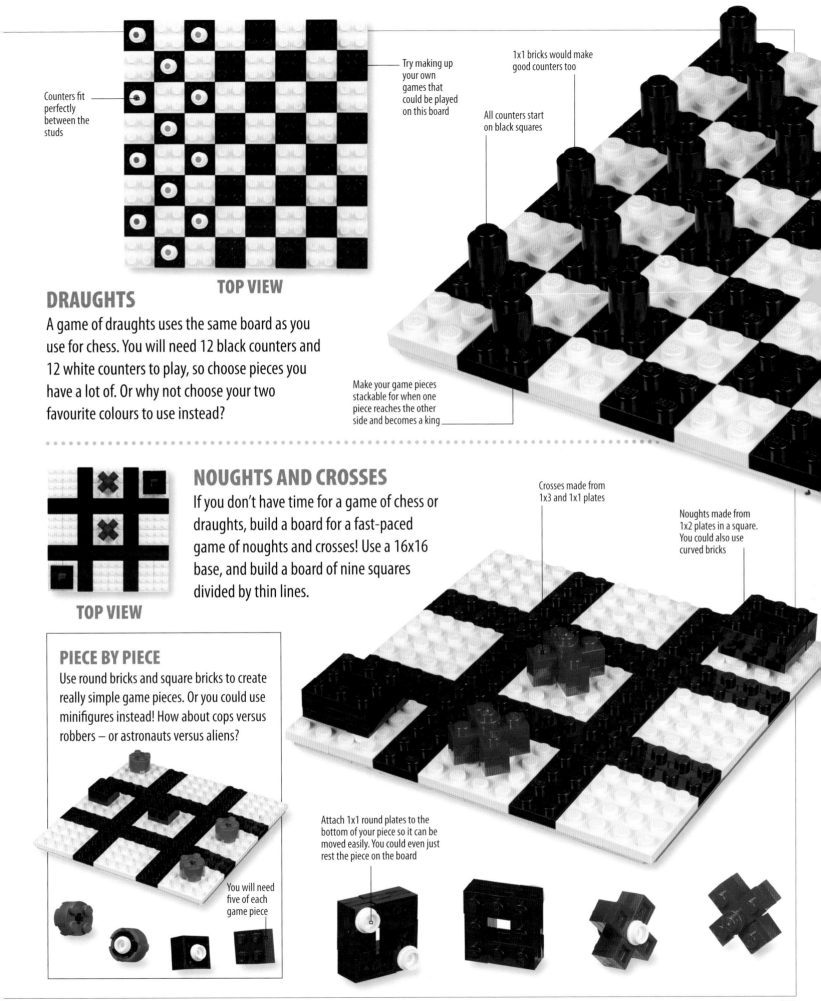

Counters fit perfectly between the studs

Try making up your own games that could be played on this board

1x1 bricks would make good counters too

All counters start on black squares

TOP VIEW

DRAUGHTS

A game of draughts uses the same board as you use for chess. You will need 12 black counters and 12 white counters to play, so choose pieces you have a lot of. Or why not choose your two favourite colours to use instead?

Make your game pieces stackable for when one piece reaches the other side and becomes a king

NOUGHTS AND CROSSES

If you don't have time for a game of chess or draughts, build a board for a fast-paced game of noughts and crosses! Use a 16x16 base, and build a board of nine squares divided by thin lines.

TOP VIEW

Crosses made from 1x3 and 1x1 plates

Noughts made from 1x2 plates in a square. You could also use curved bricks

PIECE BY PIECE

Use round bricks and square bricks to create really simple game pieces. Or you could use minifigures instead! How about cops versus robbers – or astronauts versus aliens?

You will need five of each game piece

Attach 1x1 round plates to the bottom of your piece so it can be moved easily. You could even just rest the piece on the board

MORE BOARD GAMES

Now that you can build board games out of bricks, you and your friends will never be bored again! You can make all your favourite games, and even make up your own. Before you start building, try to organise the pieces you need. Think about how many people are going to play and what colours you want to use. You could even use your favourite minifigures as pieces.

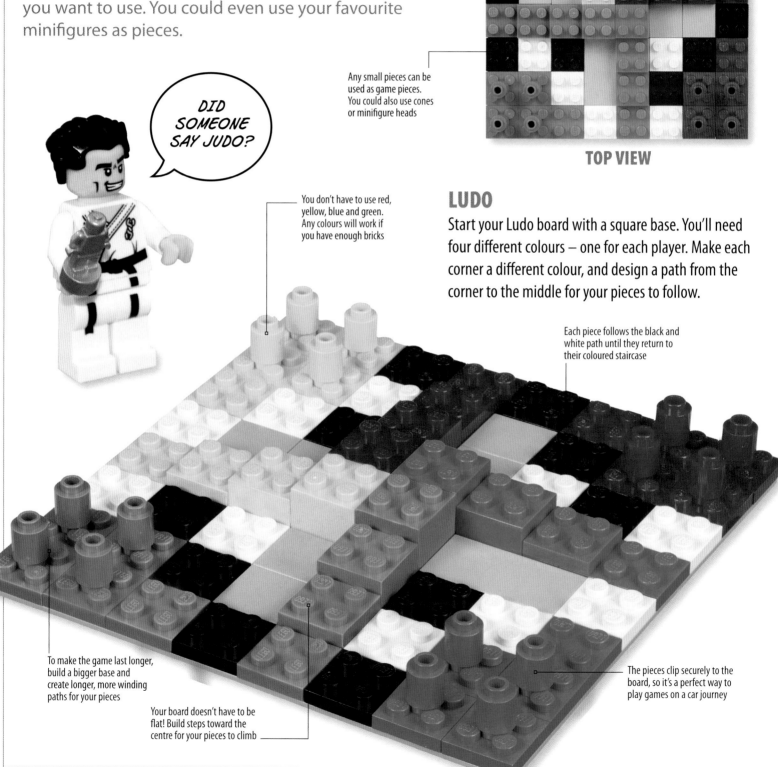

DID SOMEONE SAY JUDO?

Any small pieces can be used as game pieces. You could also use cones or minifigure heads

TOP VIEW

You don't have to use red, yellow, blue and green. Any colours will work if you have enough bricks

LUDO

Start your Ludo board with a square base. You'll need four different colours – one for each player. Make each corner a different colour, and design a path from the corner to the middle for your pieces to follow.

Each piece follows the black and white path until they return to their coloured staircase

To make the game last longer, build a bigger base and create longer, more winding paths for your pieces

Your board doesn't have to be flat! Build steps toward the centre for your pieces to climb

The pieces clip securely to the board, so it's a perfect way to play games on a car journey

SUMMIT

Try making up your own game. This one's called Summit because the aim of the game is to reach the top of the mountain. Build your board like a spiralling pyramid, with a path that gets a step higher each time it goes round a corner.

The winner is the first to reach the square at the top

TOP VIEW

COLOUR CRAZY

Choose one or two colours to use as the default board. This model uses red and white. Every so often, substitute a different colour for a square on the board to add rewards and pitfalls to the game.

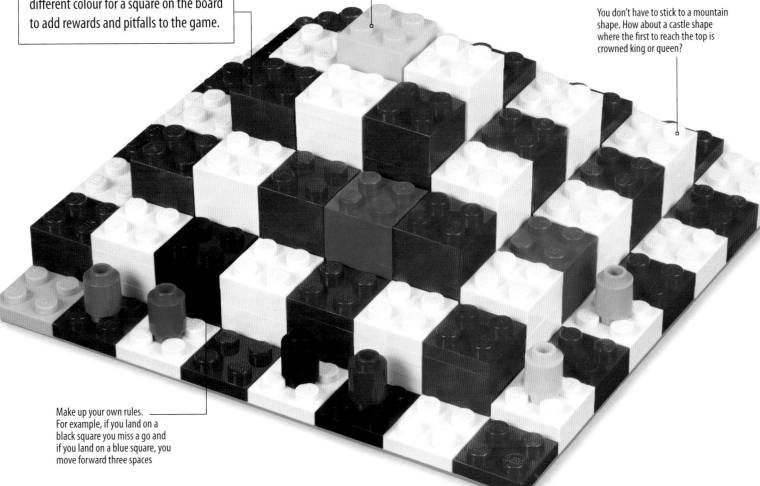

You could place a flag or a treasure piece at the summit

You don't have to stick to a mountain shape. How about a castle shape where the first to reach the top is crowned king or queen?

Make up your own rules. For example, if you land on a black square you miss a go and if you land on a blue square, you move forward three spaces

BUILDING REALITY

You may have built lots of fantasy models to play with, from flying saucers to pirate ships. But now it's time to face reality! Recreating everyday household items is a different challenge, since you can pick up the real thing and take a good look before planning the best way to make it. Create life-sized models or minifigure-scale objects – it's up to you!

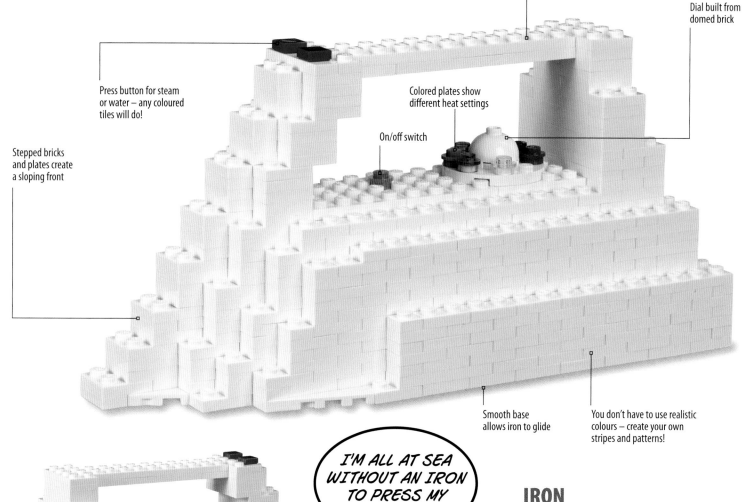

Handle must be strong enough to support the iron. The more bricks and plates you add, the more stable it will be!

Dial built from domed brick

Press button for steam or water – any coloured tiles will do!

Colored plates show different heat settings

On/off switch

Stepped bricks and plates create a sloping front

Smooth base allows iron to glide

You don't have to use realistic colours – create your own stripes and patterns!

REAR SIDE VIEW

I'M ALL AT SEA WITHOUT AN IRON TO PRESS MY CLOTHES!

IRON

Copying the curved and sloping shape of an iron with LEGO pieces is a challenge, but it can be done! Add dials, lights and buttons to bring your model to life – without the fear of burning your clothes! Just make sure any real iron is turned off and unplugged before you touch it!

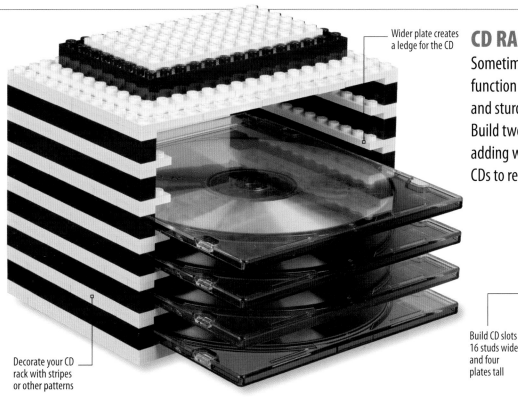

Wider plate creates a ledge for the CD

CD RACK

Sometimes LEGO builds are so realistic, they can function like the real thing! This CD rack is big and sturdy enough to hold your CD collection. Build two walls on opposite sides of a base, adding wider plates at regular intervals for your CDs to rest on.

Build CD slots 16 studs wide and four plates tall

REAR SIDE VIEW

Decorate your CD rack with stripes or other patterns

HEADPHONES

Headphones are delicate because they are quite thin. To make your model sturdy, use overlapping bricks to lock the model together. Build the strap and headphones separately and then join them together.

Measure the width of your head to make sure your headphones fit

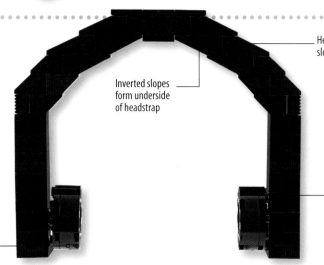

Headstrap made from 2x2 bricks, slopes and inverted slopes

Inverted slopes form underside of headstrap

LISTEN UP

Smooth ear pieces are made by attaching curved bricks to 4x4 round plates. These are connected to the headstrap using bricks with holes and LEGO Technic pins.

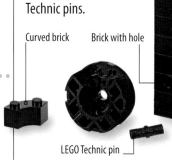

Curved brick   Brick with hole

LEGO Technic pin

Corner bricks surround a central column of two stacks of 1x1 bricks

Holes in the bricks mean that these models don't hold real-life salt and pepper!

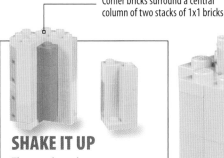

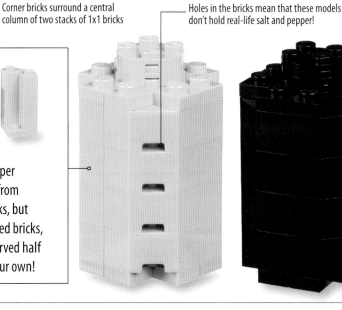

SHAKE IT UP

These salt and pepper shakers are made from angled corner bricks, but you could use curved bricks, square bricks or curved half arches to create your own!

SALT AND PEPPER

These shakers can be the beginning of your LEGO dining experience. Try and recreate what might be on a dining table, from crockery to silverware, or even a candelabra!

YOUR OWN DESIGNS

Now it's time to create some beautiful household objects using your own imagination! Instead of copying something directly, build a LEGO masterpiece of your own design. Use your favourite colours to build a decorative sculpture, or think up original designs for a set of coasters that you can use – for cold drinks only!

Mixing round and rectangular bricks helps create a curve

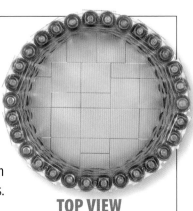

BUILDING BRIEF

Objective: Create objects of your own design
Use: Decorative, storage
Features: Life-size, beautiful, functional, unusual shapes, fun patterns
Extras: Paper tray, place mats, jewellery

This sculpture is delicate. Can you think of a way to make it more stable?

Secure the round plates and cones with 1x2 bricks and plates

COLOURFUL SCULPTURE

Stack rows of round plates, rectangular plates, cones and bricks to make your sculpture as tall or short as you like. Choose your own colours and patterns to match the colour of the room you will display the sculpture in. You could even try building different shaped sculptures.

BACK TO BASICS
Build a circular base using plates covered with tiles. At four points around the edge, position 1x2 plates and jumper plates, to which you can attach the circular sides.

TOP VIEW

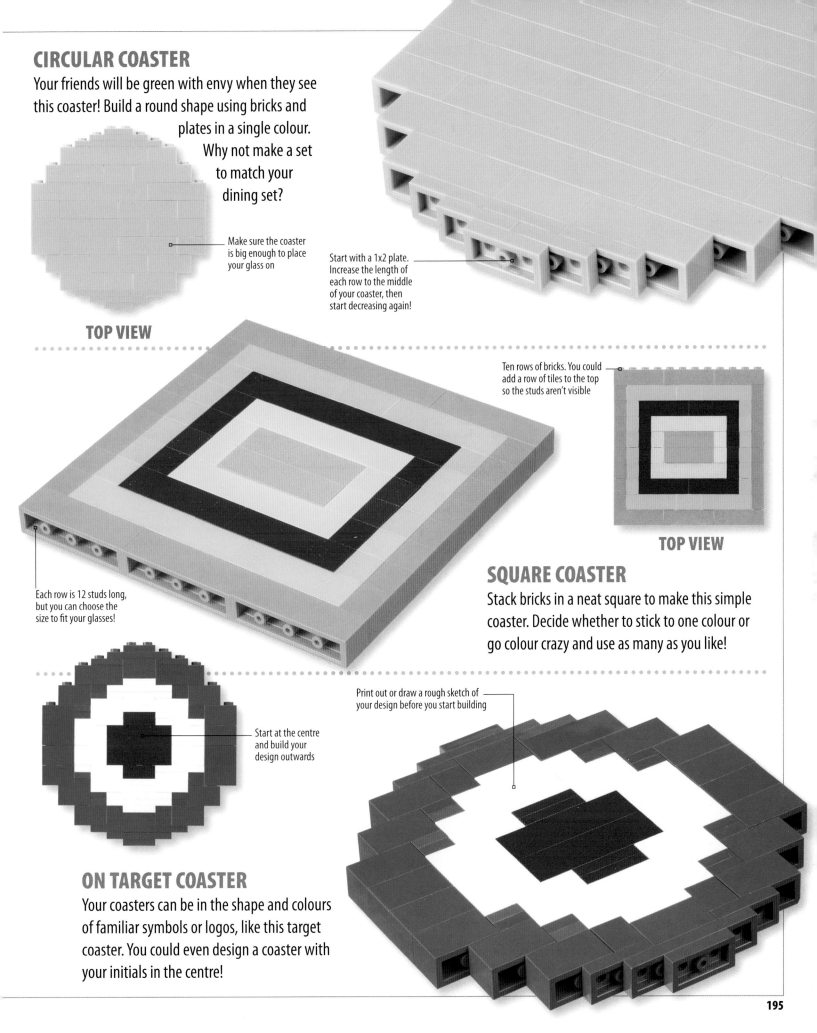

CIRCULAR COASTER

Your friends will be green with envy when they see this coaster! Build a round shape using bricks and plates in a single colour. Why not make a set to match your dining set?

Make sure the coaster is big enough to place your glass on

TOP VIEW

Start with a 1x2 plate. Increase the length of each row to the middle of your coaster, then start decreasing again!

Ten rows of bricks. You could add a row of tiles to the top so the studs aren't visible

TOP VIEW

SQUARE COASTER

Stack bricks in a neat square to make this simple coaster. Decide whether to stick to one colour or go colour crazy and use as many as you like!

Each row is 12 studs long, but you can choose the size to fit your glasses!

Print out or draw a rough sketch of your design before you start building

Start at the centre and build your design outwards

ON TARGET COASTER

Your coasters can be in the shape and colours of familiar symbols or logos, like this target coaster. You could even design a coaster with your initials in the centre!

MEET THE BUILDER

ANDREW WALKER

Location: UK
Age: 45
LEGO Speciality: City, trains and still life

How old were you when you started using LEGO bricks?

I'm pretty sure I always had LEGO bricks to play with. I think they must have belonged to my older sisters and brothers. We kept them in an old baby bath, and I remember always rummaging around in it looking for the parts I needed to build. However, when I was 13 my brother sold all the family LEGO pieces so I was without it for many years. I have only started building again in the last five years.

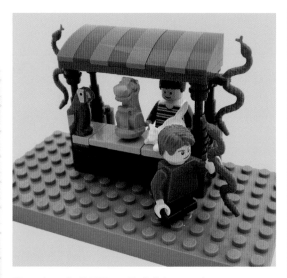

This market stall sells LEGO pets. The little boy seems happy with his new pet snake!

This is a model of Stephenson's Rocket, one of the first steam trains. The most difficult part of the building process was mounting the barrel and getting the piston to work.

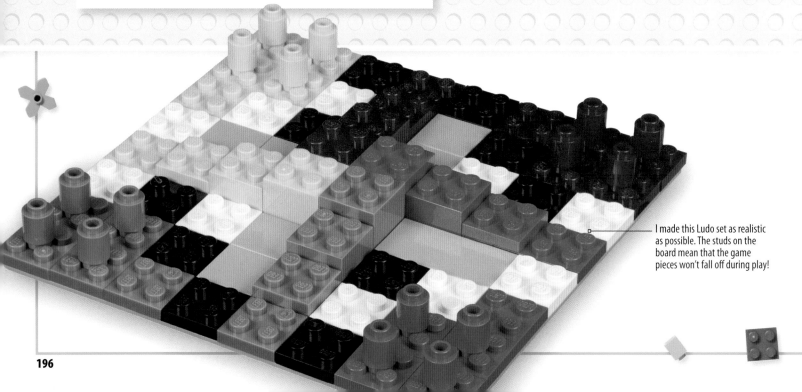

I made this Ludo set as realistic as possible. The studs on the board mean that the game pieces won't fall off during play!

What are you inspired by?

I'm inspired most often by recreating memories, whether it's a train I've ridden on or a cinema I used to visit when I was young. I also enjoy recreating scenes and models from films.

What is the biggest or most complex model you've made?

One of the great things about LEGO bricks is that you can build together: I recently worked with five other LEGO enthusiasts at a model railway exhibition to build a train layout 19ft 8in (6m) wide and 6ft 6in (2m) deep. We all brought our small individual models to build a lively and exciting town and railway. It looked great and all the visitors enjoyed our collaboration.

What things have gone wrong and how have you dealt with them?

I have often built the body of a train only to find out that when I put the wheels on it it won't go round the track or connect to any of the carriages or wagons! If you build your train too long it will overhang and hit everything else as it goes round the corner, so you need to be aware of the size and shape of your track. The wheels on trains are also important – if attached in the wrong place the train will not be able to travel around the track. To avoid this, always start with the wheels and base of your model. Check how it goes around the track and connects to the rest of your rolling stock, and then build the body of your model.

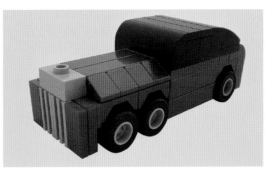

This model of a classic car takes us into the future of personal transport. It has a distinctive classic long nose and front grille, and I've added six wheels, a bulbous cabin, smooth sides and curved boot.

This space display, called Asteroid 478, was designed around many space vehicles. The command centre has solar panels, radar, communication dishes, sliding doors and its own repair robots.

If you had all the LEGO bricks (and time!) in the world, what would you build?

One of my favourite landmarks is the Eiffel Tower. I know the LEGO Group has built an official model, but I would like to make one at minifigure scale with working lifts.

What is your favourite creation?

I have made a model of the "Mole" tunnelling machine from *Thunderbirds*. I love how the body fits together and the LEGO bricks come together to make a round shape.

I really enjoyed building somewhere for my collectible minifigures to stay. It's great to display your favourites!

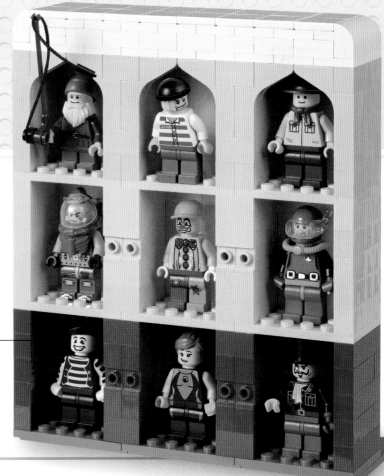

What are some of your top LEGO building tips?

Try to keep up to date with new developments. The LEGO Group are continually bringing out new bricks, which really helps you when trying to build something from real life. Some of my favourite recent bricks include: the headlight brick, which enables other bricks to be connected in different ways and can help you build in close quarters; bricks with side studs, which revolutionise how we can build details into our models; and the 1x1 plate with side ring which enables the bottom of two bricks to be joined together.

Which model were you most proud of as a young LEGO builder?

When I was about seven years old, I won a town themed building competition in a local department store. I built a jail in a town scene and enjoyed spending the prize money on more LEGO bricks!

The little figures on this clock tower are supposed to be like those that come out when the clock strikes the hour. When the LEGO Group released the trophies I knew what I had to make!

Building this underground rescue vehicle with drill presented some interesting challenges: using curved pieces to create a round body and using LEGO Technic beams to attach it to the base.

The hungry penguins are robbing the fish stall! Sometimes finding just the right minifigure head for your scene can be difficult, but this minifigure has the perfect expression!

ONE OF THE GREAT THINGS ABOUT LEGO BRICKS IS THAT YOU CAN BUILD TOGETHER.

What else do you enjoy making, apart from practical makes?

Practical items are really amazing to make. I also enjoy building town scenes, with all the cars, trains, buildings and people needed to make an accurate mini model of real life.

What is your favourite LEGO building technique or technique you use the most?

In the AFOL (Adult Fans Of LEGO) forums we refer to SNOT (Studs Not On Top) – the ability to build shapes that are smooth, round and flat, without any studs showing. This is how I like to build.

How much time do you spend building?

I usually build for one or two hours a day, depending on what project I have on the go. Sometimes I might also have to do some sorting or tidying up.

How many LEGO bricks do you have?

I must have over 50,000 by now.

Do you plan out your build? If so, how?

Planning is often very helpful. I use the LEGO Group's Digital Designer virtual building software, which helps me go over designs and particular techniques until I am happy. I also use spreadsheets to help me plan out the number of bricks I need to buy. However, if I have to make something using only the bricks I have already then I just start building and use trial and error to work it out.

My creation of this iconic British train is one of my most recent builds. Getting the doors at the rear right were the final piece of the build.

Using parts from some of the LEGO Group's most recent sets I tried to recreate my own car with a minifigure inside. With models like this, you may have to compromise or adapt to get your model to fit together.

What is your favourite LEGO brick or piece?

I think my favourite at the moment is the 1x1 slope that has been introduced over the last couple of years.

This treasure chest is the perfect place to hide all your favourite LEGO pieces! Building using specific colour design requires a little extra planning to make sure that the pieces colour coordinate but also fit together securely

DK

LONDON, NEW YORK
MELBOURNE, MUNICH and DEHLI

Editor   Shari Last
Additional Editors   Simon Beecroft, Jo Casey, Hannah Dolan,
Emma Grange, Catherine Saunders, Lisa Stock, Victoria Taylor
Senior Editor   Laura Gilbert
Designer   Owen Bennett
Additional Designers   Guy Harvey, Lynne Moulding, Robert Perry,
Lisa Sodeau, Ron Stobbart, Rhys Thomas, Toby Truphet
Senior Designer   Nathan Martin
Design Manager   Ron Stobbart
Art Director   Lisa Lanzarini
Publishing Manager   Catherine Saunders
Publisher   Simon Beecroft
Publishing Director   Alex Allan
Production Editor   Sean Daly
Production Controller   Nick Seston

Photography by Gary Ombler,
Brian Poulsen and Tim Trøjborg

This edition published in 2013
First published in Great Britain in 2011 by Dorling Kindersley Limited
80 Strand, London WC2R 0RL
Penguin Group (UK)

037—176214—Oct/11

Page design copyright © 2011, 2013 Dorling Kindersley Limited.

A CIP catalogue record for this book is available from the British Library.

ISBN: 978-1-4093-4165-9

Reproduced by MDP in the UK
Printed and bound in China by South China Printing Co. Ltd.

Discover more at
www.dk.com
www.LEGO.com

Acknowledgements
Dorling Kindersley would like to thank: Stephanie Lawrence,
Randi Sørensen and Corinna van Delden at the LEGO Group;
Sebastiaan Arts, Tim Goddard, Deborah Higdon, Barney Main,
Duncan Titmarsh (www.bright-bricks.com) and Andrew Walker
for their amazing models; Jeff van Winden for additional building;
Daniel Lipkowitz for his fantastic text; Gary Ombler, Brian Poulsen
and Tim Trøjborg for their brilliant photography; Rachel Peng and
Bo Wei at IM Studios; and Sarah Harland for editorial assistance.